Data Labeling in Machine Learning with Python

Explore modern ways to prepare labeled data for training and fine-tuning ML and generative AI models

Vijaya Kumar Suda

Data Labeling in Machine Learning with Python

Group Product Manager: Niranjan Naikwadi

Publishing Product Manager: Sanjana Gupta

Book Project Manager: Hemangi Lotlikar

Content Development Editor: Shreya Moharir

Technical Editor: Rahul Limbachiya

Copy Editor: Safis Editing

Proofreader: Safis Editing

Indexer: Tejal Soni

Production Designer: Joshua Misquitta

DevRel Marketing Coordinator: Vinishka Kalra

First published: January 2024
Production reference: 1300124

Published by Packt Publishing Ltd.
Grosvenor House
11 St Paul's Square
Birmingham
B3 1RB, UK.

ISBN 978-1-80461-054-1

www.packtpub.com

Acknowledgments

I extend my heartfelt gratitude to my mother, Rajya Lakshmi Suda, and dedicate this work to the cherished memory of my father, Koteswara Rao Suda. Their sacrifices and unwavering determination have been a profound source of inspiration.

Special thanks to my wife, Radhika, for her enduring support and patience throughout the writing of this book.

To my son, Chandra Suda (Rise Global Winner 2023), and daughter, Akshaya, your talents and creativity have shown me the beautiful evolution of skill.

I am deeply appreciative of my siblings, Rama Devi, Swarna Kumar, and Dr. Sri Kumar, for their continuous support.

A sincere acknowledgment to my mentors and managers, Kevin Fleck and Des Quinta, for their invaluable support and motivation throughout the writing process of this book.

Finally, I want to thank the Packt Publishing team, especially Shreya and Hemangi, for their fantastic support, which made the writing process an absolute pleasure.

Contributors

About the author

Vijaya Kumar Suda is a seasoned data and AI professional, boasting over two decades of expertise collaborating with global clients. Having resided and worked in diverse locations such as Switzerland, Belgium, Mexico, Bahrain, India, Canada, and the USA, Vijaya has successfully assisted customers spanning various industries. Currently serving as a senior data and AI consultant at Microsoft, he is instrumental in guiding industry partners through their digital transformation endeavors using cutting-edge cloud technologies and AI capabilities. His proficiency encompasses architecture, data engineering, machine learning, generative AI, and cloud solutions. Vijaya also shares his insights through engaging videos on the cloud, data, and AI on his YouTube channel, *Cloud & Data Science* (`https://youtu.be/piVqFcuBV2c`).

About the reviewers

Pritesh Kanani is a full stack developer with experience in data wrangling and supervised machine learning. He helped a major oil and gas company with building a tool to monitor drilling operations and handling thousands of high frequency data streams. He completed a post-graduation course in applied AI and is currently utilizing his full stack data science and cloud computing skills at a leading nuclear and renewable energy organization in Ontario, Canada.

Sourav Roy is a passionate data enthusiast, an experienced machine learning practitioner, and an expert book reviewer with a focus on literature linked to data. He possesses a diverse skill set in data engineering and data analytics, which allows him to combine technical proficiency with a deep passion in his work on data-centric books. Sourav obtained a master's degree in data science and analytics from Queen's University. He is presently employed as a data engineer in the banking sector.

Mitesh Mangaonkar is an engineering leader pioneering generative AI to transform data platforms. As a tech lead at Airbnb, he builds cutting-edge data pipelines leveraging big technologies and modern data stacks to power trust and safety products. Previously, at AWS, Mitesh helped Fortune 500 companies migrate their data warehouses to the cloud and engineered highly scalable, resilient systems. An innovator at heart, he combines deep data engineering expertise with a passion for AI to create the next generation of data products. Mitesh is an influential voice shaping the future of data engineering and governance.

Table of Contents

Part 1: Labeling Tabular Data

1

Exploring Data for Machine Learning   3

5

Labeling Image Data Using Rules   115

6

Labeling Image Data Using Data Augmentation   135

Part 3: Labeling Text, Audio, and Video Data

7

Labeling Text Data   161

8

Exploring Video Data   199

9

Labeling Video Data   225

10

Exploring Audio Data   255

11

Labeling Audio Data   289

12

Hands-On Exploring Data Labeling Tools   317

Index   361

Other Books You May Enjoy   374

Preface

In today's data-driven era, where more than 2.5 quintillion bytes of data are produced daily in various forms such as text, image, audio, and video, data stands as the cornerstone of the AI revolution. However, the majority of real-world data available for training supervised machine learning models lacks labels, or we encounter limited labeled data. This presents a significant challenge, as labeled data is essential for training any supervised machine learning model and fine-tuning large language models in the age of generative AI.

To address the scarcity of labeled data and facilitate the preparation of labeled data for training supervised machine learning models and fine-tuning large language models, this book introduces various methods for programmatic data labeling using Python libraries and methods, including semi-supervised and unsupervised learning.

This book guides you through the process of loading and analyzing tabular data, images, videos, audio, and text using various Python libraries, the OpenAI API, LangChain, and Azure Machine Learning. It explores techniques such as weak supervision, pseudo-labeling, and K-means clustering for classification and labeling, while also providing data augmentation methods to enhance accuracy. Utilizing the Azure OpenAI API and LangChain, the book demonstrates the automation of data analysis using natural language without the need to acquire any programming skills. It also encompasses the classification and data labeling of text data using OpenAI and **large language models** (LLMs). This book covers a wide variety of open source data annotation tools, along with Azure Machine Learning, and compares the pros and cons of these tools.

Real-world examples from various industries are incorporated to illustrate the application of these methods to tabular, text, image, video, and audio data.

By the conclusion of this book, you will have acquired the skills to explore different types of data using Python and OpenAI LLMs. You will have learned how to prepare data with labels, whether for training machine learning models or unlocking insights about the data to leverage for business use cases across industries.

Who this book is for

This book is for aspiring AI engineers, machine learning engineers, data scientists, and data engineers who want to learn about data labeling methods and algorithms for model training. Data enthusiasts and Python developers will be able to use this book to learn about data exploration and annotation using Python libraries.

What this book covers

Chapter 1, Exploring Data for Machine Learning, provides an overview of data analysis and visualization methods using various Python libraries. Additionally, it deep dives into unlocking data insights with natural language using OpenAI LLMs.

Chapter 2, Labeling Data for Classification, covers the process of labeling tabular data for training classification models. Various methods, such as Snorkel Python functions, semi-supervised learning, and clustering data using K-means, are explored.

Chapter 3, Labeling Data for Regression, addresses the labeling of tabular data for training regression models. Techniques include leveraging summary statistics, creating pseudo labels, employing data augmentation methods, and utilizing K-means clustering.

Chapter 4, Exploring Image Data, covers the analysis and visualization of image data and feature extraction from images using various Python libraries.

Chapter 5, Labeling Image Data Using Rules, discusses labeling images based on heuristics and image properties such as aspect ratio, and also covers image classification using pre-trained classifiers such as YOLO.

Chapter 6, Labeling Image Data Using Data Augmentation, explores methods of image data augmentation for training support vector machines and Convolutional Neural Networks (CNNs), as well as addressing image data labeling.

Chapter 7, Labeling Text Data, covers generative AI and various methods for labeling text data. This includes Azure OpenAI with real-world use cases, text classification, and sentiment analysis using Snorkel and K-means clustering.

Chapter 8, Exploring Video Data, focuses on loading video data, extracting features, visualizing video data, and clustering video data using K-means clustering.

Chapter 9, Labeling Video Data, delves into labeling video data using CNNs, segmenting video data with the watershed algorithm, and capturing important features using autoencoders, accompanied by real-world examples.

Chapter 10, Exploring Audio Data, provides the fundamentals of audio data, loading and visualizing audio data, extracting features, and real-life applications.

Chapter 11, Labeling Audio Data, covers transcribing audio data using OpenAI's Whisper model, labeling the transcription, creating spectrograms for audio data classification, augmenting audio data, and using Azure Cognitive Services for speech.

Chapter 12, Hands-On Exploring Data Labeling Tools, covers various data labeling tools, including open source tools such as Label Studio, CVAT, pyOpenAnnotate, and Azure Machine Learning. It also includes a comparison of various data labeling tools for image, text, audio, and video data.

To get the most out of this book

Basic Python knowledge is beneficial but not necessary to get the most out of this book.

Software/hardware covered in the book	Operating system requirements
Python 3.9+	Windows, macOS, or Linux
Azure OpenAI subscription	
ECMAScript 11	

If you are using the digital version of this book, we advise you to type the code yourself or access the code from the book's GitHub repository (a link is available in the next section). Doing so will help you avoid any potential errors related to the copying and pasting of code.

Download the example code files

You can download the example code files for this book from GitHub at `https://github.com/PacktPublishing/Data-Labeling-in-Machine-Learning-with-Python`. If there's an update to the code, it will be updated in the GitHub repository.

We also have other code bundles from our rich catalog of books and videos available at `https://github.com/PacktPublishing/`. Check them out!

Conventions used

There are a number of text conventions used throughout this book.

`Code in text`: Indicates code words in text, database table names, folder names, filenames, file extensions, pathnames, dummy URLs, user input, and Twitter handles. Here is an example: "Now let us generate the augmented data by calling the `noise`, `scale`, and `rotation` augmentation functions, as follows."

A block of code is set as follows:

```
# Train a linear regression model on the labeled data
regressor = LinearRegression()
regressor.fit(train_data, train_labels)
```

When we wish to draw your attention to a particular part of a code block, the relevant lines or items are set in bold:

```
news_headline="Label the following news headline into 1 of the
following categories: Business, Tech, Politics, Sport, Entertainment\
n\n Headline 1: Trump is ready to contest in nov 2024 elections\
nCategory:",
```

```
response = openai.Completion.create(
engine=model_deployment_name,
prompt= news_headline,
temperature=0,
```

Any command-line input or output is written as follows:

```
pip install keras
```

Bold: Indicates a new term, an important word, or words that you see onscreen. For instance, words in menus or dialog boxes appear in **bold**. Here is an example: "Change **System preferences | Security and privacy | General**, and then select **Open anyway**."

> **Tips or important notes**
> Appear like this.

Get in touch

Feedback from our readers is always welcome.

General feedback: If you have questions about any aspect of this book, email us at customercare@packtpub.com and mention the book title in the subject of your message.

Errata: Although we have taken every care to ensure the accuracy of our content, mistakes do happen. If you have found a mistake in this book, we would be grateful if you would report this to us. Please visit www.packtpub.com/support/errata and fill in the form.

Piracy: If you come across any illegal copies of our works in any form on the internet, we would be grateful if you would provide us with the location address or website name. Please contact us at copyright@packt.com with a link to the material.

If you are interested in becoming an author: If there is a topic that you have expertise in and you are interested in either writing or contributing to a book, please visit authors.packtpub.com

Share your thoughts

Once you've read *Data Labeling in ML and AI with Python*, we'd love to hear your thoughts! Scan the QR code below to go straight to the Amazon review page for this book and share your feedback.

https://packt.link/r/1-804-61054-2

Your review is important to us and the tech community and will help us make sure we're delivering excellent quality content.

Download a free PDF copy of this book

Thanks for purchasing this book!

Do you like to read on the go but are unable to carry your print books everywhere?

Is your eBook purchase not compatible with the device of your choice?

Don't worry, now with every Packt book you get a DRM-free PDF version of that book at no cost.

Read anywhere, any place, on any device. Search, copy, and paste code from your favorite technical books directly into your application.

The perks don't stop there, you can get exclusive access to discounts, newsletters, and great free content in your inbox daily

Follow these simple steps to get the benefits:

1. Scan the QR code or visit the link below

https://packt.link/free-ebook/9781804610541

2. Submit your proof of purchase
3. That's it! We'll send your free PDF and other benefits to your email directly

Part 1: Labeling Tabular Data

This part of the book will guide you in exploring tabular data and programmatically labeling the data using Python libraries, such as Snorkel labeling functions. You will be able to achieve this without requiring any prior data science knowledge. Additionally, it covers data labeling using K-means clustering.

This part comprises the following chapters:

- *Chapter 1, Exploring Data for Machine Learning*
- *Chapter 2, Labeling Data for Classification*
- *Chapter 3, Labeling Data for Regression*

1

Exploring Data for Machine Learning

Imagine embarking on a journey through an expansive ocean of data, where within this vastness are untold stories, patterns, and insights waiting to be discovered. Welcome to the world of data exploration in **machine learning** (**ML**). In this chapter, I encourage you to put on your analytical lenses as we embark on a thrilling quest. Here, we will delve deep into the heart of your data, armed with powerful techniques and heuristics, to uncover its secrets. As you embark on this adventure, you will discover that beneath the surface of raw numbers and statistics, there exists a treasure trove of patterns that, once revealed, can transform your data into a valuable asset. The journey begins with **exploratory data analysis** (**EDA**), a crucial phase where we unravel the mysteries of data, laying the foundation for automated labeling and, ultimately, building smarter and more accurate ML models. In this age of **generative AI**, the preparation of quality training data is essential to the fine-tuning of domain-specific **large language models** (**LLMs**). Fine-tuning involves the curation of additional domain-specific labeled data for training publicly available LLMs. So, fasten your seatbelts for a captivating voyage into the art and science of data exploration for **data labeling**.

First, let's start with the question: What is data exploration? It is the initial phase of data analysis, where raw data is examined, visualized, and summarized to uncover patterns, trends, and insights. It serves as a crucial step in understanding the nature of the data before applying advanced analytics or ML techniques.

In this chapter, we will explore tabular data using various libraries and packages in Python, including Pandas, NumPy, and Seaborn. We will also plot different bar charts and histograms to visualize data to find the relationships between various features, which is useful for labeling data. We will be exploring the *Income* dataset located in this book's GitHub repository (a link for which is located in the *Technical requirements* section). A good understanding of the data is necessary in order to define business rules, identify matching patterns, and, subsequently, label the data using Python labeling functions.

By the end of this chapter, we will be able to generate summary statistics for the given dataset. We will derive aggregates of the features for each target group. We will also learn how to perform univariate and bivariate analyses of the features in the given dataset. We will create a report using the `ydata-profiling` library.

We're going to cover the following main topics:

- EDA and data labeling

- Summary statistics and data aggregates with Pandas

- Data visualization with Seaborn for univariate and bivariate analysis

- Profiling data using the `ydata-profiling` library

- Unlocking insights from data with OpenAI and LangChain

Technical requirements

One of the following Python IDE and software tools needs to be installed before running the notebook in this chapter:

- **Anaconda Navigator**: Download and install the open source Anaconda Navigator from the following URL:

  `https://docs.anaconda.com/navigator/install/#system-requirements`

- **Jupyter Notebook**: Download and install Jupyter Notebook:

  `https://jupyter.org/install`

- We can also use open source, online Python editors such as **Google Colab** (`https://colab.research.google.com/`) or **Replit** (`https://replit.com/`)

The Python source code and the entire notebook created in this chapter are available in this book's GitHub repository:

`https://github.com/PacktPublishing/Data-Labeling-in-Machine-Learning-with-Python`

You also need to create an Azure account and add an OpenAI resource for working with generative AI. To sign up for a free Azure subscription, visit `https://azure.microsoft.com/free`. To request access to the Azure OpenAI service, visit `https://aka.ms/oaiapply`.

Once you have provisioned the Azure OpenAI service, deploy the LLM model – either GPT-3.5-Turbo or GPT 4.0 – from Azure OpenAI Studio. Then copy the keys for OpenAI from OpenAI Studio and set up the following environment variables:

```
os.environ['AZURE_OPENAI_KEY'] = 'your_api_key'
os.environ['AZURE_OPENAI_ENDPOINT"] ='your_azure_openai_endpoint'
```

Your endpoint should look like this: `https://YOUR_RESOURCE_NAME.openai.azure.com/`.

EDA and data labeling

In this section, we will gain an understanding of what EDA is. We will see why we need to perform it and discuss its advantages. We will also look at the life cycle of an ML project and learn about the role of data labeling in this cycle.

EDA comprises **data discovery**, **data collection**, **data cleaning**, and **data exploration**. These steps are part of any machine learning project. The data exploration step includes tasks such as data visualization, summary statistics, correlation analysis, and data distribution analysis. We will dive deep into these steps in the upcoming sections.

Here are some real-world examples of EDA:

- **Customer churn analysis**: Suppose you work for a telecommunications company and you want to understand why customers are churning (canceling their subscriptions); in this case, conducting EDA on customer churn data can provide valuable insights.

- **Income data analysis**: EDA on the *Income* dataset with predictive features such as education, employment status, and marital status helps to predict whether the salary of a person is greater than $50K.

EDA is a critical process for any ML or data science project, and it allows us to understand the data and gain some valuable insights into the data domain and business.

In this chapter, we will use various Python libraries, such as Pandas, and call the `describe` and `info` functions on Pandas to generate data summaries. We will discover anomalies in the data and any outliers in the given dataset. We will also figure out various data types and any missing values in the data. We will understand whether any data type conversions are required, such as converting `string` to `float`, for performing further analysis. We will also analyze the data formats and see whether any transformations are required to standardize them, such as the date format. We will analyze the counts of different labels and understand whether the dataset is balanced or imbalanced. We will understand the relationships between various features in the data and calculate the correlations between features.

To summarize, we will understand the patterns in the given dataset and also identify the relationships between various features in the data samples. Finally, we will come up with a strategy and domain rules for data cleaning and transformation. This helps us to predict labels for unlabeled data.

We will plot various data visualizations using Python libraries such as `seaborn` and `matplotlib`. We will create bar charts, histograms, heatmaps, and various charts to visualize the importance of features in the dataset and how they depend on each other.

Understanding the ML project life cycle

The following are the major steps in an ML project:

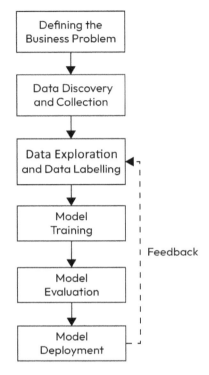

Figure 1.1 – ML project life cycle diagram

Let's look at them in detail.

Defining the business problem

The first step in every ML project is to understand the business problem and define clear goals that can be measured at the end of the project.

Data discovery and data collection

In this step, you identify and gather potential data sources that may be relevant to your project's objectives. This involves finding datasets, databases, APIs, or any other sources that may contain the data needed for your analysis and modeling.

The goal of **data discovery** is to understand the landscape of available data and assess its quality, relevance, and potential limitations.

Data discovery can also involve discussions with domain experts and stakeholders to identify what data is essential for solving business problems or achieving the project's goals.

After identifying various sources for data, data engineers will develop data pipelines to extract and load the data to the target data lake and perform some data preprocessing tasks such as data cleaning, de-duplication, and making data readily available to ML engineers and data scientists for further processing.

Data exploration

Data exploration follows data discovery and is primarily focused on understanding the data, gaining insights, and identifying patterns or anomalies.

During data exploration, you may perform basic statistical analysis, create data visualizations, and conduct initial observations to understand the data's characteristics.

Data exploration can also involve identifying missing values, outliers, and potential data quality issues, but it typically does not involve making systematic changes to the data.

During data exploration, you assess the available labeled data and determine whether it's sufficient for your ML task. If you find that the labeled data is small and insufficient for model training, you may identify the need for additional labeled data.

Data labeling

Data labeling involves acquiring or generating more labeled examples to supplement your training dataset. You may need to manually label additional data points or use programming techniques such as data augmentation to expand your labeled dataset. The process of assigning labels to data samples is called **data annotation** or data labeling.

Most of the time, it is too expensive or time-consuming to outsource the manual data labeling task. Also, data is often not allowed to be shared with external third-party organizations due to data privacy. So, automating the data labeling process with an in-house development team using Python helps to label the data quickly and at an affordable cost.

Most of the data science books available on the market are lacking information about this important step. So, this book aims to address the various methods to programmatically label data using Python as well as the annotation tools available on the market.

After obtaining a sufficient amount of labeled data, you proceed with traditional data preprocessing tasks, such as handling missing values, encoding features, scaling, and feature engineering.

Model training

Once the data is adequately prepared, then that dataset is fed into the model by ML engineers to train the model.

Model evaluation

After the model is trained, the next step is to evaluate the model on a validation dataset to see how good the model is and avoid bias and overfitting.

You can evaluate the model's performance using various metrics and techniques and iterate on the model-building process as needed.

Model deployment

Finally, you deploy your model into production and monitor for continuous improvement using **ML Operations** (**MLOps**). MLOps aims to streamline the process of taking ML models to production and maintaining and monitoring them.

In this book, we will focus on data labeling. In a real-world project, the datasets that sources provide us with for analytics and ML are not clean and not labeled. So, we need to explore unlabeled data to understand correlations and patterns and help us define the rules for data labeling using Python labeling functions. Data exploration helps us to understand the level of cleaning and transformation required before starting data labeling and model training.

This is where Python helps us to explore and perform a quick analysis of raw data using various libraries (such as Pandas, Seaborn, and ydata-profiling libraries), otherwise known as EDA.

Introducing Pandas DataFrames

Pandas is an open source library used for data analysis and manipulation. It provides various functions for data wrangling, cleaning, and merging operations. Let us see how to explore data using the `pandas` library. For this, we will use the *Income* dataset located on GitHub and explore it to find the following insights:

- How many unique values are there for age, education, and profession in the *Income* dataset? What are the observations for each unique age?

- Summary statistics such as mean value and quantile values for each feature. What is the average age of the adult for the income range > \$50K?

- How is income dependent on independent variables such as age, education, and profession using bivariate analysis?

Let us first read the data into a DataFrame using the `pandas` library.

A DataFrame is a structure that represents two-dimensional data with columns and rows, and it is similar to a SQL table. To get started, ensure that you create the `requirements.txt` file and add the required Python libraries as follows:

```
≡ requirements.txt  ×

Ch01 >  ≡ requirements.txt
    1      ydata-profiling
    2      pandas
    3      numpy
    4      matplotlib
    5      seaborn
```

Figure 1.2 – Contents of the requirements.txt file

Next, run the following command from your Python notebook cell to install the libraries added in the `requirements.txt` file:

```
%pip install -r requirements.txt
```

Now, let's import the required Python libraries using the following `import` statements:

```
# import libraries for loading dataset
import pandas as pd
import numpy as np
# import libraries for plotting
import matplotlib.pyplot as plt
import seaborn as sns
from matplotlib import rcParams
%matplotlib inline
plt.style.use('dark_background')
# ignore warnings
import warnings
warnings.filterwarnings('ignore')
```

Next, in the following code snippet, we are reading the `adult_income.csv` file and writing to the DataFrame (`df`):

```
# loading the dataset
df = pd.read_csv("<your file path>/adult_income.csv",
encoding='latin-1)'
```

Now the data is loaded to `df`.

Let us see the size of the DataFrame using the following code snippet:

```
df.shape
```

We will see the shape of the DataFrame as a result:

$$(32561, \ 15)$$

Figure 1.3 – Shape of the DataFrame

So, we can see that there are 32,561 observations (rows) and 15 features (columns) in the dataset.

Let us print the 15 column names in the dataset:

```
df.columns
```

We get the following result:

```
Index(['age', 'workclass', 'fnlwgt', 'education', 'education.num',
       'marital.status', 'occupation', 'relationship', 'race', 'sex',
       'capital.gain', 'capital.loss', 'hours.per.week', 'native.country',
       'income'],
      dtype='object')
```

Figure 1.4 – The names of the columns in our dataset

Now, let's see the first five rows of the data in the dataset with the following code:

```
df.head()
```

We can see the output in *Figure 1.5*:

	age	workclass	fnlwgt	education	education.num	marital.status	occupation	relationship	race	sex	capital.gain	capital.loss	hours.per.week
0	90	?	77053	HS-grad	9	Widowed	?	Not-in-family	White	Female	0	4356	40
1	82	Private	132870	HS-grad	9	Widowed	Exec-managerial	Not-in-family	White	Female	0	4356	18
2	66	?	186061	Some-college	10	Widowed	?	Unmarried	Black	Female	0	4356	40
3	54	Private	140359	7th-8th	4	Divorced	Machine-op-inspct	Unmarried	White	Female	0	3900	40
4	41	Private	264663	Some-college	10	Separated	Prof-specialty	Own-child	White	Female	0	3900	40

Figure 1.5 – The first five rows of data

Let's see the last five rows of the dataset using `tail`, as shown in the following figure:

```
df.tail()
```

We will get the following output.

	age	workclass	fnlwgt	education	education.num	marital.status	occupation	relationship	race	sex	capital.gain	capital.loss	hours.per.week
32556	22	Private	310152	Some-college	10	Never-married	Protective-serv	Not-in-family	White	Male	0	0	40
32557	27	Private	257302	Assoc-acdm	12	Married-civ-spouse	Tech-support	Wife	White	Female	0	0	38
32558	40	Private	154374	HS-grad	9	Married-civ-spouse	Machine-op-inspct	Husband	White	Male	0	0	40
32559	58	Private	151910	HS-grad	9	Widowed	Adm-clerical	Unmarried	White	Female	0	0	40
32560	22	Private	201490	HS-grad	9	Never-married	Adm-clerical	Own-child	White	Male	0	0	20

Figure 1.6 – The last five rows of data

As we can see, `education` and `education.num` are redundant columns, as `education.num` is just the ordinal representation of the `education` column. So, we will remove the redundant `education.num` column from the dataset as one column is enough for model training. We will also drop the `race` column from the dataset using the following code snippet as we will not use it here:

```
# As we observe education and education.num both are the same , so we
can drop one of the columns
df.drop(['education.num'], axis = 1, inplace = True)
df.drop(['race'], axis = 1, inplace = True)
```

Here, `axis = 1` refers to the columns axis, which means that you are specifying that you want to drop a column. In this case, you are dropping the columns labeled `education.num` and `race` from the DataFrame.

Now, let's print the columns using `info()` to make sure the `race` and `education.num` columns are dropped from the DataFrame:

```
df.info()
```

We will see the following output:

```
<class 'pandas.core.frame.DataFrame'>
RangeIndex: 32561 entries, 0 to 32560
Data columns (total 13 columns):
 #   Column          Non-Null Count  Dtype
---  ------          --------------  -----
 0   age             32561 non-null  int64
 1   workclass       32561 non-null  object
 2   fnlwgt          32561 non-null  int64
 3   education       32561 non-null  object
 4   marital.status  32561 non-null  object
 5   occupation      32561 non-null  object
 6   relationship    32561 non-null  object
 7   sex             32561 non-null  object
 8   capital.gain    32561 non-null  int64
 9   capital.loss    32561 non-null  int64
 10  hours.per.week  32561 non-null  int64
 11  native.country  32561 non-null  object
 12  income          32561 non-null  object
dtypes: int64(5), object(8)
memory usage: 3.2+ MB
```

Figure 1.7 – Columns in the DataFrame

We can see in the preceding data there are now only 13 columns as we deleted 2 of them from the previous total of 15 columns.

In this section, we have seen what a Pandas DataFrame is and loaded a CSV dataset into one. We also saw the various columns in the DataFrame and their data types. In the following section, we will generate the summary statistics for the important features using Pandas.

Summary statistics and data aggregates

In this section, we will derive the summary statistics for numerical columns.

Before generating summary statistics, we will identify the categorical columns and numerical columns in the dataset. Then, we will calculate the summary statistics for all numerical columns.

We will also calculate the mean value of each numerical column for the target class. Summary statistics are useful to gain insights about each feature's mean values and their effect on the target label class.

Let's print the categorical columns using the following code snippet:

```
#categorical column
catogrical_column = [column for column in df.columns if df[column].
dtypes=='object']
print(catogrical_column)
```

We will get the following result:

```
['workclass', 'education', 'marital.status', 'occupation', 'relationship', 'sex', 'native.country', 'income']
```

Figure 1.8 – Categorical columns

Now, let's print the `numerical` columns using the following code snippet:

```
#numerical_column
numerical_column = [column for column in df.columns if df[column].
dtypes !='object']
print(numerical_column)
```

We will get the following output:

```
['age', 'fnlwgt', 'capital.gain', 'capital.loss', 'hours.per.week']
```

Figure 1.9 – Numerical columns

Summary statistics

Now, let's generate summary statistics (i.e., mean, standard deviation, minimum value, maximum value, and lower (25%), middle (50%), and higher (75%) percentiles) using the following code snippet:

```
df.describe().T
```

We will get the following results:

	count	mean	std	min	25%	50%	75%	max
age	32561.0	38.581647	13.640433	17.0	28.0	37.0	48.0	90.0
fnlwgt	32561.0	189778.366512	105549.977697	12285.0	117827.0	178356.0	237051.0	1484705.0
capital.gain	32561.0	1077.648844	7385.292085	0.0	0.0	0.0	0.0	99999.0
capital.loss	32561.0	87.303830	402.960219	0.0	0.0	0.0	0.0	4356.0
hours.per.week	32561.0	40.437456	12.347429	1.0	40.0	40.0	45.0	99.0

Figure 1.10 – Summary statistics

As shown in the results, the mean value of `age` is 38.5 years, the minimum age is 17 years, and the maximum age is 90 years in the dataset. As we have only five numerical columns in the dataset, we can only see five rows in this summary statistics table.

Data aggregates of the feature for each target class

Now, let's calculate the average age of the people for each income group range using the following code snippet:

```
df.groupby("income")["age"].mean()
```

We will see the following output:

```
income
<=50K    36.783738
>50K     44.249841
Name: age, dtype: float64
```

Figure 1.11 – Average age by income group

As shown in the results, we have used the groupby clause on the target variable and calculated the mean of the age in each group. The mean age is 36.78 for people with an income group of less than or equal to $50K. Similarly, the mean age is 44.2 for the income group greater than $50K.

Now, let's calculate the average hours per week of the people for each income group range using the following code snippet:

```
df.groupby("income")["hours.per.week"]. mean()
```

We will get the following output:

```
income
<=50K    38.840210
>50K     45.473026
Name: hours.per.week, dtype: float64
```

Figure 1.12 – Average hours per week by income group

As shown in the results, the average hours per week for the income group =< $50K is 38.8 hours. Similarly, the average hours per week for the income group > $50K is 45.47 hours.

Alternatively, we can write a generic reusable function for calculating the **mean** of any numerical column group by the categorical column as follows:

```
def get_groupby_stats(categorical, numerical):
    groupby_df = df[[categorical, numerical]].groupby(categorical).
        mean().dropna()
    print(groupby_df.head)
```

If we want to get aggregations of multiple columns for each target income group, then we can calculate aggregations as follows:

```
columns_to_show = ["age", "hours.per.week"]
df.groupby(["income"])[columns_to_show].agg(['mean', 'std', 'max', 'min'])
```

We get the following results:

income	age mean	std	max	min	hours.per.week mean	std	max	min
<=50K	36.783738	14.020088	90	17	38.840210	12.318995	99	1
>50K	44.249841	10.519028	90	19	45.473026	11.012971	99	1

Figure 1.13 – Aggregations for multiple columns

As shown in the results, we have calculated the summary statistics for age and hours per week for each income group.

We learned how to calculate the aggregate values of features for the target group using reusable functions. This aggregate value gives us a correlation of those features for the target label value.

Creating visualizations using Seaborn for univariate and bivariate analysis

In this section, we are going to explore each variable separately. We are going to summarize the data for each feature and analyze the pattern present in it.

Univariate analysis is an analysis using individual features. We will also perform a bivariate analysis later in this section.

Univariate analysis

Now, let us do a univariate analysis for the age, education, work class, hours per week, and occupation features.

First, let's get the counts of unique values for each column using the following code snippet:

```
df.nunique()
```

```
df.nunique() |
✓  0.4s

age                    73
workclass               9
fnlwgt              21648
education              16
marital.status          7
occupation             15
relationship            6
sex                     2
capital.gain          119
capital.loss           92
hours.per.week         94
native.country         42
income                  2
dtype: int64
```

Figure 1.14 – Unique values for each column

As shown in the results, there are 73 unique values for `age`, 9 unique values for `workclass`, 16 unique values for `education`, 15 unique values for `occupation`, and so on.

Now, let us see the unique values count for `age` in the DataFrame:

```
df["age"].value_counts()
```

The result is as follows:

36	898
31	888
34	886
23	877
35	876
	...
83	6
88	3
85	3
86	1
87	1

```
Name: age, Length: 73, dtype: int64
```

Figure 1.15 – Value counts for age

We can see in the results that there are 898 observations (rows) with the age of 36. Similarly, there are 6 observations with the age of 83.

Histogram of age

Histograms are used to visualize the distribution of continuous data. Continuous data is data that can take on any value within a range (e.g., age, height, weight, temperature, etc.).

Let us plot a histogram using Seaborn to see the distribution of age in the dataset:

```
#univariate analysis
sns.histplot(data=df['age'],kde=True)
```

We get the following results:

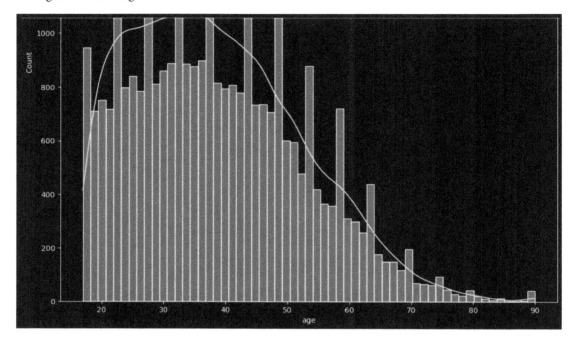

Figure 1.16 – The histogram of age

As we can see in the age histogram, there are many people in the age range of 23 to 45 in the given observations in the dataset.

Bar plot of education

Now, let us check the distribution of education in the given dataset:

```
df['education'].value_counts()
Let us plot the bar chart for education.
colors = ["white","red", "green", "blue", "orange", "yellow", "purple"]
df.education.value_counts().plot.bar(color=colors,legend=True)
```

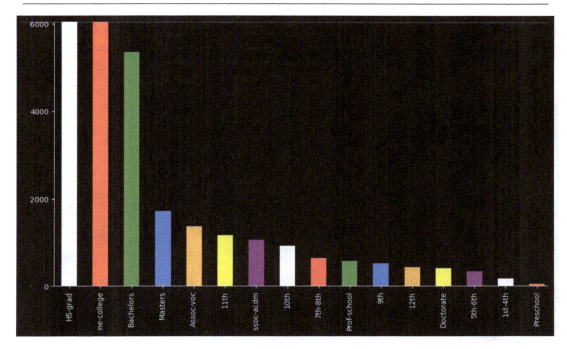

Figure 1.17 – The bar chart of education

As we see, the HS.grad count is higher than that for the Bachelors degree holders. Similarly, the Masters degree holders count is lower than the Bachelors degree holders count.

Bar chart of workclass

Now, let's see the distribution of workclass in the dataset:

```
df['workclass'].value_counts()
```

Let's plot the bar chart to visualize the distribution of different values of `workclass`:

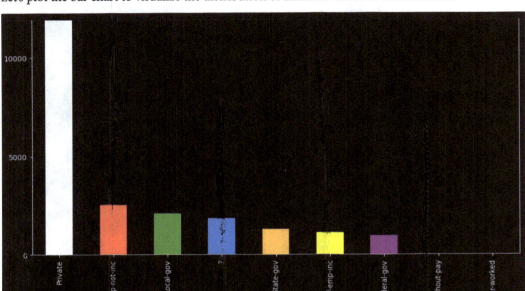

Figure 1.18 – Bar chart of workclass

As shown in the `workclass` bar chart, there are more private employees than other kinds.

Bar chart of income

Let's see the unique value for the `income` target variable and see the distribution of `income`:

```
df['income'].value_counts()
```

The result is as follows:

```
<=50K      24720
>50K        7841
Name: income, dtype: int64
```

Figure 1.19 – Distribution of income

As shown in the results, there are 24,720 observations with an income greater than $50K and 7,841 observations with an income of less than $50K. In the real world, more people have an income greater than $50K and a small portion of people have less than $50K income, assuming the income is in US dollars and for 1 year. As this ratio closely reflects the real-world scenario, we do not need to balance the minority class dataset using synthetic data.

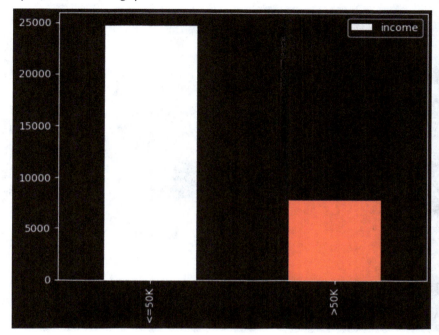

Figure 1.20 – Bar chart of income

In this section, we have seen the size of the data, column names, and data types, and the first and last five rows of the dataset. We also dropped some unnecessary columns. We performed univariate analysis to see the unique value counts and plotted the bar charts and histograms to understand the distribution of values for important columns.

Bivariate analysis

Let's do a bivariate analysis of age and income to find the relationship between them. Bivariate analysis is the analysis of two variables to find the relationship between them. We will plot a histogram using the Python Seaborn library to visualize the relationship between age and income:

```
#Bivariate analysis of age and income
sns.histplot(data=df,kde=True,x='age',hue='income')
```

The plot is as follows:

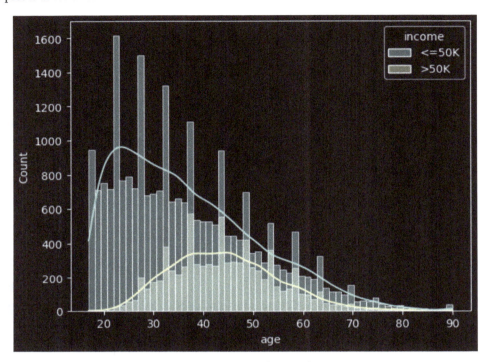

Figure 1.21 – Histogram of age with income

From the preceding histogram, we can see that income is greater than $50K for the age group between 30 and 60. Similarly, for the age group less than 30, income is less than $50K.

Now let's plot the histogram to do a bivariate analysis of education and income:

```
#Bivariate Analysis of  education and Income
sns.histplot(data=df,y='education', hue='income',multiple="dodge");
```

Here is the plot:

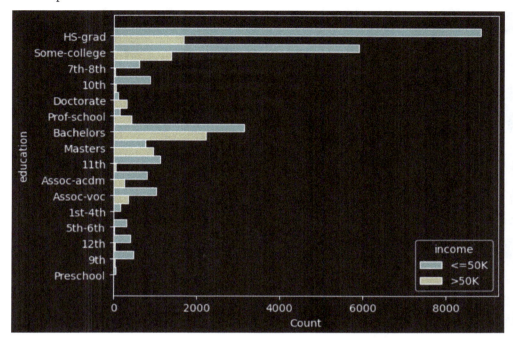

Figure 1.22 – Histogram of education with income

From the preceding histogram, we can see that income is greater than $50K for the majority of the Masters education adults. On the other hand, income is less than $50K for the majority of HS-grad adults.

Now, let's plot the histogram to do a bivariate analysis of workclass and income:

```
#Bivariate Analysis of work class and Income
sns.histplot(data=df,y='workclass', hue='income',multiple="dodge");
```

We get the following plot:

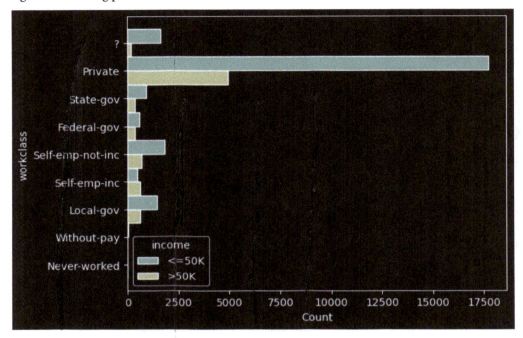

Figure 1.23 – Histogram of workclass and income

From the preceding histogram, we can see that income is greater than $50K for `Self-emp-inc` adults. On the other hand, income is less than $50K for the majority of `Private` and `Self-emp-not-inc` employees.

Now let's plot the histogram to do a bivariate analysis of `sex` and `income`:

```
#Bivariate Analysis of  Sex and Income
sns.histplot(data=df,y='sex', hue='income',multiple="dodge");
```

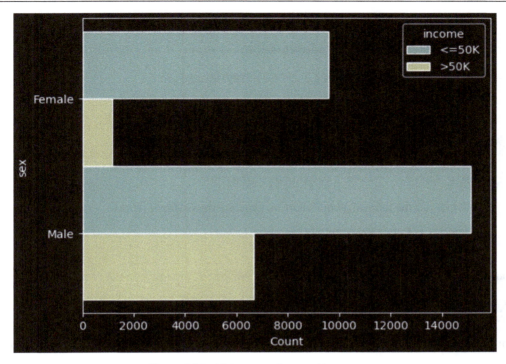

Figure 1.24 – Histogram of sex and income

From the preceding histogram, we can see that income is more than $50K for male adults and less than $50K for most female employees.

In this section, we have learned how to analyze data using Seaborn visualization libraries.

Alternatively, we can explore data using the ydata-profiling library with a few lines of code.

Profiling data using the ydata-profiling library

In this section, let us explore the dataset and generate a profiling report with various statistics using the ydata-profiling library (https://docs.profiling.ydata.ai/4.5/).

The ydata-profiling library is a Python library for easy EDA, profiling, and report generation.

Let us see how to use ydata-profiling for fast and efficient EDA:

1. Install the ydata-profiling library using pip as follows:

    ```
    pip install ydata-profiling
    ```

2. First, let us import the Pandas profiling library as follows:

    ```
    from ydata_profiling import ProfileReport
    ```

    Then, we can use Pandas profiling to generate reports.

3. Now, we will read the *Income* dataset into the Pandas DataFrame:

    ```
    df=pd.read_csv('adult.csv',na_values=-999)
    ```

4. Let us run the `upgrade` command to make sure we have the latest profiling library:

    ```
    %pip install ydata-profiling --upgrade
    ```

5. Now let us run the following commands to generate the profiling report:

    ```
    report = ProfileReport(df)
    report
    ```

We can also generate the report using the `profile_report ()` function on the Pandas DataFrame.

After running the preceding cell, all the data loaded in `df` will be analyzed and the report will be generated. The time taken to generate the report depends on the size of the dataset.

The output of the preceding cell is a report with sections. Let us understand the report that is generated.

The generated profiling report contains the following sections:

- **Overview**
- **Variables**
- **Interactions**
- **Correlations**
- **Missing values**
- **Sample**
- **Duplicate rows**

Under the **Overview** section in the report, there are three tabs:

- **Overview**
- **Alerts**
- **Reproduction**

As shown in the following figure, the **Overview** tab shows statistical information about the dataset – that is, the number of columns (number of variables) in the dataset; the number of rows (number of observations), duplicate rows, and missing cells; the percentage of duplicate rows and missing cells; and the number of Numeric and Categorical variables:

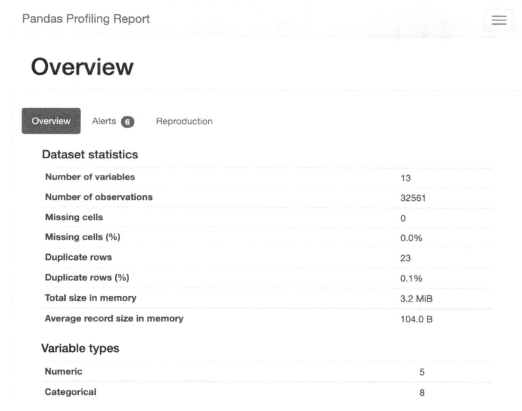

Figure 1.25 – Statistics of the dataset

The **Alerts** tab under **Overview** shows all the variables that are highly correlated with each other and the number of cells that have zero values, as follows:

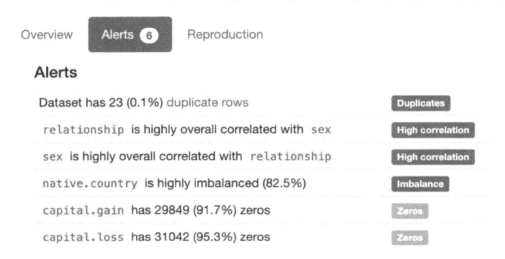

Overview

Overview   Alerts 6   Reproduction

Alerts

Dataset has 23 (0.1%) duplicate rows   `Duplicates`

`relationship` is highly overall correlated with `sex`   `High correlation`

`sex` is highly overall correlated with `relationship`   `High correlation`

`native.country` is highly imbalanced (82.5%)   `Imbalance`

`capital.gain` has 29849 (91.7%) zeros   `Zeros`

`capital.loss` has 31042 (95.3%) zeros   `Zeros`

Figure 1.26 – Alerts

The **Reproduction** tab under **Overview** shows the duration it took for the analysis to generate this report, as follows:

Overview

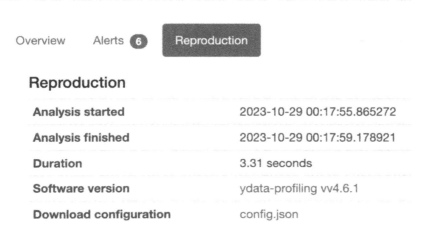

Figure 1.27 – Reproduction

Variables section

Let us walk through the **Variables** section in the report.

Under the **Variables** section, we can select any variable in the dataset under the dropdown and see the statistical information about the dataset, such as the number of unique values for that variable, missing values for that variable, the size of that variable, and so on.

In the following figure, we selected the `age` variable in the dropdown and can see the statistics about that variable:

Pandas Profiling Report

Variables

Select Columns ⌄

age
Real number (ℝ)

Distinct	73
Distinct (%)	0.2%
Missing	0
Missing (%)	0.0%
Infinite	0
Infinite (%)	0.0%
Mean	38.581647
Minimum	17
Maximum	90
Zeros	0
Zeros (%)	0.0%

Figure 1.28 – Variables

Interactions section

As shown in the following figure, this report also contains the **Interactions** plot to show how one variable relates to another variable:

Interactions

age   fnlwgt   capital.gain   capital.loss   hours.per.week

hours.per.week   age   fnlwgt   capital.gain   capital.loss

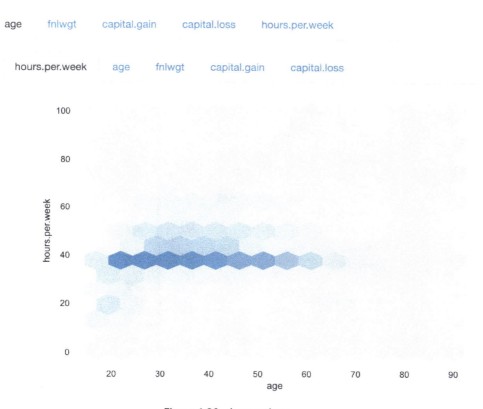

Figure 1.29 – Interactions

Correlations

Now, let's see the **Correlations** section in the report; we can see the correlation between various variables in **Heatmap**. Also, we can see various correlation coefficients in the **Table** form.

Correlations

Auto

Heatmap   Table

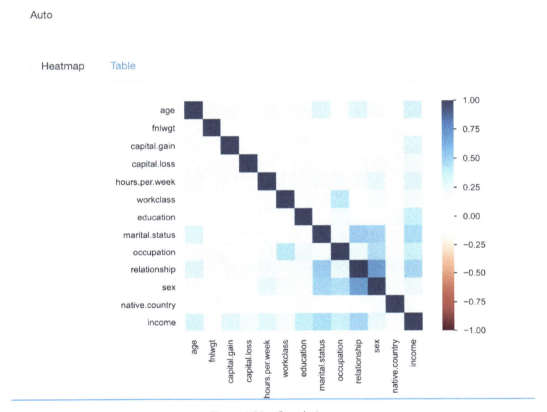

Figure 1.30 – Correlations

Heatmaps use color intensity to represent values. The colors typically range from cool to warm hues, with cool colors (e.g., blue or green) indicating low values and warm colors (e.g., red or orange) indicating high values. Rows and columns of the matrix are represented on both the x axis and y axis of the heatmap. Each cell at the intersection of a row and column represents a specific value in the data.

The color intensity of each cell corresponds to the magnitude of the value it represents. Darker colors indicate higher values, while lighter colors represent lower values.

As we can see in the preceding figure, the intersection cell between income and hours per week shows a high-intensity blue color, which indicates there is a high correlation between income and hours per week. Similarly, the intersection cell between income and capital gain shows a high-intensity blue color, indicating a high correlation between those two features.

Missing values

This section of the report shows the counts of total values present within the data and provides a good understanding of whether there are any missing values.

Under **Missing values**, we can see two tabs:

- The **Count** plot
- The **Matrix** plot

Count plot

In *Figure 1.31*, the shows that all variables have a count of 32,561, which is the count of rows (observations) in the dataset. That indicates that there are no missing values in the dataset.

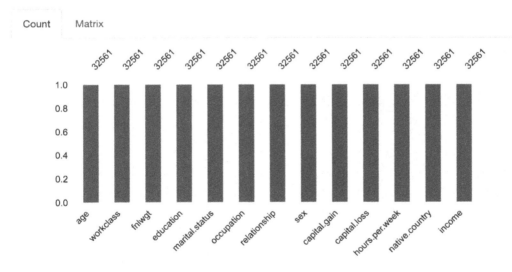

Figure 1.31 – Missing values count

Matrix plot

The following **Matrix** plot indicates where the missing values are (if there are any missing values in the dataset):

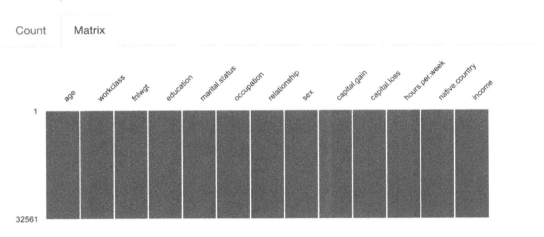

Nullity matrix is a data-dense display which lets you quickly visually pick out patterns in data completion.

Figure 1.32 – Missing values matrix

Sample data

This section shows the sample data for the first 10 rows and the last 10 rows in the dataset.

Sample

First rows   Last rows

	age	workclass	fnlwgt	education	marital.status	occupation	relationship	sex	capital.gain	capital.l
0	90	?	77053	HS-grad	Widowed	?	Not-in-family	Female	0	4356
1	82	Private	132870	HS-grad	Widowed	Exec-managerial	Not-in-family	Female	0	4356
2	66	?	186061	Some-college	Widowed	?	Unmarried	Female	0	4356
3	54	Private	140359	7th-8th	Divorced	Machine-op-inspct	Unmarried	Female	0	3900
4	41	Private	264663	Some-college	Separated	Prof-specialty	Own-child	Female	0	3900
5	34	Private	216864	HS-grad	Divorced	Other-service	Unmarried	Female	0	3770
6	38	Private	150601	10th	Separated	Adm-clerical	Unmarried	Male	0	3770
7	74	State-gov	88638	Doctorate	Never-married	Prof-specialty	Other-relative	Female	0	3683
8	68	Federal-gov	422013	HS-grad	Divorced	Prof-specialty	Not-in-family	Female	0	3683
9	41	Private	70037	Some-college	Never-married	Craft-repair	Unmarried	Male	0	3004

Figure 1.33 – Sample data

This section shows the most frequently occurring rows and the number of duplicates in the dataset.

Duplicate rows

Most frequently occurring

	age	workclass	fnlwgt	education	occupation	relationship	sex	native.country	income	# duplicates
12	19	Private	201743	Some-college	Other-service	Own-child	Female	United-States	<=50K	3
34	25	Private	195994	1st-4th	Priv-house-serv	Not-in-family	Female	Guatemala	<=50K	3
0	17	Private	183066	10th	Other-service	Own-child	Female	United-States	<=50K	2
1	17	Private	198146	11th	Sales	Own-child	Female	United-States	<=50K	2
2	18	?	137363	Some-college	?	Own-child	Female	United-States	<=50K	2
3	18	Private	194561	Some-college	Other-service	Own-child	Male	United-States	<=50K	2
4	19	?	46400	Some-college	?	Not-in-family	Female	United-States	<=50K	2
5	19	?	220517	Some-college	?	Own-child	Female	United-States	<=50K	2
6	19	Private	97261	HS-grad	Farming-fishing	Not-in-family	Male	United-States	<=50K	2
7	19	Private	138153	Some-college	Adm-clerical	Own-child	Female	United-States	<=50K	2

Figure 1.34 – Duplicate rows

We have seen how to analyze the data using Pandas and then how to visualize the data by plotting various plots such as bar charts and histograms using sns, seaborn, and pandas-ydata-profiling. Next, let us see how to perform data analysis using OpenAI LLM and the LangChain Pandas Dataframe agent by asking questions with natural language.

Unlocking insights from data with OpenAI and LangChain

Artificial intelligence is transforming how people analyze and interpret data. Exciting **generative AI** systems allow anyone to have natural conversations with their data, even if they have no coding or data science expertise. This democratization of data promises to uncover insights and patterns that may have previously remained hidden.

One pioneering system in this space is **LangChain**'s **Pandas DataFrame agent**, which leverages the power of **large language models** (**LLMs**) such as **Azure OpenAI**'s **GPT-4**. LLMs are AI systems trained on massive text datasets, allowing them to generate human-like text. LangChain provides a framework to connect LLMs with external data sources.

By simply describing in plain English what you want to know about your data stored in a Pandas DataFrame, this agent can automatically respond in natural language.

The user experience feels like magic. You upload a CSV dataset and ask a question by typing or speaking. For example, *"What were the top 3 best-selling products last year?"* The agent interprets your intent and writes and runs Pandas and Python code to load the data, analyze it, and formulate a response… all within seconds. The barrier between human language and data analysis dissolves.

Under the hood, the LLM generates Python code based on your question, which gets passed to the LangChain agent for execution. The agent handles running the code against your DataFrame, capturing any output or errors, and iterating if necessary to refine the analysis until an accurate human-readable answer is reached.

By collaborating, the agent and LLM remove the need to worry about syntax, APIs, parameters, or debugging data analysis code. The system understands what you want to know and makes it happen automatically through the magic of generative AI.

This natural language interface to data analysis opens game-changing potential. Subject-matter experts without programming skills can independently extract insights from data in their field. Data-driven decisions can happen faster. Exploratory analysis and ideation are simpler. The future where analytics is available to all AI assistants has arrived.

Let's see how the agent works behind the scenes to send a response.

When a user sends a query to the LangChain `create_pandas_dataframe_agent` agent and LLM, the following steps are performed behind the scenes:

1. The user's query is received by the LangChain agent.
2. The agent interprets the user's query and analyzes its intention.
3. The agent then generates the necessary commands to perform the first step of the analysis. For example, it could generate an SQL query that is sent to the tool that the agent knows will execute SQL queries.
4. The agent analyzes the response it receives from the tool and determines whether it is what the user wants. If it is, the agent returns the answer; if not, the agent analyzes what the next step should be and iterates again.
5. The agent keeps generating commands for the tools it can control until it obtains the response the user is looking for. It is even capable of interpreting execution errors that occur and generating the corrected command. The agent iterates until it satisfies the user's question or reaches the limit we have set.

We can represent this with the following diagram:

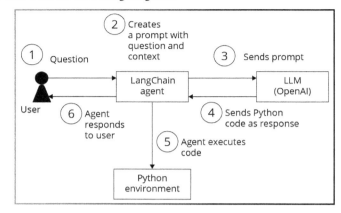

Figure 1.35 – LangChain Pandas agent flow for Data analysis

Let's see how to perform data analysis and find insights about the income dataset using the LangChain create_pandas_dataframe_agent agent and LLM.

The key steps are importing the necessary LangChain modules, loading data into a DataFrame, instantiating an LLM, and creating the DataFrame agent by passing the required objects. The agent can now analyze the data through natural language queries.

First, let's install the required libraries. To install the LangChain library, open your Python notebook and type the following:

```
%pip install langchain
%pip install langchain_experimental
```

This installs the langchain and langchain_experimental packages so you can import the necessary modules.

Let's import AzureChatOpenAI, the Pandas DataFrame agent, and other required libraries:

```
from langchain.chat_models import AzureChatOpenAI
from langchain_experimental.agents import create_pandas_dataframe_
agent
import os
import pandas as pd
import numpy as np
import seaborn as sns
import matplotlib.pyplot as plt
import openai
```

Let's configure the OpenAI endpoint and keys. Your OpenAI endpoint and key values are available in the Azure OpenAI portal:

```
openai.api_type = "azure"
openai.api_base = "your_endpoint"
openai.api_version = "2023-09-15-preview"
openai.api_key = "your_key"


# We are assuming that you have all model deployments on the same
Azure OpenAI service resource above.  If not, you can change these
settings below to point to different resources.
gpt4_endpoint = openai.api_base # Your endpoint will look something
like this: https://YOUR_AOAI_RESOURCE_NAME.openai.azure.com/
gpt4_api_key = openai.api_key # Your key will look something like
this: 00000000000000000000000000000000
gpt4_deployment_name="your model deployment name"
```

Let's load CSV data into Pandas DataFrame.

The `adult.csv` dataset is the dataset that we want to analyze and we have placed this CSV file in the same folder where we are running this Python code:

```
df = pd.read_csv("adult.csv")
```

Let's instantiate the GPT-4 LLM.

Assuming, you have deployed the GPT-4 model in Azure OpenAI Studio as per the *Technical requirements* section, here, we are passing the `gpt4` endpoint, key, and deployment name to create the instance of GPT-4 as follows:

```
gpt4 = AzureChatOpenAI(
    openai_api_base=gpt4_endpoint,
    openai_api_version="2023-03-15-preview",
    deployment_name=gpt4_deployment_name,
    openai_api_key=gpt4_api_key,
    openai_api_type = openai.api_type,
)
```

Setting the temperature to `0.0` has the model return the most accurate outputs.

Let's create a Pandas DataFrame agent. To create the Pandas DataFrame agent, we need to pass the `gpt4` model instance and the DataFrame:

```
agent = create_pandas_dataframe_agent(gpt4, df, verbose=True)
```

Pass the `gpt4` LLM instance and the DataFrame, and set `verbose` to `True` to see the output. Finally, let's ask a question and run the agent.

As illustrated in *Figure 1.36*, when we ask the following questions to the LangChain agent in the Python notebook, the question is passed to the LLM. The LLM generates Python code for this query and sends it back to the agent. The agent then executes this code in the Python environment with the CSV file, obtains a response, and the LLM converts that response to natural language before sending it back to the agent and the user:

```
agent("how many rows and how many columns are there?")
```

Output:

```
> Entering new AgentExecutor chain...
Thought: To find the number of rows and columns in the dataframe, I can use the shape attribute of the dataframe.

Action: python_repl_ast

Action Input: df.shape

Observation: (32561, 15)
Thought:The dataframe has 32561 rows and 15 columns.
Final Answer: There are 32561 rows and 15 columns in the dataframe.

> Finished chain.

{'input': 'how many rows and how many columns are there?',
 'output': 'There are 32561 rows and 15 columns in the dataframe.'}
```

Figure 1.36 – Agent response for row and column count

We try the next question:

```
agent("sample first 5 records and display?")
```

Here's the output:

```
> Entering new AgentExecutor chain...
Thought: I need to use the `head()` function to sample the first 5 records of the dataframe.

Action: python_repl_ast

Action Input: df.head(5)

Observation:   age workclass fnlwgt   education education.num marital.status \
0 90      ?  77053      HS-grad          9       Widowed
1 82  Private 132870     HS-grad          9       Widowed
2 66      ? 186061  Some-college         10        Widowed
3 54  Private 140359     7th-8th          4       Divorced
4 41  Private 264663 Some-college         10      Separated

        occupation  relationship  race   sex capital.gain \
0             ? Not-in-family White Female          0
1  Exec-managerial Not-in-family White Female          0
2             ?  Unmarried Black Female          0
3 Machine-op-inspct   Unmarried White Female          0
4    Prof-specialty   Own-child White Female        0

   capital.loss hours.per.week native.country income
0       4356         40 United-States  <=50K

4       3900         40 United-States  <=50K
Thought:I can see the first 5 records of the dataframe.
Final Answer: The first 5 records of the dataframe are displayed above.

> Finished chain.

{'input': 'sample first 5 records and display?',
 'output': 'The first 5 records of the dataframe are displayed above.'}
```

Figure 1.37 – agent response for first five records

This way, the LangChain Pandas DataFrame agent facilitates interaction with the DataFrame by interpreting natural language queries, generating corresponding Python code, and presenting the results in a human-readable format.

You can try these questions and see the responses from the agent:

- query = "calculate the average age of the people for each income group ?"
- query ="provide summary statistics for this dataset"

- query = "provide count of unique values for each column"
- query = "draw the histogram of the age"

Next, let's try the following query to plot the bar chart:

```
query = "draw the bar chart  for the column education"
results = agent(query)
```

The Langchain agent responded with a bar chart that shows the counts for different education levels, as follows.

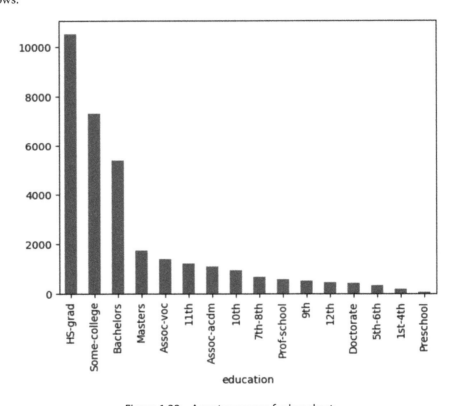

Figure 1.38 – Agent response for bar chart

The plot of the following query shows a comparison of income for different education levels – master's and HS-GRAD. And we can see the income is less than \$5,000 for education.num 8 to 10 when compared to higher education:

```
query = "Compare the income of those have Masters with those have HS-
grad using KDE plot"
results = agent(query)
```

Here's the output:

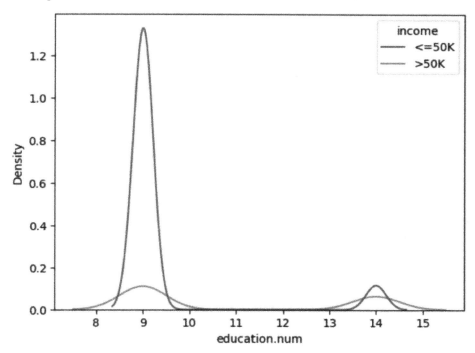

Figure 1.39 – Agent response for comparison of income

Next, let's try the following query to find any outliers in the data:

```
query = "Are there  any outliers in terms of age. Find out using Box
plot."
results = agent(query)
```

This plot shows outliers in age greater than 80 years.

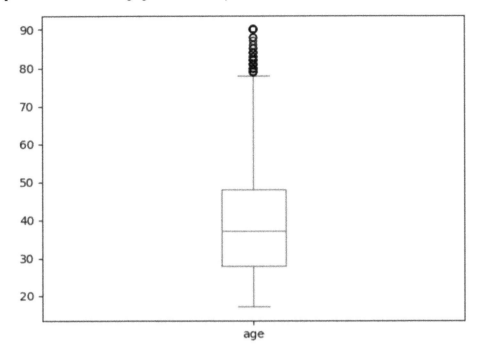

Figure 1.40 – Agent response for outliers

We have seen how to perform data analysis and find insights about the income dataset using natural language with the power of LangChain and OpenAI LLMs.

Summary

In this chapter, we have learned how to use Pandas and matplotlib to analyze a dataset and understand the data and correlations between various features. This understanding of data and patterns in the data is required to build the rules for labeling raw data before using it for training ML models and fine-tuning LLMs.

We also went through various examples for aggregating columns and categorical values using groupby and mean. Then, we created reusable functions so that those functions can be reused simply by calling and passing column names to get aggregates of one or more columns.

Finally, we saw a fast and easy exploration of data using the ydata-profiling library with simple one-line Python code. Using this library, we need not remember many Pandas functions. We can simply call one line of code to perform a detailed analysis of data. We can create detailed reports of statistics for each variable with missing values, correlations, interactions, and duplicate rows.

Once we get a good sense of our data using EDA, we will be able to build the rules for creating labels for the dataset.

In the next chapter, we will see how to build these rules using Python libraries such as `snorkel` and `compose` to label an unlabeled dataset. We will also explore other methods, such as pseudo-labeling and K-means clustering, for data labeling.

2

Labeling Data for Classification

In this chapter, we are going to learn how to label tabular data by applying business rules programmatically with Python libraries. In real-world use cases , not all of our data will have labels. But we need to prepare labeled data for training the **machine learning models** and **fine-tuning** the **foundation models**. The manual labeling of large sets of data or documents is cumbersome and expensive. In case of manual labeling, individual labels are created one by one. Also, occasionally, sharing private data with a crowd-sourcing team outside the organization is not secure.

So, programmatically labeling data is required to automate data labeling and quickly label a large-scale dataset. In case of programmatic labeling, there are mainly three approaches. In the first approach, users create **labeling functions** and apply to vast amounts of unlabeled data to auto label large training datasets. In the second approach, users apply **semi-supervised learning** to create **Pseudo-Labels**. **K-means clustering** is another way to group similar dataset and label those clusters. We will deep dive into all these three methods in this chapter and label the example tabular dataset. We will also discover how to utilize **large language models** (**LLMs**) for predicting labels in tabular data classification tasks.

By the end of this chapter, you will be able to create labeling functions and a label model, and finally, you will be able to predict labels using that label model.

In this chapter, we are going to cover the following main topics:

- Predicting labels with LLMs for tabular data

- Labeling data using a rule-based generative model

- Labeling data using semi-supervised learning

- Labeling data using K-means clustering

Technical requirements

We need to install the Snorkel library using the following command:

```
%pip install snorkel
```

You can download the dataset and Python notebook from the following link:

`https://github.com/PacktPublishing/Data-Labeling-in-Machine-Learning-with-Python/code/Ch02`

OpenAI setup requirements are same as mentioned in *Chapter 1*.

Predicting labels with LLMs for tabular data

We will explore the process of predicting labels for tabular data classification tasks using **large language models** (**LLMs**) and few-shot learning.

In the case of few-shot learning, we provide a few training data examples in the form of text along with a prompt for the model. The model adapts to the context and responds to new questions from the user.

First, let's examine how to predict labels using LLMs for tabular data.

For tabular data, the initial step involves converting the data into serialized text data using LangChain's templates. LangChain templates allow converting rows of data into fluent sentences or paragraphs by mapping columns to text snippets with variables that are filled based on cell values. Once we have the text data, we can utilize it as few-shot examples, comprising pairs of questions along with their corresponding labels (answers). Subsequently, we will send this few-shot data to the model.

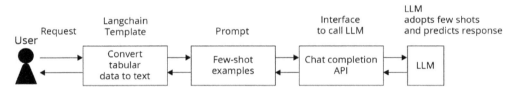

Figure 2.1 – LLM Few-shot example for predicting labels

Now we will use the LangChain template to translate the tabular data to natural language text.

Patient ID	Age	Blood pressure	Diabetes	Death_event
1	70	high	yes	yes
2	45	high	no	no
3	50	normal	yes	?

Table 2.1 – Few-shot example data in tabular format

The following is the text after converting the cell values to text using templates:

```
User message :"The age is 70 and blood pressure is high and diabetes
is yes.
Does this patient had death event? "
System: Yes
```

Similarly, we can convert the second row to text and send it as a few-shot example with a prompt to the LLM using `ChatCompletion` API.

These few shot examples are sent along with a prompt to the LLM and then the LLM responds with the predicted label, `Yes` or `No`, for new text:

```
User message :"The age is 50 and blood pressure is normal and diabetes
is yes.
Does this patient had death event? "
Then system responds "yes"
```

We have seen how to leverage few-shot learning for predicting labels for tabular data.

The serialized data and the few-shot learning examples are used to provide context to the LLM model so that it can understand the meaning of the data and learn how to classify new tabular datasets. The LLM model generates a response based on the input.

Now, let's explore a second example of predicting labels using few-shot learning and LLMs for text data.

As mentioned earlier, in the case of few-shot learning, a small set of training data examples is provided along with the prompt to the LLM.

The following code illustrates few-shot learning for predicting labels using prompts and LLMs. In this example, a system role is defined to guide the model in understanding the context and desired sentiment labels.

The user provides a new message expressing sentiments about a new house. The code then calls the `ChatCompletion` API to generate a response using the specified GPT model deployment. The system and user messages are structured to guide the model's understanding of the sentiment. The sentiment analysis output is obtained from the API response and printed.

This approach enables the model to learn from examples provided in the system role and user messages, allowing it to predict sentiment labels for the user's input:

```
# Set the system role and user message variables
system_role = """Provide text sentiment in given text:
: I like Arkansas state. Because it is natural state and beautiful!!!
positive
: I hate winters. It's freezing and bad weather.
negative"""
```

```
user_message = f"""
I love this new house.It's amazing!!!"""
```

Let's call the ChatCompletion API to send a response:

```
# Send a completion call to generate the sentiment analysis
response = openai.ChatCompletion.create(
  engine = "your gpt model deployment name",
  messages = [
  "role": "system", "content": system_role,
  "role": "user", "content": user_message,
 ]
 )


# Print the sentiment analysis output
print(response['choices'][0]['message']['content'])
```

When you check the output, you will see Positive in the response. We have seen how to send text messages as few-shot examples, along with a prompt, to the LLM using ChatCompletion API and how the LLM responds with the sentiment based on user input messages. Next, we'll discuss labeling data using Snorkel library.

Data labeling using Snorkel

In this section, we are going to learn what Snorkel is and how we can use it to label data in Python programmatically.

Labeling data is an important step of a data science project and critical for training models to solve specific business problems.

In many real-world cases, training data does not have labels, or very little data with labels is available. For example, in a housing dataset, in some neighborhoods, historical housing prices may not be available for most of the houses. Another example, in the case of finance, is all transactions may not have an associated invoice number. Historical data with labels is critical for businesses to train models and automate their business processes using **machine learning** (**ML**) and artificial intelligence. However, this requires either outsourcing the data labeling to expensive domain experts or the business waiting for a long time to get new training data with labels.

This is where Snorkel comes into the picture to help us programmatically build labels and manage the training data at a relatively lower cost than hiring domain experts. It is also faster than manual labeling. In some cases, data may be sensitive due to it including personal information such as date of birth and social security number. In such cases, the organization cannot share data outside of the organization with a third party. So, organizations prefer to label the data programmatically with a team of in-house developers to protect data privacy and comply with government and consumer data regulations.

What is Snorkel?

Snorkel is a Python open source library (https://www.snorkel.org/) that is used to create labels based on heuristics for tabular data. Using this library saves the time and cost of manual labeling. Snorkel uses a list of defined rules to label the data programmatically. With Snorkel, business knowledge is applied to generate "weak" labels for the dataset. This is also called a weak supervision model.

The weak generative model created by Snorkel generates noisy labels. These noisy labels are used to train a classifier that generalizes the model.

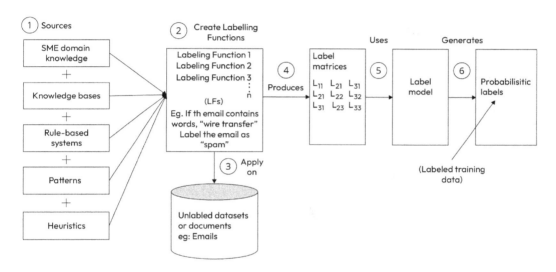

Figure 2.2 – Programmatic data labeling (preparing training data)

Here is an overview of the Snorkel system:

1. Domain specific rules are extracted from various sources such as **subject matter experts (SMEs)**, knowledge bases, legacy rule based systems, patterns and heuristics using **exploratory data analysis (EDA)**.

2. Labeling functions are created based on the rules obtained from various sources. One labeling function is created for each business rule.

3. These labeling functions are applied to the unlabeled dataset to generate the label matrix.

4. Label matrix (`i*j`) consists of `i` rows and `j` columns where `i` is the number of observations in the dataset and `j` is the number of labeling functions. Each labeling function creates one label for each row in the dataset.

5. Then, Snorkel's label model is trained on this label matrix to create a generative model. This generative label model combines the outputs of the various **labeling functions** (**LFs**) and produces a single, noise-aware probabilistic training label set.

6. Finally, this probabilistic training label set is used to train a downstream discriminative ML model such as logistic regression.

Why is Snorkel popular?

Snorkel is used by several large companies, such as Google, Apple, Stanford Medicine, and Tide, and it has proven to solve business problems on a large scale. For example, as mentioned on the *snorkel. ai* website, Google used Snorkel to replace 100K+ hand-annotated labels in critical ML pipelines for text classification. Another example is, researchers at Stanford Medicine used Snorkel to label medical imaging and monitoring datasets, converting years of work of hand-labeling into a several-hour job using Snorkel. Apple built a solution called Overton that utilizes Snorkel's framework of weak supervision to overcome cost, privacy, and cold-start issues. A UK-based fintech company, Tide, used Snorkel to label matching invoices with transactions, which otherwise would have required investing in expensive subject matter experts to hand-label historical data. Excerpts of these case studies and more can be found at `https://snorkel.ai/case-studies`.

Snorkel creates weak labels using business rules and patterns in the absence of labeled data. Using Snorkel requires relatively less development effort compared to crowdsourcing manual labeling. The cost of development also comes down due to automation using Python programming instead of hiring expensive business domain experts.

The weak labels developed by Snorkel label model can be used to train a machine learning classifier for classification and information extraction tasks. In the following sections, we are going to see the step-by-step process of generating weak labels using Snorkel. For that, first, let's load some unlabeled data from a CSV file.

In the following example, we have a limited dataset related to adult income with labels.

In this adult income dataset, we have the `income` label and features such as age, working hours, education, and work class. The `income` label class is available only for a few observations. The majority of observations are unlabeled without any value for `income`. So, our goal is to generate the labels using the Snorkel Python library.

We will come up with business rules after analyzing the correlation between each individual feature of the `income` label class. Using those business rules, we will create one labeling function for each business rule with the Snorkel Python library. Then, we will generate labels for the unlabeled income dataset by applying those labeling functions.

Loading unlabeled data

We will first load the adult income dataset for predicting weak labels. Let us load the data using Pandas into a DataFrame:

```
# loading the data set
#df = pd.read_csv("<YourPath>/adult_income.csv", encoding='latin-1)'
```

Here, don't forget to replace <YourPath> with the path in your system. The target column name is income. Let us make sure the data is loaded correctly:

```
df.head()
```

Let us model the input and output:

```
x = df.iloc[:,:-1]
y = df["income"]
```

In this section, we have loaded the income dataset from a CSV file into a Pandas DataFrame.

Creating the labeling functions

Labeling functions implement the rules that are used to create the labeling model. Let us import the following method, which is required to implement the labeling functions:

```
from snorkel.labeling import labeling_function
```

We need to create at least four labeling functions to create an accurate labeling generative model. In order to create labeling functions, let's first define the labeling rules based on the available small dataset labels. If no data is available, subject matter expert knowledge is required to define the rules for labeling. Labeling functions use the following labeling rules for the classification of income range for the given adult income dataset.

Labeling rules

The labeling rules from our small-volume income dataset are as follows:

- **Age rule**: Based on exploratory bi-variate analysis of age and income, we come up with a heuristics rule that if the age range is between 28 and 58, then income is greater than $50K; else, it is less than $50K.

- **Education rule**: Based on a bi-variate analysis of education and income, we come up with a heuristic rule that if education is bachelor's or master's, then income is > $50K; otherwise, income is < $50K.

- **Working hours rule**: Based on a bi-variate analysis of working hours and income, we come up with the heuristic rule that if working hours are greater than 40, then income is greater than $50K; otherwise, it is less than $50K

- **Work class rule**: Based on a bi-variate analysis of work class and income, we come up with the heuristic rule that if the work class is `Self-emp-inc` or `Federal-gov`, then income is greater than $50K; otherwise, it is less than $50K.

Constants

Let us define various constants that are used in our labeling functions as follows.

- Each labeling function returns either one of the following labels as output:

  - `income_high` indicates income > $50K

  - `income_low` indicates income < $50K

- Let us assign the numerical values to the output labels as follows:

  - `income_high` = 1

  - `income_low` = 0

  - `Abstain` = -1

  `Abstain` indicates that income does not fall within any range for that observation data point:

Labeling functions

Now, let's create labeling functions using these labeling rules and constants. We'll discuss each function one by one as follows.

Age rule function

The age rule function is used to check whether the age of the person is greater than 28; if so, the income is greater than $50K.

We have defined our function with the help of the `@labeling_function()` decorator. This decorator, when applied to a Python function, returns a label. Let us apply this decorator to the `age` function to return the label based on age:

```
@labeling_function()
def age(record):
    if record['age'] < 28 and record['age'] > 58:
    return income_low
    elif record['age'] >28 and record['age']< 58:
```

```
        return income_high
    else:
        return ABSTAIN
```

Later, we will apply this age rule labeling function to the unlabeled income dataset using the Pandas LF applier, which returns a label accordingly for each observation in the dataset.

Education rule function

The education rule function is used to check whether the education of the person is bachelor's or master's; if so, the income is greater than $50K.

We have defined our labeling function for education with the help of the labeling function decorator as follows:

```
@labeling_function()
def education(record):
    if record['education'] == "Bachelors" or record['education'] ==
"Masters":
        return income_high
    else:
        return income_low
```

Later, we are going to apply this labeling function to our unlabeled income dataset using the Pandas LF applier, which returns the label accordingly for each observation in the dataset.

Hours per week rule function

The hours per week rule function is used to check whether the working hours per week of the person is greater than 40; if so, the income is greater than $50K.

We have defined our labeling function for education with the help of the labeling function decorator as follows:

```
@labeling_function()
def hours_per_week(record):
    if record['hours.per.week'] > 40 or record['hours.per.week'] < 60:
    return income_high
    else:
    return income_low
```

Later, we are going to apply this labeling function to our unlabeled income dataset using the Pandas LF applier, which returns the label accordingly for each observation in the dataset.

Work class rule function

The work class rule function is used to check whether the work class of the person is greater than self-employed or federal government; if so, the income is greater than $50K.

We have defined our labeling function for the work class with the help of the labeling function decorator as follows:

```
@labeling_function()
def work_class(record):
    if record['workclass'] == "Self-emp-inc" or record['workclass'] ==
"Federal-gov":
      return income_high
    else:
      return income_low
```

Creating a label model

Now, we are going to apply all the labeling functions that we created to the unlabeled income dataset using the Pandas LF applier:

```
lfs = [age,education,hours_per_week,work_class]
from snorkel.labeling import PandasLFApplier
applier = PandasLFApplier(lfs=lfs)
L_train = applier.apply(df=x)
```

Here is the output that we got after applying the label functions (lfs) to the input data (df):

```
L_train
✓  0.0s

array([[-1,  0,  1,  0],
       [-1,  0,  1,  0],
       [-1,  0,  1,  0],
       ...,
       [ 1,  0,  1,  0],
       [-1,  0,  1,  0],
       [-1,  0,  1,  0]])
```

Figure 2.3 – Label matrix

Here, L_train is the label matrix that is returned after applying the four label functions on the unlabeled dataset. For each labeling function, one label (-1, 1, or 0) will be returned. As we have created four labeling functions, four labels will be returned for each observation. The size of the label matrix will be [n*m], where n is the number of observations and m is the number of labeling functions, which is the same as the number of labels for each observation.

Next, we will use the label matrix (`L_train`) that was returned in the previous step:

```
From snorkel.labeling.model.label_model import LabelModel
label_model = LabelModel(verbose=False)
```

Train the label model using the `L_train` label matrix:

```
label_model.fit(L_train=L_train, n_epochs=1000, seed=100)
```

Now, let us predict the labels using the trained label model.

Predicting labels

`L_train` is passed to the label model to predict the labels, as follows:

```
X['Labels'] = label_model.predict(L=L_train)
```

We get the following result:

```
x['Labels'] = label_model.predict(L=L_train)


x['Labels']


0         0
1         0
2         0
3         1
4         1
         ..
32556     0
32557     0
32558     1
32559     0
32560     0
Name: Labels, Length: 32561, dtype: int64
```

Figure 2.4 – Probabilistic labels

As we have seen, we have generated a label matrix containing labels after applying label functions to a dataset. Then, we used that label matrix to train the label model, and then finally used that generative label model to predict the noise-aware probabilistic labels. Here, the label value 0 indicates income < $50K and the label value 1 indicates income > $50K. These values are defined using the `income_high` and `income_low` constants before implementing the labeling functions.

We can further use these noise-aware probabilistic labels training set to train the discriminative ML model and then predict accurate labels.

Labeling data using the Compose library

Compose is an open source Python library developed to generate the labels for supervised machine learning. Compose creates labels from historical data using LabelMaker.

Subject matter experts or end users write labeling functions for the outcome of interest. For example, if the outcome of interest is the amount spent by customers in the last five days, then the labeling function returns the amount spent by taking the last five days of transaction data as input. We will take a look at this example as follows.

Let us first install the composeml Python package. It is an open source Python library for prediction engineering:

```
pip install composeml
```

We will create the label for the total purchase spend amount in the next five days based on the customer's transactions data history.

For this, let us first import composeml:

```
import composeml as cp
```

Then, load the sample data:

```
from demo.next_purchase import load_sample
df = load_sample()
```

Next, to start using the Compose function, we need to define the labeling function:

```
def amount_spent(df):
total = df['amount'].sum()
return total
```

Next, we will build LabelMaker to run a search to automatically extract training examples from historical data. LabelMaker generates labels using labeling functions. Now, let us build LabelMaker using the labeling function:

```
label_maker = cp.LabelMaker(
target_dataframe_name="customer_id",
time_index="transaction_time",
labeling_function=amount_spent,
window_size="5d",
)
```

Now, let us search and extract the labels using label search:

```
labels = label_maker.search(
df.sort_values('transaction_time'),
num_examples_per_instance=-1,
gap=1,
verbose=True,
)
labels.head()
```

We can transform the labels by applying a threshold to binary labels as follows:

```
labels = labels.threshold(300)
labels.head()
```

Now, the labels DataFrame contains a label for the amount (`amount_spent`) forecast to be spent in the next five days. So, we have seen that Compose is used to generate labels for the transactions by defining labeling function and LabelMaker. This labeled data will be used for supervised learning for prediction problems. More documentation about *Compose* can be found at (`https://compose.alteryx.com/en/stable/index.html`).

Labeling data using semi-supervised learning

In this section, let us see how to generate labels using semi-supervised learning.

What is semi-supervised learning?

Semi-supervised learning falls in between supervised learning and unsupervised learning:

- In the case of supervised learning, all the training dataset is labeled
- In the case of unsupervised learning, all the training dataset is unlabeled
- In the case of semi-supervised learning, a very small set of data is labeled and the majority of the dataset is unlabeled

In this case, first we will generate the pseudo-labels using a small part of the labeled dataset with supervised learning:

1. In this first step, we use this training dataset to train the supervised model and generate the additional pseudo labeled dataset:

    Training dataset = small set of labeled dataset

2. In this second step, we will use the small set of labeled dataset along with the pseudo-labeled dataset generated in the first step:

    Training dataset = small set of labeled dataset + pseudo-labeled dataset

What is pseudo-labeling?

Pseudo-labeling is a **semi-supervised machine learning** technique that generates labels for unlabeled data by leveraging a model trained on a separate small set of labeled data using supervised learning.

For this demonstration, let's download the *heart failure dataset* from GitHub repo using the link in the *Technical requirements* section.

We know our demo dataset, heart failure dataset, is already labeled. But we are going to modify the dataset by splitting it into two parts. One will have labels and the other will be unlabeled. We generate pseudo-labels for unlabeled data from a labeled dataset. Then, finally, we will combine this pseudo-labeled dataset with the initial labeled dataset to train the final model.

Let's import the libraries as follows:

```
import pandas as pd
import numpy as np

from sklearn.model_selection import train_test_split
from sklearn.ensemble import RandomForestClassifier
```

Let's download the income dataset:

```
data = pd.read_csv("<your_path>/heart_failure_dataset.csv ",
encoding='latin-1')

  y = training.DEATH_EVENT #Output for each example
  x = training.drop('DEATH_EVENT', axis=1)  #Input
```

Let's split the data with and without labels in the 30:70 ratio. Here, we want 30% of the data to have labels and 70% of the data to be unlabeled to demonstrate a real-world scenario where we have less data with labels and more data without labels:

```
x_train,x_test,y_train,_ = train_test_split(x,y,test_size=.7)
x_train.shape,y_train.shape,x_test.shape
```

Now, let's fit the data to the model and create the model. Here, we will use the Random Forest classifier. Think of Random Forest as a group of clever friends in the world of computers. Each friend knows a little something about the data we give them and can make decisions. When we put all their ideas together, we get a smart tool that can help us understand and predict things. It's like having a team of experts to guide us through the jungle of data. In this chapter, we'll explore how this friendly Random Forest can assist us in making sense of data and making better decisions.

Random Forest is a versatile ML algorithm that can be used for both regression and classification tasks. The following subsection provides an explanation of both.

Random Forest classifier

In classification tasks, the Random Forest classifier is used to predict and assign a class or category to a given input based on a set of input features. It's particularly useful for tasks such as spam detection, image classification, and sentiment analysis. The algorithm works by constructing multiple decision trees during the training process. Each decision tree is like a "vote" on which class an input should be assigned to.

The final prediction is made by taking a majority vote among all the decision trees in the forest. This ensemble approach often results in robust and accurate classification:

```
pseudomodel =  RandomForestClassifier(n_estimators = 10, criterion =
'entropy', random_state = 0)
```

We are training the pseudo-model with 30% of the labeled training data:

```
pseudomodel.fit(x_train,y_train)
```

Let us calculate the accuracy score for data label model training:

```
pseudomodel.score(x_train,y_train)
0.95
```

Now, let us use this pseudo-model to predict the labels for the 70% unlabeled data with x_test:

```
y_new =  pseudomodel.predict(x_test)
y_new.shape
```

Let us concatenate both the datasets' features and labels, that is, the original labels and pseudo-labels:

```
# Take a subset of the test set with pseudo-labels and append it onto
# the training set
from sklearn.utils import shuffle
sampled_pseudo_data = pseudo_data.sample(n=150)
temp_train = pd.concat([x, y], axis=1)
augemented_train = pd.concat([sampled_pseudo_data, temp_train])
shuffle(augemented_train)
x = augemented_train.drop('DEATH_EVENT', axis=1)
y = augemented_train.DEATH_EVENT
x_train_final, x_test_final, y_train_final, y_test_final = train_test_
split(x, y, test_size=0.3, random_state=42)
```

Now, let us create a model for the entire dataset using RandomForestClassifier:

```
finalmodel =  RandomForestClassifier(n_estimators = 10, criterion =
'entropy', random_state = 0)
 #this model is with augmented data
```

```
finalmodel.fit(x_train_final,y_train_final)
finalmodel.score(x_train_final,y_train_final)
```

We get the following result:

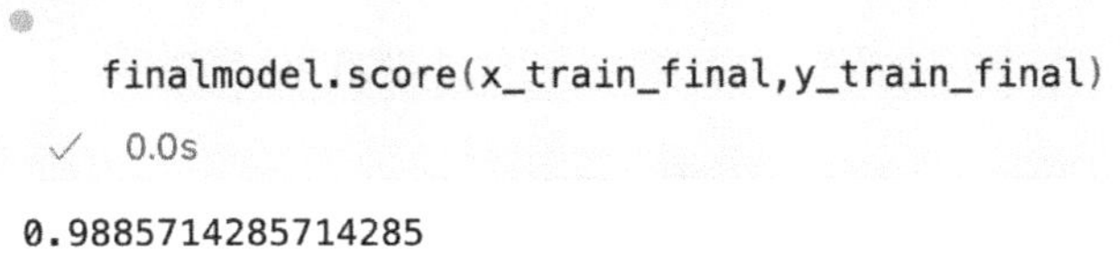

```
finalmodel.score(x_train_final,y_train_final)
✓  0.0s
```
0.9885714285714285

Figure 2.5 – final model

To summarize, we have imported the *heart failure dataset* and then changed it to split the dataset into labeled and unlabeled datasets. Then, we applied semi-supervised learning to generate pseudo-labels. After that, we combined the original and pseudo-labeled training datasets and again applied the Random Forest regressor to generate the final labels for the unseen dataset using the final model.

Labeling data using K-means clustering

In this section, we are going to learn what the K-means clustering algorithm is and how the K-means clustering algorithm is used to predict labels. Let us understand what unsupervised learning is.

What is unsupervised learning?

Unsupervised learning is a category of machine learning where the algorithm is tasked with discovering patterns, structures, or relationships within a dataset without explicit guidance or labeled outputs. In other words, the algorithm explores the inherent structure of the data on its own. The primary goal of unsupervised learning is often to uncover hidden patterns, group similar data points, or reduce the dimensionality of the data.

In the case of **unsupervised learning**, we have data with no target variable. We group observations based on similarity into different clusters. Once we have a limited number of clusters, we can register the labels for those clusters.

For example, in the case of customer segmentation, customers with a similar income range are grouped and formed into clusters, and then their spending power is associated with those clusters. Any new training data without labels can be measured for similarity to identify the cluster, and then the same label can be associated with all observations in the same cluster.

K-means clustering is a specific algorithm within the realm of unsupervised learning. It is a partitioning technique that divides a dataset into distinct, non-overlapping subsets or clusters. Now, let's dive deep into K-means clustering.

K-means clustering

Traversing the world of data is like finding your way through a maze. Imagine you have a bunch of colorful marbles and you want to group similar ones. K-means clustering is your helper in this quest. It's like a sorting magician that organizes your marbles into distinct groups, making it easier to understand them. K-means clustering is a cool trick that helps you make sense of your data by finding hidden patterns and grouping things that go together.

Let us download the *adult income* dataset, using the link in the *Technical requirements* section.

The selected features from this dataset will be used as input to the K-means algorithm, which will then partition the data into clusters based on the patterns in these selected features.

```
# Select features for clustering
  selected_features = ['hoursperweek', 'education-num']
```

selected_features is a list that contains the names of the features (columns) you want to use for clustering. In this case, the features selected are `hoursperweek` and `education-num`. These are likely columns from a dataset containing information about individuals, where `hoursperweek` represents the number of hours worked per week, and `education-num` represents the number of years of education.

When performing K-means clustering, it's common to choose relevant features that you believe might contribute to the formation of meaningful clusters. The choice of features depends on the nature of your data and the problem you're trying to solve. We will identify similar features and then group them into clusters using K-means clustering.

In the case of K-means clustering, the following sequence of steps needs to be followed:

1. First, identify the number of clusters randomly:

    ```
    n_clusters = random.randint(2,4)
    ```

    A random number of clusters (between 2 and 4) is chosen.

2. Initialize K-means with random centroids:

    ```
    kmeans = KMeans(n_clusters=n_clusters, init='random', random_
    state=0)
    kmeans.fit(X_scaled)
    ```

    The K-means algorithm is initialized with random centroids and fitted to the scaled data.

3. Perform K-means clustering and update centroids until convergence:

    ```
    while True:
        # Assign data points to clusters
        cluster_labels = kmeans.predict(X_scaled)
        # Calculate new centroids
    ```

```
new_centroids = np.array([X_scaled[cluster_labels ==
i].mean(axis=0) for i in range(n_clusters)])
```

The code calculates new centroids by computing the mean of the data points in each cluster:

```
# Check for convergence by comparing old and new centroids
if np.allclose(kmeans.cluster_centers_, new_centroids):
break
```

The loop checks for convergence by comparing the old centroids with the new centroids. If they are very close, indicating that the centroids have not changed significantly, the loop breaks, and the clustering process stops:

```
# Update centroids
kmeans.cluster_centers_ = new_centroids
# Update inertia
inertia = kmeans.inertia_
```

`kmeans.cluster_centers_` and `inertia` are updated within the loop, ensuring that the model parameters are adjusted in each iteration.

4. Calculate metrics (Dunn's Index). Inter-cluster and intra-cluster distances are calculated to compute Dunn's Index:

```
intercluster_distances = pairwise_distances(kmeans.cluster_
centers_)
```

Here, `pairwise_distances` from scikit-learn is used to calculate the distances between cluster centers (inter-cluster distances). The result is a matrix where the element at position (`i`, `j`) represents the distance between the `i`-th and `j`-th cluster centers.

```
intracluster_distances = np.array([np.max(pdist(X_
scaled[cluster_labels == i])) for i in range(n_clusters)])
```

For each cluster, `pdist` (pairwise distance) is used to calculate the distances between all pairs of data points within the cluster. `np.max` then finds the maximum distance within each cluster. This results in an array where each element represents the maximum intra-cluster distance for a specific cluster:

```
min_intercluster_distances = min(np.min(intercluster_
distances[~np.eye(n_clusters, dtype=bool)]), min_intercluster_
distances)
max_intracluster_distances = max(np.max(intracluster_distances),
max_intracluster_distances)
```

`min_intercluster_distances` is updated by finding the minimum inter-cluster distance, excluding diagonal elements (distances between a cluster and itself), and comparing it with the current minimum.

`max_intracluster_distances` is updated by finding the maximum intra-cluster distance across all clusters and comparing it with the current maximum.

Dunn's index is calculated by dividing the minimum inter-cluster distance by the maximum intra-cluster distance:

dunn_index = min_intercluster_distances / max_intracluster_distances

It is a measure of how well-separated clusters are relative to their internal cohesion:

```
# Print the results
print(f"Number of clusters: {n_clusters}")
print(f"Inertia: {inertia}")
print(f"Dunn's Index: {dunn_index}")
```

We get the following result:

```
Number of clusters: 2
Inertia: 64659.046440620616
Dunn's Index: 0.2663444503263014
```

Figure 2.6 – K-means clustering metrics

Let us understand the metrics Inertia and Dunn's index in the results.

Inertia

Inertia is nothing but the sum of the distance of all the points from the centroid.

If all the points are close to each other, that means they are similar and it is a good cluster. So, we aim for a small distance for all points from the centroid.

Dunn's index

If the clusters are far from each other, that means the different clusters are clearly separate groups of observations. So, we measure the distance between the centroids of each cluster, which is called the inter-cluster distance. A large inter-cluster distance is ideal for good clusters.

Now, let us print the cluster labels obtained in K-means clustering:

```
# Add the cluster labels as a new column to the original dataset
X['cluster_label'] = kmeans.labels_
# Print the dataset with cluster labels
X.head()
```

We get the following result:

education	education-num	marital-status	occupation	relationship	race	sex	capitalgain	capitalloss	hoursperweek	native-country	cluster_label
Bachelors	13.0	Never-married	Adm-clerical	Not-in-family	White	Male	1	0	2	United-States	2
Bachelors	13.0	Married-civ-spouse	Exec-managerial	Husband	White	Male	0	0	0	United-States	1
HS-grad	9.0	Divorced	Handlers-cleaners	Not-in-family	White	Male	0	0	2	United-States	0
11th	7.0	Married-civ-spouse	Handlers-cleaners	Husband	Black	Male	0	0	2	United-States	3
Bachelors	13.0	Married-civ-spouse	Prof-specialty	Wife	Black	Female	0	0	2	Cuba	2

Figure 2.7 – Cluster labels

We can use the cluster labels as a feature to predict the adult income using regression.

To summarize, we have seen what the K-means clustering algorithm is and how it is used to create clusters for *adult income* dataset. The selected features from this dataset will be used as input to the K-means algorithm, which will then partition the data into clusters based on the patterns in these selected features.

The complete code notebook is available in this book's GitHub repository.

Summary

In this chapter, we have seen the implementation of rules using Snorkel labeling functions for predicting the income range and labeling functions using the Compose library to predict the total amount spent by a customer during a given period. We have learned how semi-supervised learning can be used to generate pseudo-labels and data augmentation. We also learned how K-means clustering can be used to cluster the income features and then predict the income for each cluster based on business knowledge.

In the next chapter, we are going to learn how we can label data for regression using the Snorkel Python library, semi-supervised learning, and K-means clustering. Let us explore that in the next chapter.

3
Labeling Data for Regression

In this chapter, we will explore the process of labeling data for regression-based machine learning tasks, such as predicting housing prices, in situations where there is insufficient labeled data available for training. Regression tasks are tasks that involve predicting numerical values using a labeled training dataset, making them integral to fields such as finance and economics. However, real-world scenarios often present a challenge: labeled data is a precious commodity, often in short supply.

If there is a short supply of labeled data to train a machine learning model, you can still use summary statistics, semi-supervised learning, and clustering to predict the target labels for your unlabeled data. We have demonstrated this using house price data as an example and generated the predicted labels for house prices programmatically using Python. We will look at different approaches to labeling data for regression using Snorkel libraries, semi-supervised learning, data augmentation, and K-means clustering methods. In real-world projects, it is challenging to get the labeled data required for training machine learning regression models. For example, adequate data may not be available to train the model to predict house prices. In those cases, we prepare the training data by using various Python libraries.

In this chapter, we're going to cover the following main topics:

- Using rules based on summary statistics to generate house price labels for regression
- Using semi-supervised learning to label regression data for house price prediction with regression
- Generating house price data labels with data augmentation to generate synthetic data for regression
- Using K-means clustering to label the house price data for regression

By the end of this chapter, you will be able to generate labels for regression data using Python libraries programmatically. Furthermore, you'll have the expertise required to overcome regression challenges adeptly, ensuring your data-driven endeavors steer toward success.

Technical requirements

We will use the California house price dataset (`https://www.kaggle.com/datasets/camnugent/california-housing-prices`) for this chapter. You can download the `housing.csv` file from GitHub at the following path: `https://github.com/PacktPublishing/Data-Labeling-in-Machine-Learning-with-Python/tree/main/datasets`.

We also need to install Python 3.7+ and set up any of the following Python editors:

- The VS Code IDE
- Anaconda
- Jupyter Notebook
- Replit

We recommend following the complete code on GitHub to follow along with the chapter.

Using summary statistics to generate housing price labels

In this section, we are going to generate house price labels using summary statistics of a small set of available labeled housing price data. This is useful in real-world projects when there is insufficient labeled data for regression tasks. In such scenarios, we will generate labeled data by creating some rules based on summary statistics.

We decode the significance of the data's underlying trends. By computing the mean of each feature within the labeled training dataset, we embark on a journey to quantify the essence of the data. This approach ingeniously leverages distance metrics to unveil the closest match for a label, bestowing unlabeled data points with the wisdom of their labeled counterparts.

Let's load the data from the `housing.csv` file using pandas:

```
import pandas as pd
# Load the labeled data
df_labeled = pd.read_csv('housing.csv')
```

Here's the output:

latitude	housing_median_age	total_rooms	total_bedrooms	population	households	median_income	median_house_value
37.88	41.0	880.0	129.0	322.0	126.0	8.3252	452600.0
37.86	21.0	7099.0	1106.0	2401.0	1138.0	8.3014	358500.0

Figure 3.1 – Snippet of the DataFrame

After loading the labeled data using `pd.read_csv`, we then compute the summary statistics for each feature by target label using the `groupby()` and `describe()` methods. This gives us the mean, standard deviation, minimum, maximum, and quartile values for each feature by target label:

```
# Compute the summary statistics for each feature by target label
summary_stats = df.groupby('median_house_value').describe()
```

Here's the output:

median_house_value	longitude								latitude		...	households	
	count	mean	std	min	25%	50%	75%	max	count	mean	...	75%	max
358500.0	1.0	-122.22	NaN	-122.22	-122.22	-122.22	-122.22	-122.22	1.0	37.86	...	1138.0	1138.0
452600.0	1.0	-122.23	NaN	-122.23	-122.23	-122.23	-122.23	-122.23	1.0	37.88	...	126.0	126.0

Figure 3.2 – Summary statistics of the house price dataset

Finding the closest labeled observation to match the label

We then loop through each row in the unlabeled data and compute the distances to each target label's summary statistics using Euclidean distance. We select the target label with the minimum distance as the predicted target label and assign it to the current row:

```
# Load the unlabeled data
df_unlabeled = pd.read_csv(''housing_unlabled.csv')
```

The Euclidean distance is the distance between two points on a plane. Here, the distance between two points `(x1, y1)` and `(x2, y2)` is `d = √[(x2 - x1)2 + (y2 - y1)2]`. This is used to find similar points, that is, the closest point to an unlabeled data point in the labeled data points, so that we can assign the corresponding label from the labeled dataset to the unlabeled data point. unlabeled dataset) is calculated by combining the distance between all the features in the row. We assign the target label of a row with the minimum distance from the predicted target label to the current row in the unlabeled dataset. This helps us to assign labels to the unlabeled dataset based on the closest match to the label in the training dataset using distance metrics.

Here, the outermost `for` loop reads one row at a time from unlabeled data and then performs the following steps on that row in the inner `for` loop:

```
# Predict the target label for each data point in the unlabeled data
for i, row in df_unlabeled.iterrows():
```

The outermost `for` loop reads one row at a time from unlabeled data and then performs the following steps on that row in the inner `for` loop:

```
# Compute the distances to each target label's summary statistics
dists = {}
```

The `for target` loop iterates over each target label in the `summary_stats` DataFrame. The `index` attribute of a DataFrame returns the row labels, which in this case are the target labels:

```
for target in summary_stats.index:
```

The following line initializes the `dist` variable to 0, which we will use to accumulate the distance between the current unlabeled data point and the current target label's summary statistics:

```
dist = 0
for col in df_unlabeled.columns:
```

The `for col` loop iterates over each column in the `df_unlabeled` DataFrame. We want to compute the distance between the current unlabeled data point and each target label's summary statistics for each feature.

The following line checks if the current column is not the target column. We don't want to compute the distance between the current unlabeled data point and the summary statistics of the target column, as this would not make sense:

```
if col != 'median_house_value':
```

The following line computes the squared distance between the current unlabeled data point's feature value and the corresponding feature's mean value in the current target label's summary statistics. We square the distance to make it positive and exaggerate the differences:

```
dist += (row[col] - summary_stats.loc[target, (col, 'mean')]) ** 2
```

The following line saves the computed distance in the `dists` dictionary for the current target label:

```
dists[target] = dist
# Select the target label with the minimum distance
predicted_target = min(dists, key=dists.get)
# Assign the predicted target label to the current row
df_unlabeled.at[i, 'median_house_value'] = predicted_target
```

By the end of this inner loop, the `dists` dictionary will contain the squared distances between the current unlabeled data point and each target label's summary statistics. We will then select the target label with the minimum distance as the predicted target label for the current data point.

The same process continues for each row of the unlabeled data to compute distances from each of the target label's features mean values in the summary statistics to the corresponding column in the unlabeled data.

Finally, we save the labeled data to a new CSV file using the `to_csv()` method, `df_unlabeled.to_csv('housing_result.csv')`.

latitude	housing_median_age	total_rooms	total_bedrooms	population	households	median_income	median_house_value
47.86	20.0	7099.0	1106.0	2401.0	1138.0	8.3014	358500

Figure 3.3 – Labeled data with predicted median house value

Now, we can see that `median_house_value` is assigned to the row in the unlabeled dataset. Note that this approach assumes that the summary statistics of the labeled data can be used to predict the target labels of the unlabeled data accurately. Therefore, it is essential to validate the accuracy of the predictions before using them in practice.

Using semi-supervised learning to label regression data

In this section, we are going to use semi-supervised learning to label the regression data. Semi-supervised learning is a type of machine learning that combines both labeled and unlabeled data to improve the accuracy of a predictive model. In semi-supervised learning, a small amount of labeled data is used with a much larger amount of unlabeled data to train the model. The idea is that the unlabeled data can provide additional information about the underlying patterns in the data that can help the model to learn more effectively. By using both labeled and unlabeled data, semi-supervised learning can improve the accuracy of machine learning models, especially when labeled data is scarce or expensive to obtain.

Now, let's look in detail at the pseudo-labeling method and how it is used for data labeling.

Pseudo-labeling

Pseudo-labeling is a technique used in semi-supervised learning where a model trained on labeled data is used to predict the labels of the unlabeled data. These predicted labels are called pseudo-labels. The model then combines the labeled and pseudo-labeled data to retrain and improve the accuracy of the model. Pseudo-labeling is a way to leverage the unlabeled data to improve the performance of the model, especially when labeled data is limited.

The pseudo-labeling process involves the following steps:

1. **Train a model on labeled data**: Train a supervised learning model on the labeled data using a training algorithm. The model is fitted to the training set using the provided labels.

2. **Predict labels for unlabeled data**: Use the trained model to predict the labels for the unlabeled data. These predicted labels are called pseudo-labels.

3. **Combine labeled and pseudo-labeled data**: Combine the labeled data with the pseudo-labeled data to form a new, larger training set. The pseudo-labeled data is treated as if it were labeled data.

4. **Retrain the model**: Retrain the model using the combined dataset. The model is updated using both the labeled and pseudo-labeled data to improve the model's accuracy.

5. **Repeat steps 2-4**: Iterate the process by reusing the updated model to predict labels for new, previously unlabeled data, and combining the newly labeled data with the existing labeled data for the next round of model retraining, and the process is repeated until convergence.

Pseudo-labeling can be an effective way to leverage the large amount of unlabeled data that is typically available in many applications. By using this unlabeled data to improve the accuracy of the model, pseudo-labeling can help to improve the performance of supervised machine learning models, especially when enough labeled training data is not easily available.

Let's use the house price dataset to predict the labels for regression:

```
import pandas as pd
from sklearn.model_selection import train_test_split
from sklearn.linear_model import LinearRegression
import numpy as np
```

Let's load the house price dataset and then split the labeled data into the `labeled_data` DataFrame and unlabeled data into the `unlabeled_data` DataFrame, as follows:

```
# Load the data
data = pd.read_csv("housing_data.csv")

# Split the labeled data into training and testing sets
train_data, test_data, train_labels, test_labels = \
    train_test_split(labeled_data.drop('price', axis=1), \
        labeled_data['price'], test_size=0.2)
```

This code snippet is used to divide the labeled data into two parts: a training set and a testing set. The training set contains the features (input data) and the corresponding labels (output data) that we will use to train our machine learning model. The testing set is a small portion of the data that we will use to evaluate the model's performance. The `train_test_split` function from the `sklearn.model_selection` library helps us achieve this division while specifying the size of the testing set (in this case, 20% of the data). Let's train the model using the training dataset for regression, as follows:

```
# Train a linear regression model on the labeled data
regressor = LinearRegression()
regressor.fit(train_data, train_labels)
```

In this code snippet, we're building and training a linear regression model using the labeled data. First, we import the `LinearRegression` class from the `sklearn.linear_model` library. Then, we create an instance of the linear regression model named `regressor`. Finally, we train the model using the training data (`train_data`) as the input features and the corresponding labels (train_labels) as the desired outputs. The model learns from this data to make predictions later. Now, let's predict the labels using the regressor for the unlabeled dataset, as follows:

```
# Use the trained model to predict the labels of the unlabeled data
predicted_labels = regressor.predict(
    unlabeled_data.drop('price', axis=1))
```

In this code snippet, we're employing the trained linear regression model to predict labels for unlabeled data points. We initialize an empty list, predicted_labels, to store the predictions. By applying the predict method of the trained regressor model, we generate predictions based on the features (input data) in the unlabeled_data. The price column is excluded since it's the target variable we want to predict. The predicted_labels list now holds the predicted outcomes of the regression model for the unlabeled data. Now we will combine this predicted labeled data with the labeled data and train the model, as follows:

```
# Combine the labeled and newly predicted data
new_data = pd.concat([labeled_data, unlabeled_data], ignore_index=True)
new_data['price'] = pd.concat([train_labels, \
    pd.Series(predicted_labels)], ignore_index=True)
```

In this code snippet, we're creating a new dataset, new_data, by combining the labeled and the newly predicted data. First, we use pd.concat to concatenate the labeled_data and unlabeled_data dataframes, creating a continuous dataset. The ignore_index=True argument ensures that the index is reset for the new dataset.

Next, we're populating the 'price' column in the new_data DataFrame. We achieve this by concatenating the train_labels (from the labeled data) with the predicted labels stored in the predicted_labels list. This step ensures that our new dataset has complete labels for all data points, combining both known and predicted values:

```
# Train a new model on the combined data
new_train_data, new_test_data, new_train_labels, new_test_labels = \
    train_test_split(new_data.drop('price', axis=1), \
    new_data['price'], test_size=0.2)
new_regressor = LinearRegression()
new_regressor.fit(new_train_data, new_train_labels)
```

In this code snippet, we're training a new linear regression model on the combined dataset that includes both the labeled and predicted data. First, we split the combined data into new training and testing sets using the train_test_split function, similar to what we did before. The new training data is stored in new_train_data, and the corresponding labels are stored in new_train_labels.

Next, we create a new instance of the linear regression model called new_regressor. Finally, we train the new model using new_train_data as input features and new_train_labels as the desired outputs. This step ensures that our new model is fine-tuned to predict the combined data, leveraging both labeled and predicted information:

```
# Evaluate the performance of the new model on the test data
score = new_regressor.score(new_test_data, new_test_labels)
print("R^2 Score: ", score)
```

Here's the output:

```
# Evaluate the performance of the new model on the test data

score = new_regressor.score(new_test_data, new_test_labels)

print("R^2 Score: ", score)
✓  0.0s

R^2 Score:   0.6905783112767134
```

Figure 3.4 – Performance of the model after adding pseudo-labeled data

In this code snippet, we're evaluating the performance of the new linear regression model on the test data that it hasn't seen during training. The R-squared(coefficient of determination) score is calculated using the `score` method of the `new_regressor` model. The R^2 score is a measure of how well the model's predictions match the actual data values. Higher R^2 scores indicate better predictive accuracy.

As we can see, the R^2 score is higher (0.6905783112767134) with the combined dataset than with the original labeled trained dataset (0.624186740765541). Finally, we use this model to predict the labels. Now, let's see another method, data augmentation, to generate synthetic data with labels for regression.

Using data augmentation to label regression data

Data augmentation can be used to generate additional labeled data for regression tasks where labeled data is limited. Here is a way to use data augmentation to label regression data:

1. **Collect labeled data**: Collect the limited labeled data available for the regression task.

2. **Define data augmentation techniques**: Define a set of data augmentation techniques that can be used to generate new data points from the available labeled data. For regression tasks, common data augmentation techniques include adding noise, scaling, and rotating the data.

3. **Generate augmented data**: Use data augmentation techniques to generate new data points from the available labeled data. The new data points will have labels based on the labels of the original data points.

4. **Train the model**: Train a regression model using the augmented data and the original labeled data. This step involves fitting a model to the combined dataset using a supervised learning algorithm.

5. **Evaluate the model**: Evaluate the performance of the trained model on a validation set. This step involves testing the accuracy of the model's predictions on new, unseen data.

6. **Fine-tune the model**: Fine-tune the model based on the performance on the validation set. This step involves adjusting the model's hyperparameters to improve its performance on the validation set.

7. **Test the model**: Finally, test the model's performance on a test set to evaluate its generalization performance.

By using data augmentation to generate additional labeled data, it is possible to train a more accurate regression model even when limited labeled data is available. However, it is important to be careful when using data augmentation techniques to ensure that the generated data is meaningful and representative of the original data distribution.

In the context of numerical data, we should focus on the following data augmentation techniques that are relevant and meaningful for the given dataset. For example, we can consider the following:

- **Adding noise**: Adding random noise to numerical features and labels can simulate variations and uncertainties in the data

- **Scaling**: Scaling numerical features can simulate changes in units or magnitudes

- **Jittering**: Introducing small perturbations to numerical values can account for measurement errors or fluctuations

- **Outlier injection**: Introducing outliers can help the model become more robust to extreme values

- **Shuffling**: Randomly shuffling the order of data points can prevent the model from learning any sequence-related bias

Remember that the choice of data augmentation techniques should be based on the characteristics of your dataset and the problem you're trying to solve. The techniques should add meaningful variations that align with the nature of your data.

Let's see how we generate augmented data for the house price dataset to predict labels. Let's import the necessary libraries, load the house price dataset, and define the `noise`, `scale`, and `rotate` data augmentation functions, as follows:

```
import pandas as pd
import numpy as np
from sklearn.linear_model import LinearRegression
from sklearn.metrics import mean_squared_error
from sklearn.model_selection import train_test_split
import random
```

Then we load the labeled data stored in a CSV file named `labeled_data.csv` with columns for the features and a column named `price` for the target variable:

```
# Load the available labeled data
df = pd.read_csv("labeled_data.csv")
```

The following code defines two data augmentation techniques that add noise. It generates new data points by applying these augmentation techniques to the labeled data:

```
# Define the data augmentation techniques
def add_noise(x, std):
    noise = np.random.normal(0, std, len(x))
    return x + noise



# Define the range of data augmentation parameters
noise_range = [0.1, 0.2, 0.3]
```

The range of data augmentation parameters for noise range is defined, and for each available data point, it generates multiple augmented data points with different parameter values:

```
# Generate augmented data
augmented_data = []
for _, row in df.iterrows():
    for noise in noise_range:
        new_row = row.copy()
        new_row["price"] = add_noise(row["price"], noise)
        augmented_data.append(new_row)
```

By iterating through each value in `noise_range` and adding noise to each data point's `price` feature, the code generates multiple data points with different levels of noise. This process results in more labeled data points for the machine learning model to learn from and improves the model's accuracy.

`noise_range` is a list of standard deviation values for generating different levels of noise. It could be any list of values to add different levels of noise to the data points:

- `for noise in noise_range` creates a loop that iterates through each value in the `noise_range` list.
- `new_row = row.copy()` creates a copy of the original data point (i.e., row).
- `new_row["price"] = add_noise(row["price"], noise)` adds noise to the copied data point's `price` feature using the `add_noise()` function. The `add_noise()` function adds random noise to each data point based on the standard deviation provided in the `noise` variable.

- `augmented_data.append(new_row)` appends the newly generated data point to the `augmented_data` list. The `augmented_data` list contains all the newly generated data points for all levels of noise in the `noise_range` list.

Similarly, let's define another data augmentation scale function:

```
def scale(x, factor):
    return x * factor

scale_range = [0.5, 0.75, 1.25, 1.5]
```

The range of parameters for `scale_range` is defined, and for each available data point, it generates multiple augmented data points with different parameter values:

```
for scale_factor in scale_range:
    new_row = row.copy()
    new_row["price"] = scale(row["price"], scale_factor)
    augmented_data.append(new_row)
```

In this code snippet, we're utilizing data augmentation to generate augmented data by applying scaling to the `price` feature. For each scale factor within the specified `scale_range`, we duplicate the current data row by creating a copy of it using `row.copy()`. Then, we apply scaling to the `price` feature using `scale_factor`, effectively modifying the price values while preserving the data's relationships.

Finally, the augmented row is added to the list of augmented data stored in the `augmented_data` list. This approach empowers us to explore how varying scales affect the `price` feature and enrich our dataset with diverse instances for improved model training and testing:

```
# Combine the original data and the augmented data
combined_data = pd.concat([df, pd.DataFrame(augmented_data)])
```

Here's the augmented data:

```
Original Data:
[[-1.2223e+02  3.7880e+01  4.1000e+01  8.8000e+02  1.2900e+02  3.2200e+02
   1.2600e+02  8.3252e+00  4.5260e+05]
 [-1.2222e+02  3.7860e+01  2.1000e+01  7.0990e+03  1.1060e+03  2.4010e+03
   1.1380e+03  8.3014e+00  3.5850e+05]]

Augmented Data:
[[-1.22251751e+02  3.78676351e+01  4.10211854e+01  7.97660895e+02
   1.44116754e+02  2.53714573e+02 -9.99873136e+01  8.32521386e+00
   4.48916551e+05]
 [-1.22216317e+02  3.78600629e+01  2.08620374e+01  7.25418012e+03
   1.11195936e+03  2.32858094e+03  1.09139398e+03  8.30215604e+00
   3.69155898e+05]]
```

Figure 3.5 – Original data and augmented data

The code then combines the original labeled data with the augmented data, splits it into training and testing sets, trains a linear regression model on the combined data, and evaluates the model's performance on the test set using mean squared error as the evaluation metric:

```
# Split the data into training and testing sets
X = combined_data.drop("price", axis=1)
y = combined_data["price"]
X_train, X_test, y_train, y_test = train_test_split(X, y, \
    test_size=0.2, random_state=42)

# Train a linear regression model
model = LinearRegression()
model.fit(X_train, y_train)

# Evaluate the model
y_pred = model.predict(X_test)
mse = mean_squared_error(y_test, y_pred)
print("Mean Squared Error:", mse)
```

By iterating through each value in `noise_range` and adding noise to each available data point, it generates multiple augmented data points with different levels of noise. This process results in more labeled data points for the machine learning model to learn from and improves the model's accuracy. Similarly, scale factor and rotation degree are used to generate labeled data using data augmentation to predict house prices using regression.

In this section, we have seen how to generate the augmented data using noise and scale techniques for regression. Now, let's see how we can use the K-means clustering unsupervised learning method to label the house price data.

Using k-means clustering to label regression data

In this section, we are going to use the unsupervised K-means clustering method to label the regression data. We use K-means to cluster data points into groups or clusters based on their similarity.

Once the clustering is done, we can compute the average label value for each cluster by taking the mean of the labeled data points that belong to that cluster. This is because the labeled data points in a cluster are likely to have similar label values since they are similar in terms of their feature values.

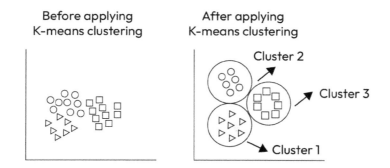

Figure 3.6 – Basic k-means clustering with no. of clusters =3

For example, let's say we have a dataset of house prices with which we want to predict the price of a house based on features such as size, location, number of rooms, and so on. We have some labeled data points that consist of the features and their corresponding prices, but we also have some unlabeled data points with the same features.

We can use K-means clustering to cluster the labeled and unlabeled data points into groups based on their features. Then, we can compute the average price for each cluster by taking the mean of the labeled data points in that cluster.

Finally, we can use these average prices to predict the prices of the unlabeled data points based on their cluster assignment.

We can use these predicted labels to create a new dataset by combining the labeled and unlabeled data. We then train a new model on the combined data and evaluate its performance on the test data:

```python
import numpy as np
from sklearn.cluster import KMeans
from sklearn.metrics import mean_squared_error

# Define labelled and unlabelled data
labelled_data = np.array([
[-122.23, 37.88, 41.0, 880.0, 129.0, 322.0, 126.0, 8.3252, 452600.0],
[-122.22, 37.86, 21.0, 7099.0, 1106.0, 2401.0, 1138.0, 8.3014,
358500.0]
])

unlabelled_data = np.array([
[-122.22, 47.86, 20.0, 7099.0, 1106.0, 2401.0, 1138.0, 8.3014, 0.0]
])

# Extract features and labels from labelled data
labelled_features = labelled_data[:, :-1]
labelled_labels = labelled_data[:, -1]
```

Here, we import the necessary libraries and define the labeled and unlabeled data arrays:

```
# Train K-means clustering model
n_clusters = 2 # Number of clusters (you can adjust this)
kmeans_model = KMeans(n_clusters=n_clusters)
kmeans_model.fit(labelled_features)
```

We specify the number of clusters (`n_clusters`) and use k-means clustering to fit the model to the labeled features:

```
# Predict cluster labels for unlabelled data
unlabelled_clusters = kmeans_model.predict(unlabelled_data[:, :-1])
```

We predict cluster labels for the unlabeled data using the trained k-means model:

```
# Calculate average prices for each cluster
cluster_avg_prices = []
for cluster_idx in range(n_clusters):
    cluster_mask = (kmeans_model.labels_ == cluster_idx)
    cluster_avg_price = np.mean(labelled_labels[cluster_mask])
    cluster_avg_prices.append(cluster_avg_price)
```

We calculate the average prices for each cluster by iterating through cluster indices and calculating the mean of the labeled prices for each cluster.

The line `cluster_mask = (kmeans_model.labels_ == cluster_idx)` creates a boolean mask that identifies the data points in a specific cluster.

Here's a breakdown of what each part of the line does:

- `kmeans_model.labels_`: This is an attribute of the K-means model that contains the cluster labels assigned to each data point during the clustering process. Each value in `kmeans_model.labels_` corresponds to the cluster label assigned to the corresponding data point in the order they appear in the input data.

- `cluster_idx`: This is the index of the cluster you're interested in, ranging from 0 to the number of clusters minus one. It's used to specify which cluster you want to create the mask for.

- `kmeans_model.labels_ == cluster_idx`: This part creates a boolean array where each element is `True` if the corresponding data point's cluster label is equal to `cluster_idx`, and `False` otherwise. Essentially, it's checking which data points belong to the specific cluster of interest.

- `cluster_mask`: This is the resulting boolean mask that identifies the data points belonging to the cluster with the index `cluster_idx`.

In summary, the line `cluster_mask = (kmeans_model.labels_ == cluster_idx)` creates a mask that helps you filter and select the data points in a specific cluster based on their assigned cluster labels. This mask can then be used to perform various operations on the data points belonging to that cluster. Predicted prices are assigned to the unlabeled data based on the calculated cluster average prices:

```
# Assign predicted prices to unlabeled data
predicted_prices = np.array([cluster_avg_prices[cluster] \
    for cluster in unlabelled_clusters])
```

Finally, we display the predicted prices for the unlabeled data using the K-means clustering technique, providing insights into the potential housing prices for the unlabeled samples.:

```
print("Predicted Prices for Unlabelled Data:", predicted_prices)
```

Here's the output for the predicted labels:

```
Predicted Prices for Unlabelled Data: [358500.]
```

Figure 3.7 – Predicted price for unlabeled data based on the mean value of the labeled data cluster

As shown in the output, we can predict the house price for unlabeled data using K-means clustering when there is a scarce training dataset. Then, we can combine the predicted labeled dataset and the original training dataset to fit the model using regression:

```
# Combine the labeled and newly predicted data
new_data = pd.concat([labeled_data, unlabeled_data], ignore_index=True)
new_data['price'] = pd.concat([train_labels, \
    pd.Series(predicted_labels)], ignore_index=True)

# Train a new model on the combined data
new_train_data, new_test_data, new_train_labels, new_test_labels = \
    train_test_split(new_data.drop('price', axis=1), \
    new_data['price'], test_size=0.2)
new_regressor = LinearRegression()
new_regressor.fit(new_train_data, new_train_labels)

# Evaluate the performance of the new model on the test data
score = new_regressor.score(new_test_data, new_test_labels)
print("R^2 Score: ", score)
```

Overall, we have seen how clustering can be used in unsupervised learning to generate labels for unlabeled data. By computing the average label value for each cluster, we can effectively assign labels to the unlabeled data points based on their similarity to the labeled data.

Summary

In this chapter, we have explored a range of techniques to tackle the challenge of data labeling in regression tasks. We began by delving into the power of summary statistics, harnessing the mean of each feature in the labeled dataset to predict labels for unlabeled data. This technique not only simplifies the labeling process but also introduces a foundation for accurate predictions.

Further enriching our labeling arsenal, we ventured into semi-supervised learning, leveraging a small set of labeled data to generate pseudo-labels. The amalgamation of genuine and pseudo-labels in model training not only extends our labeled data but also equips our models to make more informed predictions for unlabeled data.

Data augmentation has emerged as a vital tool in enhancing regression data. Techniques such as scaling and noise injection have breathed new life into our dataset, providing varied instances that empower models to discern patterns better and boost prediction accuracy.

The utilization of k-means clustering rounded off our exploration, as we ventured into grouping data into clusters and assigning labels based on cluster mean values. This approach not only saves time but also bolsters the prediction precision of our models.

The key takeaways from this chapter are that summary statistics simplify data labeling by leveraging means and distances. Semi-supervised learning merges genuine and pseudo-labels for comprehensive training. Data augmentation techniques such as scaling and noise addition enrich and diversify datasets. K-means clustering optimizes labeling by grouping data into clusters and assigning cluster-wide mean labels.

These acquired skills bestow resilience and versatility to our regression models, instilling them with the ability to handle real-world, unlabeled data effectively. In the next chapter, we'll delve into the exploratory data analysis of image data in machine learning.

Part 2:
Labeling Image Data

In this part of the book, you will learn how to analyze image data, extract features from images, and label images using Python libraries such as Snorkel. The content also covers various methods of image data augmentation, along with the utilization of **support vector machine (SVM)**, **convolutional neural network (CNN)**, and pre-trained models such as YOLO for image classification and labeling.

This part comprises the following chapters:

- *Chapter 4, Exploring Image Data*
- *Chapter 5, Labeling Image Data Using Rules*
- *Chapter 6, Labeling Image Data Using Data Augmentation*

4
Exploring Image Data

In this chapter, we will learn how to explore image data using various packages and libraries in Python. We will also see how to visualize images using Matplotlib and analyze image properties using NumPy.

Image data is widely used in machine learning, computer vision, and object detection across various real-world applications.

The chapter is divided into three key sections covering visualizing image data, analyzing image size and aspect ratios, and performing transformations on images. Each section focuses on a specific aspect of image data analysis, providing practical insights and techniques to extract valuable information.

In the first section, *Visualizing image data*, we will utilize the Matplotlib, Seaborn, **Python Imaging Library** (**PIL**), and NumPy libraries and explore techniques such as plotting histograms of pixel values for grayscale images, visualizing color channels in RGB images, adding annotations to enhance image interpretation, and performing image segmentation. Additionally, we will dive into feature extraction using the **Histogram of Oriented Gradients** (**HOG**). Through practical examples and hands-on exercises, this section equips you with essential skills for visually analyzing and interpreting image data using Python libraries. Whether you're a beginner or seeking to deepen your image processing expertise, this section provides valuable insights and practical knowledge.

Moving on to the second *Analyzing image size and aspect ratio* section, we delve into the importance of understanding the dimensions and proportions of images. We demonstrate how Python libraries such as **Python Imaging Library** (**PIL**) and OpenCV can be utilized to extract and analyze image size and aspect ratios. By studying these attributes, we can derive meaningful insights about the composition and structure of images, which can inform data-labeling decisions and contribute to accurate classification or object detection tasks.

The final *Performing transformations on images* section explores the concept of data augmentation through transformations. We delve into how various image transformations, such as rotations, translations, and shearing, can be applied using libraries such as OpenCV and scikit-image. These transformations not only enhance the diversity and size of the dataset but also enable the creation of augmented images that capture different orientations, perspectives, or variations. We discuss how these transformed images can be leveraged for data labeling and improving model performance.

Throughout the chapter, we emphasize the practical implementation of these techniques using Python. By leveraging the rich ecosystem of image processing libraries and visualization tools, we empower readers to perform exploratory data analysis specifically tailored for image datasets. The insights gained from visualizing image data, analyzing size and aspect ratios, and performing transformations lay a strong foundation for effective data labeling and building robust machine learning models.

Whether you are an aspiring data scientist, an image processing enthusiast, or a professional looking to enhance your data labeling skills, this chapter provides valuable guidance and hands-on examples to explore, analyze, and label image data effectively using Python.

By the end of this chapter, we will have covered the following topics:

- Visualizing image data

- Analyzing image size and aspect ratios

- Performing transformations on images

Technical requirements

In this chapter, you'll need VS Code, Keras, CV2, and OpenCV. A Python notebook with the example code used in this chapter can be downloaded from `https://github.com/PacktPublishing/Data-Labeling-in-Machine-Learning-with-Python/tree/main/code//Ch04`.

You will find the results of all code blocks in the notebook in this GitHub repository. As well as this, you will need the environment setup outlined in the *Preface* of the book.

Visualizing image data using Matplotlib in Python

In this section, we explore the power of visualization tools and techniques to gain meaningful insights into the characteristics and patterns of image data. Using Python libraries such as Matplotlib and Seaborn, we learn how to create visualizations that showcase image distributions, class imbalances, color distributions, and other essential features. By visualizing the image data, we can uncover hidden patterns, detect anomalies, and make informed decisions for data labeling.

Exploratory Data Analysis (EDA) is an important step in the process of building computer vision models. In EDA, we analyze the image data to understand its characteristics and identify patterns and relationships that can inform our modeling decisions.

Some real-world examples of image data analysis and AI applications are as follows:

- **Autonomous vehicles**: Image data plays a crucial role in enabling autonomous vehicles to perceive their surroundings. Cameras mounted on vehicles capture images of the road and surroundings, and machine learning algorithms analyze these images to detect and recognize objects such as pedestrians, vehicles, and traffic signs.

- **Medical image analysis**: In the field of medical imaging, machine learning is used for tasks such as tumor detection, organ segmentation, and disease diagnosis. Radiological images, such as X-rays, MRIs, and CT scans, are analyzed to identify anomalies and assist healthcare professionals in making informed decisions.

- **Retail and e-commerce**: Object detection is employed in retail for inventory management and customer experience improvement. For example, automated checkout systems use computer vision to recognize and tally products in a shopping cart, enhancing the efficiency of the checkout process.

- **Security and surveillance**: Image data is utilized in security systems for surveillance and threat detection. Machine learning models can analyze video feeds to identify and alert authorities about suspicious activities, intruders, or unusual behavior in public spaces.

- **Facial recognition**: Facial recognition technology relies on image data to identify and verify individuals. This is used in various applications, including smartphone authentication, access control systems, and law enforcement for criminal identification.

- **Augmented Reality (AR)**: AR applications overlay digital information onto the real world. Image data is essential for tracking and recognizing objects and surfaces, enabling realistic and interactive AR experiences.

- **Quality control in manufacturing**: Computer vision is employed in manufacturing to inspect products for defects and ensure quality. Automated systems analyze images of products on assembly lines, identifying any deviations from the desired specifications.

- **Satellite image analysis**: Satellite imagery is used for various purposes, including land cover classification, environmental monitoring, and disaster response. Machine learning algorithms can analyze satellite images to identify changes in landscapes, detect deforestation, or assess the impact of natural disasters.

These examples illustrate the diverse applications of image data in machine learning, computer vision, and object detection, showcasing its significance in solving real-world problems across different domains.

The following are some steps to follow when conducting EDA for image data.

Loading the data

The first step in any EDA process is to load the image data into your **Integrated Development Environment** (**IDE**) workspace, such as VS Code, Jupyter Notebook, or any other Python editor. Depending on the format of the data, you may need to use a library such as OpenCV or PIL to read in the images.

Checking the dimensions

The next step is to check the dimensions of the images. Image dimensions can affect the performance of your model, as larger images require more memory and computation. You should also check that all the images have the same dimensions, as this is a requirement for most computer vision models. If the images are not of the same size, then preprocessing is required to convert them to the same size.

Visualizing the data

Visualization is a powerful tool for understanding image data. You can use the Matplotlib or Seaborn libraries to visualize the data in various ways. You can plot histograms of pixel values to see their distributions or use scatter plots to visualize the relationship between pixel values. We will cover this later in this chapter.

Checking for outliers

Outliers can have a significant impact on your model's performance. You should check for outliers in your image data by plotting boxplots and examining the distribution of pixel values. In the context of image data, outliers are data points (in this case, images) that significantly deviate from the expected or normal distribution of the dataset. Outliers in image data are images that have distinct characteristics or patterns that are different from the majority of images in the dataset. Images with pixel values that are much higher or lower than the typical range for the dataset can be considered outliers. These extreme values might be due to sensor malfunctions, data corruption, or other anomalies. Images with color distributions that significantly differ from the expected color distributions of the dataset can be considered outliers. These might be images with unusual color casts, saturation, or intensity.

Performing data preprocessing

Preprocessing is an important step in EDA, as it can help to reduce noise and improve the quality of the images. Common preprocessing techniques include resizing, normalization, data augmentation, image segmentation, and feature extraction.

In image data, preprocessing involves several steps.

1. Image resizing

The first step in preprocessing image data is resizing the images. Image resizing is essential because we need all the images to be of the same size. If we do not make sure to resize the images, we may end up with images of different sizes, which can lead to issues during training.

2. Image normalization

The next step in preprocessing image data is normalization. Normalization is essential because it helps to reduce the effect of lighting and color variations on the images. Normalization involves scaling the pixel values of the images to a specific range. The most common method of normalization is to scale the pixel values to the range [0,1]. Scaling pixel values to the range [0, 1] during image dataset normalization has several significant advantages and implications that make it a common and effective practice in various image processing and machine learning tasks. Here's why this range is significant. Normalizing images to a common range ensures that all pixel values across different images have the same scale. This makes it easier for algorithms to compare and process images, as they don't need to deal with varying pixel value ranges. The range [0, 1] is well suited for numerical stability in computations. Many machine learning algorithms and image processing techniques work best when dealing with values that are not too large or too small. Scaling to [0, 1] helps prevent numerical instability and issues such as exploding gradients during training.

3. Image augmentation

Image augmentation is a technique used to increase the size of the training dataset by creating additional images. Image augmentation involves applying various transformations to the original images, such as rotation, flipping, zooming, and shearing. It is used in image classification and object detection tasks. Image augmentation is essential because it helps to reduce overfitting and improves the generalization of the model. Overfitting is a common problem in machine learning and deep learning where a model learns the training data so well that it starts capturing noise and random fluctuations in the data instead of the underlying patterns. It helps produce robust models. Excessive augmentation can lead to unrealistic models or overfitting, which can result in reduced generalization ability, limiting the model's usefulness in real-world scenarios.

Adding more training data is one way to help reduce overfitting. However, in many situations, collecting a large amount of new, diverse data can be impractical or expensive. This is where data augmentation comes in. Data augmentation involves applying various transformations to the existing training data to artificially increase its size and diversity. Here's how data augmentation helps reduce overfitting, particularly in the context of image datasets:

- **Improved generalization**: Augmentation helps the model generalize better to unseen data by exposing it to a diverse range of transformations. This can enhance the model's ability to handle variations in object appearance.

- **Robustness to variations**: Models trained with augmented data are often more robust to changes in lighting, orientation, and other factors that may be present in real-world scenarios.

- **Data efficiency**: Augmentation allows for the creation of a larger effective training dataset without collecting additional labeled samples. This can be particularly beneficial when the available labeled data is limited.

- **Mitigating overfitting**: Augmentation introduces variability, helping to prevent overfitting. Models trained on augmented data are less likely to memorize specific training examples and are more likely to learn generalizable features.

- **Considerations**: While augmentation is generally beneficial, it's essential to apply transformations that make sense for the specific task. For example, randomly flipping images horizontally makes sense for many tasks, but randomly rotating images might not be suitable for tasks with strict orientation requirements.

4. Image segmentation

Image segmentation is the process of dividing an image into multiple meaningful segments or regions. Image segmentation is essential in medical image analysis, where we need to identify the different organs or tissues in the image. Image segmentation is also used in object detection, where we need to identify the different objects in an image.

5. Feature extraction

Feature extraction is the process of extracting relevant features or information from the image data. Feature extraction is essential because it helps to reduce the dimensionality of the image data, which can improve the performance of machine learning algorithms. Feature extraction involves applying various filters to the images, such as edge detection, texture analysis, and color segmentation. Examples of color features are color histograms that represent the distribution of color intensities in an image. Similarly, shape features include the Hough transform that detects and represents shapes such as lines and circles.

To summarize, data exploration and preprocessing are essential steps in the machine learning pipeline. In image data, we need to resize the images, normalize the pixel values, apply image augmentation, perform image segmentation, and extract relevant features from the images. By following these preprocessing steps, we can improve the performance of the machine learning algorithm and achieve better results.

Checking for class imbalance

In many image classification problems, the classes may not be evenly represented in the dataset. You should check for class imbalance by counting the number of images in each class and visualizing the distribution of classes. If there is an imbalance, we augment the minority class data by applying transformations such as rotations, flips, crops, and color variations. This increases the diversity of the minority class without needing to generate entirely new samples.

Identifying patterns and relationships

The goal of EDA is to identify patterns and relationships in the data that can inform your modeling decisions. You can use techniques such as clustering to identify patterns in the data or examine the relationship between different features using scatter plots or correlation matrices. Clustering, in the context of image dataset analysis, is a technique used to group similar images together based on their inherent patterns and characteristics. It's a data exploration method that aids in understanding the structure of image data by identifying groups or clusters of images that share similar visual traits. Clustering algorithms analyze the visual properties of images, such as pixel values or extracted features, to group images that are visually similar into clusters. Images that share common visual traits are grouped together, forming distinct clusters.

Evaluating the impact of preprocessing

Finally, you should evaluate the impact of preprocessing on your image data. You can compare the performance of your model on preprocessed and unprocessed data to determine the effectiveness of your preprocessing techniques.

In summary, EDA is an important step in the process of building computer vision models. By visualizing the data, checking for outliers and class imbalance, identifying patterns and relationships, and evaluating the impact of preprocessing, you can gain a better understanding of your image data and make informed decisions about your modeling approach.

Practice example of visualizing data

Let's see an example of visualizing image data using Matplotlib. In the following code, we first load the image using the PIL library:

```
import matplotlib.pyplot as plt
import numpy as np
from PIL import Image

# Load an image
img = Image.open('../images/roseflower.jpeg')
```

Then we convert it to a NumPy array using the np.array function:

```
# Convert image to numpy array
img_array = np.array(img)
```

Next, plot the result with the following commands:

```
# Plot the image
plt.imshow(img_array)
plt.show()
```

We get the following result:

Figure 4.1 – Visualizing image data

We then use the `imshow` function from Matplotlib to plot the image. Converting images to NumPy arrays during EDA offers several benefits that make data manipulation, analysis, and visualization more convenient and efficient. NumPy is a powerful numerical computing library in Python that provides support for multi-dimensional arrays and a wide range of mathematical operations. Converting images to NumPy arrays is common during EDA as NumPy arrays provide direct access to individual pixels in an image, making it easier to analyze pixel values and perform pixel-level operations. Many data analysis and visualization libraries in Python, including Matplotlib and scikit-learn, work seamlessly with NumPy arrays. This allows you to take advantage of a rich ecosystem of tools and techniques for image analysis.

There are many different ways to visualize image data using Matplotlib. We'll now review a few commonly encountered examples.

Grayscale image: To display a grayscale image, we can simply set the cmap parameter of the imshow function to 'gray':

```python
import numpy as np
from PIL import Image
import matplotlib.pyplot as plt

img_color = Image.open('../images/roseflower.jpeg')

# Convert the image to grayscale
img_gray = img_color.convert('L')

# Convert the image to a NumPy array
img_gray_array = np.array(img_gray)

# Display the image using matplotlib
plt.imshow(img_gray_array, cmap='gray')
# Show the plot
plt.show()
```

The following figure is the result of this code:

Figure 4.2 – Grayscale image

Histogram of pixel values: We can use a histogram to visualize the distribution of pixel values in an image. This can help us understand the overall brightness and contrast of the image:

```
import numpy as np
from PIL import Image
import matplotlib.pyplot as plt

# Load an image
img_color = Image.open('../images/roseflower.jpeg')

# Convert image to numpy array
img_array = np.array(img_color)

# Plot the histogram
plt.hist(img_array.ravel(), bins=256)
plt.show()
```

The resulting graph is as follows:

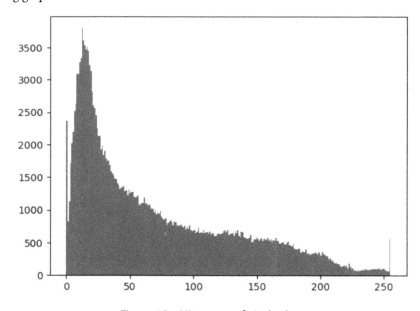

Figure 4.3 – Histogram of pixel values

Multiple images side by side: We can use subplots to display multiple images side by side for comparison:

```
import matplotlib.pyplot as plt
import numpy as np
from PIL import Image
```

```
# Load two images
img1 = Image.open('./images/roseflower.jpeg')
img2 = Image.open('./images/roseflower.jpeg')

# Convert images to numpy arrays
img1_array = np.array(img1)
img2_array = np.array(img2)

# Plot the images side-by-side
fig, axes = plt.subplots(nrows=1, ncols=2)
axes[0].imshow(img1_array)
axes[1].imshow(img2_array)
plt.show()
```

We get the stunning result as follows:

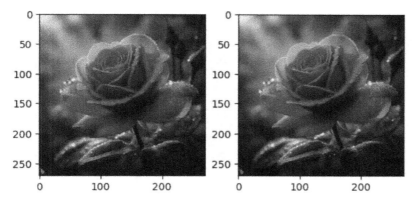

Figure 4.4 – Multiple images side by side

Color channel visualization: For color images, we can plot each color channel separately to see how they contribute to the overall image. In an image dataset, a color channel refers to a single component of color information in each pixel of an image. Color images are composed of multiple color channels, where each channel represents a specific color aspect or color space. The combination of these color channels creates the full-color representation of an image. Common color spaces include **Red, Green, Blue (RGB)**, **Hue, Saturation, Value (HSV)**, and **Cyan, Magenta, Yellow, Key/Black (CMYK)**.

In general, RGB color channels are visualized using the appropriate colormap to represent their respective colors. When visualizing individual color channels (red, green, and blue) separately, it's common to use colormaps that highlight the specific color information.

Here are typical colormaps used for visualizing individual RGB channels:

- **Red channel**: The 'Reds' colormap is often used to visualize the red channel. It ranges from dark to light red, with the darker values representing lower intensity and the lighter values representing higher intensity.

- **Green channel**: The 'Greens' colormap is commonly used to visualize the green channel. Similar to 'Reds', it ranges from dark to light green.

- **Blue channel**: The 'Blues' colormap is used for visualizing the blue channel. It ranges from dark to light blue.

Here's an example of how you might visualize individual RGB channels using these colormaps:

```python
import matplotlib.pyplot as plt
import numpy as np
from PIL import Image

# Load a color image
img = Image.open('../images/roseflower.jpeg')

# Split the image into RGB channels
r, g, b = img.split()

# Convert channels to numpy arrays
r_array = np.array(r)
g_array = np.array(g)
b_array = np.array(b)

# Plot each channel separately
fig, axes = plt.subplots(nrows=1, ncols=3)
axes[0].imshow(r_array, cmap='Reds') # Use 'Reds' colormap for the red
channel
axes[1].imshow(g_array, cmap='Greens') # Use 'Greens' colormap for the
green channel
axes[2].imshow(b_array, cmap='Blues') # Use 'Blues' colormap for the
blue channel
plt.show()
```

As a result, we see the following channels:

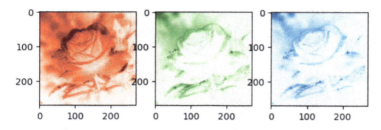

Figure 4.5 – Color channel visualization

Practice example for adding annotations to an image

We can add annotations to an image to highlight specific regions of interest, such as marking key features within an image, perhaps facial landmarks on a person's face (eyes, nose, mouth), to emphasize important attributes for analysis or recognition. Annotations can also be used to highlight regions that exhibit anomalies, defects, or irregularities in industrial inspection images, medical images, and quality control processes, along with identifying and marking specific points of interest, such as landmarks on a map. Let's see annotations at work:

```
import matplotlib.pyplot as plt
import numpy as np
from PIL import Image

# Load an image
img = Image.open('../images/roseflower.jpeg')

# Convert image to numpy array
img_array = np.array(img)

# Plot the image with annotations
plt.imshow(img_array)
plt.scatter(100, 200, c='r', s=50)
plt.annotate("Example annotation", (50, 50), fontsize=12, color='w')
plt.show()
```

We get the following result as output:

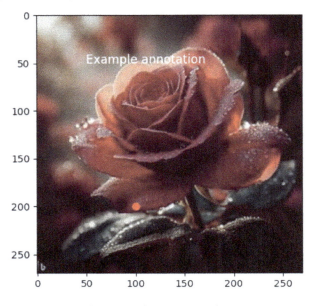

Figure 4.6 – Image annotation

These are just a few examples of the many ways that we can use Matplotlib to visualize image data. With some creativity and experimentation, we can create a wide variety of visualizations to help us understand our image data better.

Practice example of image segmentation

The following simple code snippet demonstrates how to perform basic image segmentation using the CIFAR-10 dataset and a simple thresholding technique:

```
import numpy as np
import matplotlib.pyplot as plt
from keras.datasets import cifar10

# Load the CIFAR-10 dataset
(x_train, _), (_, _) = cifar10.load_data()

# Select a sample image for segmentation
sample_image = x_train[0]  # You can choose any index here

# Convert the image to grayscale (optional)
gray_image = np.mean(sample_image, axis=2)
```

```
# Apply a simple thresholding for segmentation
threshold = 100
segmented_image = np.where(\
    gray_image > threshold, 255, 0).astype(np.uint8)

# Plot the original and segmented images
plt.figure(figsize=(8, 4))
plt.subplot(1, 2, 1)
plt.imshow(sample_image)
plt.title('Original Image')

plt.subplot(1, 2, 2)
plt.imshow(segmented_image, cmap='gray')
plt.title('Segmented Image')

plt.tight_layout()
plt.show()
```

The result is as follows:

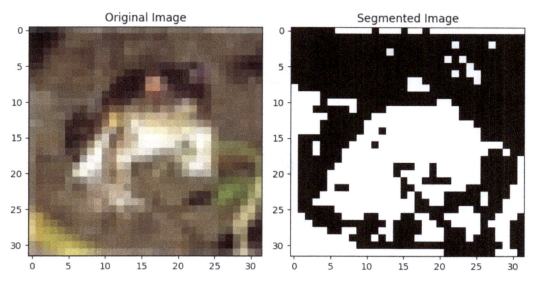

Figure 4.7 – Image segmentation

This example uses a basic thresholding technique to segment the image based on pixel intensity values.

Practice example for feature extraction

Feature extraction from an image dataset such as CIFAR-10 involves transforming raw image data into a set of relevant features that can be used as input for machine learning models. Here's a simple example using the **Histogram of Oriented Gradients (HOG)** feature extraction technique:

```python
import numpy as np
import matplotlib.pyplot as plt
from skimage.feature import hog
from skimage import exposure
from keras.datasets import cifar10

# Load the CIFAR-10 dataset
(x_train, _), (_, _) = cifar10.load_data()

# Select a sample image for feature extraction
sample_image = x_train[0]  # You can choose any index here

# Convert the image to grayscale (optional)
gray_image = np.mean(sample_image, axis=2)

# Apply Histogram of Oriented Gradients (HOG) feature extraction
hog_features, hog_image = hog( \
    gray_image,pixels_per_cell=(8, 8),\
    cells_per_block=(2, 2), visualize=True)

# Plot the original image and its HOG representation
plt.figure(figsize=(8, 4))
plt.subplot(1, 2, 1)
plt.imshow(gray_image, cmap='gray')
plt.title('Original Grayscale Image')

plt.subplot(1, 2, 2)
plt.imshow(hog_image, cmap='gray')
plt.title('HOG Feature Extraction')

plt.tight_layout()
plt.show()
```

We get the following output:

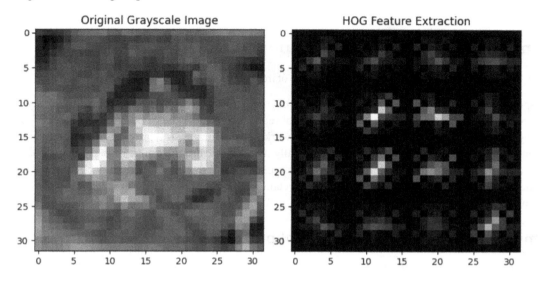

Figure 4.8 – HOG feature extraction

Imagine you have a picture, and you want to understand what's in the picture by looking at the patterns of lines and edges. HOG is a way to do that by focusing on the directions of lines and edges in an image.

In the preceding code block, the hog function internally performs the following four steps to generate the HOG image:

1. **Divide the image into small cells**: First, the function takes the image and divide it into small boxes called cells. Think of these like little squares placed over the image.

2. **Calculate gradients**: Inside each cell, we look at how the colors change. If the colors change significantly, it means there's probably an edge or a line. We figure out the direction of this color change, and this is called a gradient. Imagine drawing little arrows to show the directions of these color changes.

3. **Group arrows into directions**: Now, we group these little arrows with similar directions together. This is like saying, "Hey, there are a lot of edges going this way, and a lot of edges going that way."

4. **Make a histogram of the directions**: A histogram is like a chart that shows how many times something happens. Here, we make a histogram that shows how many arrows are pointing in each direction. This tells us which directions of edges and lines are more common in that cell.

In this section, we have seen how to visualize the image data and plot various features including color pixel histograms, grayscale images, RGB color channels, image segmentation, and annotations on images.

In the next section, we will examine the importance of image size and aspect ratio distribution in image data models.

Analyzing image size and aspect ratio

It is very important to understand the distribution of image sizes and aspect ratios in image data models.

Aspect ratio, in the context of image dataset EDA, refers to the proportional relationship between the width and height of an image. It's a numerical representation that helps describe the shape of an image. Aspect ratio is especially important when working with images, as it provides insights into how elongated or compressed an image appears visually. Mathematically, the aspect ratio is calculated by dividing the width of the image by its height. It's typically expressed as a ratio or a decimal value. A square image has an aspect ratio of 1:1, while a rectangular image would have an aspect ratio different from 1:1.

Impact of aspect ratios on model performance

Let's understand the impact of aspect ratios on the model performance using the following points:

- **Object recognition**: In object recognition tasks, maintaining the correct aspect ratio is essential for accurate detection. If the aspect ratio is distorted during preprocessing or augmentation, it may lead to misinterpretation of object shapes by the model.

- **Training stability**: Ensuring consistent aspect ratios across the training dataset can contribute to training stability. Models may struggle if they encounter variations in aspect ratios that were not present in the training data.

- **Bounding-box accuracy**: In object detection, bounding boxes are often defined by aspect ratios. Deviations from the expected aspect ratios can impact the accuracy of bounding box predictions.

Let's consider a scenario where we have an image represented by a matrix with dimensions $M \times N$, where M is the number of rows (height) and N is the number of columns (width). The image size, aspect ratio, and pixel aspect ratio can be calculated as follows:

- **Image size**: Image size is the total number of pixels in the image and is calculated by multiplying the number of rows (M) by the number of columns (N).

  Image size = $M \times N$

  Example: If we have an image with dimensions `300×200`, the image size would be `300×200=60,000` pixels.

- **Aspect ratio**: The aspect ratio is the ratio of the width to the height of the image and is calculated by dividing the number of columns (N) by the number of rows (M).

Aspect ratio = N/M

Example: For an image with dimensions 300×200, the aspect ratio would be 200/300, which simplifies to 2/3.

- **Pixel Aspect Ratio (PAR)**: It is the ratio of the width of a pixel to its height. This is especially relevant when dealing with non-square pixels.

  PAR = *Height of pixel/ Width of pixel*

  Example: If the pixel aspect ratio is 3/4, it means that the width of a pixel is three-quarters of its height.

These mathematical examples provide a basic understanding of how image size, aspect ratio, and pixel aspect ratio can be calculated using simple formulas.

Now, let's delve into the concepts of padding, cropping, and aspect ratio evaluation metrics in the context of image data analysis in machine learning:

- **Padding** involves adding extra pixels around the edges of an image. This is often done to ensure that the spatial dimensions of the input images remain consistent, especially when applying convolutional operations in neural networks. Padding can be applied symmetrically, adding pixels equally on all sides, or asymmetrically, depending on the requirements of the model.

  Example: Suppose you have an image of size 200×200 pixels, and you want to apply a 3×3 convolutional filter. Without padding, the output size would be 198×198. To maintain the spatial size, you can add a border of one pixel around the image, resulting in a 202×202 image after padding.

- **Cropping** involves removing portions of an image, typically from the borders. This is often done to focus on specific regions of interest or to resize the image. Cropping can help eliminate irrelevant information and reduce the computational load.

  Example: If you have an image of size 300×300 pixels and you decide to crop the central region, you might end up with a 200×200 pixel image by removing 50 pixels from each side.

- Aspect ratio evaluation metrics are measures used to assess the similarity between the aspect ratio of predicted bounding boxes and the ground truth bounding boxes in object detection tasks. Common metrics include **Intersection over Union (IoU)** and F1 score.

In image classification, aspect ratio evaluation metrics play a crucial role in gauging the accuracy of predicted bounding boxes compared to the ground truth bounding boxes in object detection tasks. One widely employed metric is IoU, calculated by dividing the area of overlap between the predicted and ground truth bounding boxes by the total area covered by both. The resulting IoU score ranges from 0 to 1, where a score of 0 indicates no overlap, and a score of 1 signifies perfect alignment. Additionally, the F1 score, another common metric, combines precision and recall, providing a balanced assessment of the model's performance in maintaining accurate aspect ratios across predicted and true bounding boxes. These metrics collectively offer valuable insights into the effectiveness of object detection models in preserving the spatial relationships of objects within an image.

Example: Let's say that in an object detection task, you have a ground-truth bounding box with an aspect ratio of 2 : 1 for a specific object. If your model predicts a bounding box with an aspect ratio of 1.5 : 1, you can use IoU to measure how well the predicted box aligns with the ground truth. If the IoU metric is high, it indicates good alignment; if it's low, there may be a mismatch in aspect ratios.

Understanding and effectively applying padding, cropping, and aspect ratio evaluation metrics are crucial aspects of preprocessing and evaluating image data in machine learning models, particularly in tasks such as object detection where accurate bounding box predictions are essential.

Image resizing

Image resizing is the process of changing the dimensions of an image while preserving its aspect ratio. It is a common preprocessing step in computer vision applications, including object detection, image classification, and image segmentation.

The primary reasons for resizing images are as follows:

- To fit the image into a specific display size or aspect ratio, such as for web pages or mobile applications.

- To reduce the computational complexity of processing the image, such as for real-time computer vision applications or when the image size is too large to fit into memory.

- When resizing an image, we need to decide on a new size for the image. The new size can be specified in terms of pixels or as a scaling factor. In the latter case, we multiply the original image dimensions by a scaling factor to obtain the new dimensions.

There are two primary methods for resizing an image: interpolation and resampling:

Interpolation is a technique for estimating the pixel values in the resized image. It involves computing a weighted average of the pixel values in the original image surrounding the target pixel location. There are several interpolation methods available, including nearest neighbor, bilinear, bicubic, and Lanczos resampling.

Lanczos resampling is a method used in digital image processing for resizing or resampling images. It is a type of interpolation algorithm that aims to produce high-quality results, particularly when downscaling images. The Lanczos algorithm is named after Cornelius Lanczos, a Hungarian mathematician and physicist. The Lanczos resampling algorithm involves applying a sinc function (a type of mathematical function) to the pixel values in the original image to calculate the values of pixels in the resized image. This process is more complex than simple interpolation methods such as bilinear or bicubic, but it tends to produce better results, especially when reducing the size of an image.

The following is a simple example in Python using the Pillow library (a fork of PIL) to demonstrate nearest neighbor, bilinear, bicubic, and Lanczos resampling methods:

```
from PIL import Image

# Open an example image
```

```
image_path = "../images/roseflower.jpeg"
image = Image.open(image_path)

# Resize the image using different interpolation methods
nearest_neighbor_resized = image.resize((100, 100), \
    resample=Image.NEAREST)
bilinear_resized = image.resize((100, 100), \
    resample=Image.BILINEAR)
bicubic_resized = image.resize((100, 100), \
    resample=Image.BICUBIC)
lanczos_resized = image.resize((100, 100), \
    resample=Image.LANCZOS)

# Save the resized images
nearest_neighbor_resized.save("nearest_neighbor_resized.jpg")
bilinear_resized.save("bilinear_resized.jpg")
bicubic_resized.save("bicubic_resized.jpg")
lanczos_resized.save("lanczos_resized.jpg")
```

We get the following output:

Bicubic_resized_image.jpg   Bilinear_resized_image.jpg

Lanczos_resized_image.jpg   Nearest_neighbor_image.jpg

Figure 4.9 – The results of each interpolation method

Let's delve into the details of each interpolation method:

- **Nearest neighbor method** (`Image.NEAREST`): This method chooses the nearest pixel value to the interpolated point:

  - **Usage** (`resample=Image.NEAREST`): Simple and fast. Often used for upscaling pixel art images.

  - **Visual effect**: Results in blocky or pixelated images, especially noticeable during upscaling.

- **Bilinear method** (`Image.BILINEAR`): Uses a linear interpolation between the four nearest pixels:

  - **Usage** (`resample=Image.BILINEAR`): Commonly used for general image resizing

  - **Visual effect**: Smoother than nearest neighbor but may result in some loss of sharpness

- **Bicubic method** (`Image.BICUBIC`): Employs a cubic polynomial for interpolation:

  - **Usage** (`resample=Image.BICUBIC`): Typically used for high-quality downsampling

  - **Visual effect**: Smoother than bilinear; often used for photographic images, but can introduce slight blurring

- **Lanczos method** (`Image.LANCZOS`): Applies a `sinc` function as the interpolation kernel:

  - **Usage** (`resample=Image.LANCZOS`): Preferred for downscaling images and maintaining quality.

  - **Visual effect**: Generally produces the highest quality, especially noticeable in downscaling scenarios. May take longer to compute.

- **Choosing the right method**:

  - **Quality versus speed**: Nearest neighbor is the fastest but may result in visible artifacts. Bicubic and Lanczos are often preferred for quality, sacrificing a bit of speed.

  - **Downscaling versus upscaling**: Bicubic and Lanczos are commonly used for downscaling, while bilinear might be sufficient for upscaling.

  If the images do not show noticeable differences, it could be due to factors such as the original image's characteristics, the magnitude of resizing, or the viewer's display capabilities. Generally, for high-quality resizing, especially downscaling, Lanczos interpolation tends to provide superior results. If the images are small or the differences subtle, the choice of method may have less impact.

- **Resampling**: Resampling is the process of selecting a subset of the pixels from the original image to create the resized image. This method can result in loss of information or artifacts in the image due to the removal of pixels.

In Python, we can use the Pillow library for image resizing. Here is some example code for resizing an image using the Pillow library:

```
 #resizing Image
from PIL import Image
# Open image
img = Image.open('../images/roseflower.jpeg')
# Resize image
new_size = (200, 200)
resized_img = img.resize(new_size)
resized_img.save("resized_image.jpg")
```

We get the following result:

Figure 4.10 – Resized image (200*200)

In the preceding code, we first open an image using the `Image.open()` function from the Pillow library. We then define the new size of the image as a tuple `(500, 500)`. Finally, we call the `resize()` method on the image object with the new size tuple as an argument, which returns a new resized image object. We then save the resized image using the `save()` method with the new filename.

Let's see one more example of resizing images using Python. We first import the necessary libraries: `os` for file and directory operations and `cv2` for image loading and manipulation:

```
import os
import cv2
```

We define the path to the image directory and get a list of all image filenames in the directory using a list comprehension:

```
# Define the path to the image directory
img_dir = '../Images/resize_images'

# Get a list of all image filenames in the directory
img_files = [os.path.join(img_dir, f) \
```

```
    for f in os.listdir(img_dir) \
    if os.path.isfile(os.path.join(img_dir, f))]
```

We define the new size of the images using a tuple (224, 224) in this example. You can change the tuple to any other size you want:

```
# Define the new size of the images
new_size = (224, 224)
```

We then resize the image as follows:

```
# Loop through all the image files
for img_file in img_files:
    # Load the image using OpenCV
    img = cv2.imread(img_file)

    # Resize the image
    resized_img = cv2.resize(img, new_size)

    # Save the resized image with the same filename
    cv2.imwrite(img_file, resized_img)
```

Here's the output of the resized images in the relevant directory:

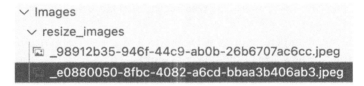

Figure 4.11 – Resized images in the directory

We loop through all the image files using a for loop. For each image file, we load the image using OpenCV (cv2.imread()), resize the image using cv2.resize(), and save the resized image with the same filename using cv2.imwrite().

The cv2.resize() function takes three parameters: the image to resize, the new size of the image as a tuple (width, height), and an interpolation method. The default interpolation method is cv2.INTER_LINEAR, which produces good results in most cases.

Resizing an image is a common preprocessing step in image classification and object detection tasks. It is often necessary to resize images to a fixed size to ensure that all images have the same size and aspect ratio, which makes it easier to train machine learning models on the images. Resizing can also help to reduce the computational cost of processing images, as smaller images require less memory and computing resources than larger images.

In summary, image resizing is the process of changing the dimensions of an image while preserving its aspect ratio. It is a common preprocessing step in computer vision applications and can be performed using interpolation or resampling techniques. In Python, we can use the Pillow library for image resizing.

Image normalization

Image normalization is a preprocessing technique that is commonly used in computer vision applications. The goal of image normalization is to transform the pixel values of an image that are within a certain range or have certain statistical properties. Normalization is used to reduce the impact of variations in lighting conditions or to standardize the color or brightness of images.

Normalization techniques typically involve scaling the pixel values of an image to fall within a certain range or modifying the distribution of pixel values to have certain statistical properties. There are many different techniques for image normalization, and the choice of technique depends on the specific application and the characteristics of the image data.

Here are some common techniques for image normalization.

Min-max normalization: This technique scales the pixel values of an image so that they fall within a specified range, typically `[0, 1]` or `[-1, 1]`. This can be done using the following formula:

```
normalized_image = (image - min_value) / (max_value - min_value)
```

Here, `min_value` and `max_value` are the minimum and maximum pixel values in the image, respectively.

Z-score normalization: This technique modifies the distribution of pixel values in an image to have a mean of 0 and a standard deviation of 1. This can be done using the following formula:

```
normalized_image = (image - mean_value) / std_value
```

Here, `mean_value` and `std_value` are the mean and standard deviation of the pixel values in the image, respectively.

Histogram equalization: This technique modifies the distribution of pixel values in an image to be more uniform. This can be done by computing the **cumulative distribution function** (**CDF**) of the pixel values and mapping the pixel values to new values based on the CDF:

```
import cv2

# Load image
img = cv2.imread("image.jpg", 0)

# Apply histogram equalization
equalized_img = cv2.equalizeHist(img)
```

In the preceding code, we first load an image using the OpenCV library. We then apply histogram equalization using the `equalizeHist()` function, which returns a new image with a more uniform distribution of pixel values. OpenCV is a powerful and widely used open source library that plays a crucial role in image recognition and computer vision tasks. Its importance stems from its comprehensive collection of tools, functions, and algorithms designed to handle various aspects of image processing, analysis, and recognition.

Let's see an example of image normalization using Python. We first import the necessary libraries: `os` for file and directory operations, `cv2` for image loading and manipulation, and `numpy` for mathematical operations:

```
import os
import cv2
import numpy as np
```

We define the path to the image directory and get a list of all image filenames in the directory using a list comprehension:

```
# Define the path to the image directory
img_dir = 'path/to/image/directory'
# Get a list of all image filenames in the directory
img_files = [os.path.join(img_dir, f) \
    for f in os.listdir(img_dir) \
    if os.path.isfile(os.path.join(img_dir, f))]
```

We loop through all the image files using a `for` loop. For each image file, we load the image using OpenCV (`cv2.imread()`):

```
# Loop through all the image files
for img_file in img_files:
    # Load the image using OpenCV
    img = cv2.imread(img_file)
```

We convert the image to `float32` data type using `astype(np.float32)`. This is necessary for the next step of normalization:

```
    # Convert the image to float32 data type
    img = img.astype(np.float32)
```

We normalize the image pixels to have zero mean and unit variance using the following formula: `img -= np.mean(img); img /= np.std(img)`. This is also known as standardization or z-score normalization. This step is important for machine learning models that are sensitive to the scale of input features, as it ensures that the pixel values have a similar scale across all images:

```
    # Normalize the image pixels to have zero mean and unit variance
    img -= np.mean(img)
    img /= np.std(img)
```

Finally, we save the normalized image with the same filename using `cv2.imwrite()`:

```
# Save the normalized image with the same filename
cv2.imwrite(img_file, img)
```

Image normalization is a critical step in many computer vision applications, as it can help to reduce the impact of variations in lighting conditions and standardize the color and brightness of images. By transforming the pixel values of an image, we can make it easier for machine learning algorithms to learn from the image data and improve the accuracy of our models.

Performing transformations on images – image augmentation

In the realm of image processing and deep learning, the ability to effectively work with image data is paramount. However, acquiring a diverse and extensive dataset can be a challenge. This is where the concept of image augmentation comes into play. Image augmentation is a transformative technique that holds the power to enhance the richness of a dataset without the need to amass additional images manually. This section delves into the intricacies of image augmentation – an indispensable tool for improving model performance, enhancing generalization capabilities, and mitigating overfitting concerns.

Image augmentation is a technique for artificially increasing the size of a dataset by generating new training examples from existing ones. It is commonly used in deep learning applications to prevent overfitting and improve generalization performance.

The idea behind image augmentation is to apply a variety of transformations to existing images to create new, slightly modified versions of the original images. By doing so, we can effectively increase the size of our dataset without having to collect and label new images manually. For example, in medical image analysis, acquiring a large number of high-quality medical images with accurate annotations is often difficult due to patient privacy concerns and the expertise required for labeling. Image augmentation techniques can help to generate diverse training examples to train accurate diagnostic models. Another scenario is when dealing with rare events or anomalies, such as defects in manufacturing or diseases in agriculture, where collecting a sufficient number of real-world instances can be challenging. Image augmentation allows the generation of various scenarios of these rare events, improving the model's ability to detect them.

There are several types of image augmentation techniques that can be used. The most commonly used techniques include the following:

- **Rotation**: Rotating the image by a specified angle in degrees
- **Flipping**: Flipping the image horizontally or vertically
- **Zooming**: Zooming in or out on the image by a specified factor

- **Shearing**: Shearing the image in the *x* or *y* direction by a specified factor

- **Shifting**: Shifting the image horizontally or vertically by a specified number of pixels

These techniques can be applied in various combinations to generate a large number of new images from a small set of original images. For example, we can rotate an image by 45 degrees, flip it horizontally, and shift it vertically, resulting in a new image that is quite different from the original but still retains some of its features.

One important consideration when using image augmentation is to ensure that the generated images are still representative of the underlying dataset. For example, if we are training a model to recognize handwritten digits, we should ensure that the generated images are still recognizable as digits and not some random patterns.

Overall, image augmentation is a powerful technique that can be used to increase the size of a dataset and improve the performance of deep learning models. The Keras library provides a convenient way to apply various image augmentation techniques to a dataset, as we will see in the following code example.

Let us see some example Python code for image augmentation. We first import the necessary libraries: `keras.preprocessing.image` for image augmentation and `os` for file and directory operations:

Step 1: Import the necessary libraries for image augmentation

The following code snippet shows how to import the libraries:

```
# import the necessary libraries
from keras.preprocessing.image import ImageDataGenerator
import os
```

We define the path to the image directory as follows:

```
# Define the path to the image directory
img_dir = 'path/to/image/directory'
```

Step 2: Create an instance of ImageDataGenerator

We create an instance of the `ImageDataGenerator` class, which allows us to define various types of image augmentation techniques. In this example, we use rotation, horizontal and vertical shifts, shear, zoom, and horizontal flipping:

```
# Create an instance of the ImageDataGenerator class
datagen = ImageDataGenerator(
    rotation_range=30,
    width_shift_range=0.2,
    height_shift_range=0.2,
    shear_range=0.2,
    zoom_range=0.2,
```

```
        horizontal_flip=True,
        fill_mode='nearest')
```

Step 3: Load each image from the directory and convert the image to an array

We get a list of all image filenames in the directory using a list comprehension. We then loop through all the image files using a `for` loop. For each image file, we load the image using Keras' `load_img` function and convert it to an array using Keras' `img_to_array` function:

```
# Get a list of all image filenames in the directory
img_files = [os.path.join(img_dir, f) \
    for f in os.listdir(img_dir) \
    if os.path.isfile(os.path.join(img_dir, f))]


# Loop through all the image files
for img_file in img_files:
    # Load the image using Keras' load_img function
    img = load_img(img_file)

    # Convert the image to an array using Keras' img_to_array function
    img_arr = img_to_array(img)
```

We reshape the array to have a batch dimension of 1, which is required by the `flow` method of the `ImageDataGenerator` class:

```
    # Reshape the array to have a batch dimension of 1
    img_arr = img_arr.reshape((1,) + img_arr.shape)
```

Step 4: Regenerate five augmented images for each input image

We then regenerate our augmented images as follows:

```
    # Generate 5 augmented images for each input image
    i = 0
    for batch in datagen.flow( \
        img_arr, batch_size=1, save_to_dir=img_dir, \
        save_prefix='aug_', save_format='jpg' \
    ):
        i += 1
        if i == 5:
            break
```

You can see five augmented images generated for the flow in the GitHub repository in the directory as follows:

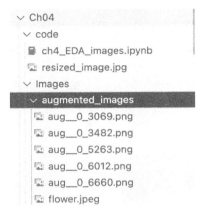

Figure 4.12 – Augmented images

We use the flow method to generate five augmented images for each input image. The flow method takes the array of input images, a batch size of 1, and various parameters defined in *step 3*. It returns a generator that generates augmented images on the fly. We save each augmented image with a filename prefix of aug_ using the save_to_dir, save_prefix, and save_format parameters.

In this section, we learned how to transform a dataset using data augmentation and saw some commonly used data augmentation techniques for generating additional data for training.

Summary

In this chapter, we learned how to review images after loading an image dataset and explore them using a tool called Matplotlib in Python. We also found out how to change the size of pictures using two handy tools called PIL and OpenCV. And just when things were getting interesting, we discovered a cool trick called data augmentation that helps us make our dataset bigger and teaches our computer how to understand different versions of the same picture.

But wait, there's more to come! In the next chapter, we are going to see how to label our image data using Snorkel based on rules and heuristics. Get ready for some more fun as we dive into the world of labeling images!

5

Labeling Image Data Using Rules

In this chapter, we will explore data labeling techniques tailored specifically for image classification, using Python. Our primary objective is to clarify the path you need to take to generate precise labels for these images in the dataset, relying on meticulously crafted rules founded upon various image properties. You will be empowered with the ability to dissect and decode images through manual inspection, harnessing the formidable Python ecosystem.

In this chapter, you will learn the following:

- How to create labeling rules based on manual inspection of image visualizations in Python
- How to create labeling rules based on the size and aspect ratio of images
- How to apply transfer learning to label image data, using pre-trained models such as **YOLO V3**

The overarching goal is to empower you with the ability to generate precise and reliable labels for your data. We aim to equip you with a versatile set of labeling strategies that can be applied across various machine learning projects.

We will also introduce transformations such as **shearing** and **flipping** for image labeling. We will provide you with the knowledge and techniques required to harness these transformations effectively, giving your labeling process a dynamic edge. we'll delve into the intricacies of **size, aspect ratio, bounding box, polygon annotation**, and **polyline annotation**. You'll learn how to derive labeling rules based on these quantitative image characteristics, providing a systematic and reliable approach to labeling data.

Technical requirements

Complete code notebooks for the examples used in this chapter are available on GitHub at `https://github.com/PacktPublishing/Data-Labeling-in-Machine-Learning-with-Python`.

The sample image dataset used in this chapter is available on GitHub at `https://github.com/PacktPublishing/Data-Labeling-in-Machine-Learning-with-Python/tree/main/images`.

Labeling rules based on image visualization

Image classification is the process of categorizing an image into one or more classes based on its content. It is a challenging task due to the high variability and complexity of images. In recent years, machine learning techniques have been applied to image classification with great success. However, machine learning models require a large amount of labeled data to train effectively.

Image labeling using rules with Snorkel

Snorkel is an open source data platform that provides a way to generate large amounts of labeled data using weak supervision techniques. Weak supervision allows you to label data with noisy or incomplete sources of supervision, such as heuristics, rules, or patterns.

Snorkel primarily operates within the paradigm of weak supervision rather than traditional semi-supervised learning. Snorkel is a framework designed for weak supervision, where the labeling process may involve noisy, limited, or imprecise rules rather than a large amount of labeled data.

In Snorkel, users create **labeling functions** (**LFs**) that express heuristic or rule-based labeling strategies. These LFs might not be perfect, and there can be conflicts or noise in the generated labels. Snorkel's labeling model then learns to denoise and combine these weak labels to create more accurate and reliable labeling for the training data.

While semi-supervised learning typically involves having a small amount of labeled data and a large amount of unlabeled data, Snorkel focuses on the weak supervision scenario, allowing users to leverage various sources of noisy or incomplete supervision to train machine learning models.

In summary, Snorkel is more aligned with the principles of weak supervision, where the emphasis is on handling noisy or imprecise labels generated by heuristic rules, rather than being strictly categorized as a semi-supervised learning framework.

In this section, we will explore the concept of weak supervision and how to generate labels using Snorkel.

Weak supervision

Weak supervision is a technique for generating large amounts of labeled data using noisy or incomplete sources of supervision. The idea is to use a set of LFs that generate noisy labels for each data point. These labels are then combined to generate a final label for each data point. The key advantage of weak supervision is that it allows you to generate labeled data quickly and at a low cost.

Snorkel is a framework that provides a way to generate labels using weak supervision. It provides a set of tools to create LFs, combine them, and train a model to learn from the generated labels. Snorkel uses a technique called data programming to combine the LFs and generate a final label for each data point.

An LF is a function that generates a noisy label for a data point. The label can be any value, including continuous or discrete values. In the context of image classification, an LF is a function that outputs a label of 1 if the image contains the object of interest, and 0 otherwise.

LFs are created using heuristics, rules, or patterns. The key idea is to define a set of rules that capture the relevant information for each data point.

Now, let us see how to define the rules and an LF based on the manual visualization of an image's object color for plant disease labeling.

Rules based on the manual visualization of an image's object color

In this section, let us see how we can use LFs that look for specific visual features that are characteristic of images of a plant's leaves, which we are interested in classifying as "healthy" or "deceased". For instance, we could use an LF that checks whether the image has a certain color distribution, or whether it contains specific shapes that are common in those images.

Snorkel's LFs can be used to label images based on various properties, such as the presence of certain objects, colors, textures, and shapes. Here's an example of Python code that uses Snorkel LFs to detect images based on their color distribution.

Creating labeling rules based on manual inspection of image visualizations is a manual process that often involves the expertise of a human annotator. This process is commonly used in scenarios where there is no existing labeled dataset, and you need to create labels for machine learning or analysis tasks.

Here's a general outline of how you can create labeling rules based on the manual inspection of image visualizations in Python:

1. **Collect a representative sample**: Begin by selecting a representative sample of images from your dataset. This sample should cover the range of variations and categories you want to classify.

2. **Define the labeling criteria**: Clearly define the criteria or rules to label images based on their visual properties. For example, if you're classifying images to identify plant diseases from images of leaves, agricultural experts visually inspect leaf images for discoloration, spots, or unusual patterns. Rules can be defined based on the appearance and location of symptoms. We will use this example for our demonstration shortly.

3. **Create a labeling interface**: You can use existing tools or libraries to create a labeling interface where human annotators can view images and apply labels based on the defined criteria. Libraries such as Labelbox and Supervisely or custom interfaces, using Python web frameworks such as Flask or Django, can be used for this purpose.

4. **Annotate the images**: Have human annotators manually inspect each image in your sample and apply labels according to the defined criteria. This step involves the human annotators visually inspecting the images and making classification decisions, based on their expertise and the provided guidelines.

5. **Collect annotations**: Collect the annotations generated by the human annotators. Each image should have a corresponding label or class assigned based on the visual inspection.

6. **Analyze and formalize rules**: After collecting a sufficient number of annotations, analyze the patterns and decisions made by the annotators. Try to formalize the decision criteria based on the annotations. For example, you might observe that images with certain visual features were consistently labeled as a specific class.

7. **Convert rules to code**: Translate the formalized decision criteria into code that can automatically classify images based on those rules. This code can be written in Python and integrated into your machine learning pipeline or analysis workflow.

8. **Test and validate rules**: Apply the automated labeling rules to a larger portion of your dataset to ensure that they generalize well. Validate the rules by comparing the automated labels with ground truth labels if available, or by reviewing a subset of the automatically labeled images manually.

9. **Iterate and refine**: Iteratively refine the labeling rules based on feedback, error analysis, and additional manual inspection if necessary. This process may involve improving the rules, adding more criteria, or adjusting thresholds.

Creating labeling rules based on manual inspection is a labor-intensive process but can be essential to generate labeled data when no other options are available. The quality of your labeled dataset and the effectiveness of your rules depend on the accuracy and consistency of the human annotators, as well as the clarity of the defined criteria.

Real-world applications

Manual inspection of images for classification, along with the definition of rules or patterns, is common in various real-world applications. Here are some practical examples:

- **Medical image classification**:

    - **Example**: Classifying X-ray or MRI images as "normal" or "abnormal."

    - **Rules/patterns**: Radiologists visually inspect images for abnormalities, such as tumors, fractures, or anomalies in anatomy. Rules can be based on the presence, size, or location of these features.

- **Plant disease detection**:

    - **Example**: Identifying plant diseases from images of leaves.

    - **Rules/patterns**: Agricultural experts visually inspect leaf images for discoloration, spots, or unusual patterns. Rules can be defined based on the appearance and location of symptoms.

- **Food quality inspection**:

  - **Example**: Classifying food products as "fresh" or "spoiled" from images.
  - **Rules/patterns**: Food inspectors visually inspect images of fruits, vegetables, or packaged goods for signs of spoilage, mold, or other quality issues. Rules can be based on color, texture, or shape.

- **Defect detection in manufacturing**:

  - **Example**: Detecting defects in manufactured products from images.
  - **Rules/patterns**: Quality control inspectors visually inspect images of products for defects such as cracks, scratches, or missing components. Rules can be defined based on the location and characteristics of defects.

- **Traffic sign recognition**:

  - **Example**: Recognizing traffic signs from images captured by autonomous vehicles.
  - **Rules/patterns**: Engineers visually inspect images for the presence of signs and their shapes, colors, and symbols. Rules can be defined based on these visual cues.

- **Wildlife monitoring**:

  - **Example**: Identifying and tracking animals in camera trap images.
  - **Rules/patterns**: Wildlife experts visually inspect images for the presence of specific animal species, their behavior, or the time of day. Rules can be based on the appearance and context of animals.

- **Historical document classification**:

  - **Example**: Classifying historical documents based on content or era.
  - **Rules/patterns**: Archivists visually inspect scanned documents for handwriting style, language, content, or visual elements such as illustrations. Rules can be defined based on these characteristics.

- **Security and surveillance**:

  - **Example**: Identifying security threats or intruders in surveillance camera footage.
  - **Rules/patterns**: Security personnel visually inspect video feeds for unusual behavior, suspicious objects, or unauthorized access. Rules can be defined based on these observations.

In all these examples, experts or human annotators visually examine images, identify relevant patterns or features, and define rules or criteria for classification. These rules are often based on domain knowledge and experience. Once established, the rules can be used to create LFs and classify images automatically, assist in decision-making, or prioritize further analysis.

A practical example of plant disease detection

Let us see the example LF for plant disease detection. In this code, we have created a rule to classify healthy and diseased plants, based on the color distribution of leaves. One rule is if `black_pixel_ percentage` in the plant leaves is greater than the threshold value, then we classify that plant as a diseased plant.

The following are the two different types of plant leaves.

Figure 5.1 – Healthy and diseased plant leaves

We calculate the number of black color pixels in a leaf image and then calculate the percent of black pixels:

Percent of black pixels = count of black pixels in a leaf image/total number of pixels in a leaf image

We are going to use the rule that if the black pixel percent in a plant leave image is greater than the threshold value (in this example, 10%), then we classify that plant as a diseased plant and label it as a "diseased plant."

Similarly, if the black pixel percentage is less than 10%, then we classify that plant as a healthy plant and label it as a "healthy plant."

The following code snippet shows how to calculate the black pixel percentage in an image using Python libraries:

```
# Convert the image to grayscale
gray_image = cv2.cvtColor(resized_image, cv2.COLOR_BGR2GRAY)
```

This line converts the original color image to grayscale using OpenCV's cvtColor function. Grayscale images have only one channel (compared to the three channels in a color image), representing the intensity or brightness of each pixel. Converting to grayscale simplifies subsequent processing:

```
# Apply thresholding to detect regions with discoloration
_, binary_image = cv2.threshold(gray_image, 150, 255,\
    cv2.THRESH_BINARY_INV)
```

In this line, a thresholding operation is applied to the grayscale image, gray_image. Thresholding is a technique that separates pixels into two categories, based on their intensity values – those above a certain threshold and those below it. Here's what each parameter means:

- gray_image: The grayscale image to be thresholded.

- 150: The threshold value. Pixels with intensities greater than or equal to 150 will be set to the maximum value (255), while pixels with intensities lower than 150 will be set to 0.

- 255: The maximum value to which pixels above the threshold are set.

- cv2.THRESH_BINARY_INV: The thresholding type. In this case, it's set to "binary inverted," which means that pixels above the threshold will become 0, and pixels below the threshold will become 255.

The result of this thresholding operation is stored in binary_image, which is a binary image where regions with discoloration are highlighted:

```
# Calculate the percentage of black pixels (discoloration) in the
image
white_pixel_percentage = \
    (cv2.countNonZero(binary_image) / binary_image.size) * 100
```

The cv2.countNonZero(binary_image) function counts the number of non-zero (white) pixels in the binary image. Since we are interested in black pixels (discoloration), we subtract this count from the total number of pixels in the image.

binary_image.size: This is the total number of pixels in the binary image, which is equal to the width multiplied by the height.

By dividing the count of non-zero (white) pixels by the total number of pixels and multiplying by 100, we obtain the percentage of white pixels in the image. This percentage represents the extent of discoloration in the image.

To calculate the percentage of black pixels (discoloration), you can use the following code:

```
black_pixel_percentage = 100 - white_pixel_percentage
```

Overall, this code snippet is a simple method to quantitatively measure the extent of discoloration in a grayscale image, by converting it into a binary image and calculating the percentage of black pixels. It can be useful for tasks such as detecting defects or anomalies in images. Adjusting the threshold value (in this case, 150) can change the sensitivity of the detection.

Let us create the labeling function to classify the plant as `Healthy` or `Diseased`, based on the threshold value of `black_pixel_percentage` in the leaf images, as follows.

```
# Define a labeling function to classify images as "Healthy"
@labeling_function()
def is_healthy(record):
# Define a threshold for discoloration (adjust as needed)
threshold = 10
# Classify as "Healthy" if the percentage of discoloration is below
the threshold
if record['black_pixel_percentage'] < threshold:
    return 1 # Label as "Healthy"
else:
    return 0 # Label as "Diseased"
```

This LF returns labels 0 (a diseased plant) or 1 (a healthy plant) based on the *black* color pixels percentage in the image. The complete working code for this plant disease labeling is available in the GitHub repo.

In the next section, let us see how we can apply labels using image properties such as size and aspect ratio.

Labeling images using rules based on properties

Let us see an example of Python code that demonstrates how to classify images using rules, based on image properties such as size and aspect ratio.

Here, we will define rules such as if the black color distribution is greater than 50% in leaves, then that is a diseased plant. Similarly, in case of detecting a bicycle with a person, if the aspect ratio of an image is greater than some threshold value, then that image has a bicycle with a person.

In computer vision and image classification, the **aspect ratio** refers to the ratio of the width to the height of an image or object. It is a measure of how elongated or stretched an object or image appears along its horizontal and vertical dimensions. Aspect ratio is often used as a feature or criterion in image analysis and classification. It's worth noting that aspect ratio alone is often not sufficient for classification, and it is typically used in conjunction with other features, such as **contour height**, **texture**, and **edge**, to achieve accurate classification results. Image properties such as bounding boxes, polygon annotations, and polyline annotations are commonly used in computer vision tasks for object detection and image segmentation. These properties help you to label and annotate objects within an image. Here's an explanation of each feature along with Python code examples to demonstrate how to work with them:

Bounding boxes

A bounding box is a rectangular region that encloses an object of interest within an image. It is defined by four values – (x_min, y_min) for the top-left corner and (x_max, y_max) for the bottom-right corner. Bounding boxes are often used for object detection and localization. Here is an example of Python code to create and manipulate bounding boxes:

```python
# Define a bounding box as (x_min, y_min, x_max, y_max)
bounding_box = (100, 50, 300, 200)

# Access individual components
x_min, y_min, x_max, y_max = bounding_box

# Calculate width and height of the bounding box
width = x_max - x_min
height = y_max - y_min

# Check if a point (x, y) is inside the bounding box
x, y = 200, 150
is_inside = x_min <= x <= x_max and y_min <= y <= y_max


print(f"Width: {width}, Height: {height}, Is Inside: {is_inside}")
```

Polygon annotation

A polygon annotation is a set of connected vertices that outline the shape of an object in an image. It is defined by a list of (x, y) coordinates representing the vertices. Polygon annotations are used for detailed object segmentation. Here is some example Python code to work with polygon annotations:

```python
# Define a polygon annotation as a list of (x, y) coordinates
polygon = [(100, 50), (200, 50), (250, 150), (150, 200)]

# Calculate the area of the polygon (using shoelace formula)
def polygon_area(vertices):
    n = len(vertices)
    area = 0
    for i in range(n):
        j = (i + 1) % n
        area += (vertices[i][0] * vertices[j][1]) - \
            (vertices[j][0] * vertices[i][1])
    area = abs(area) / 2
    return area
```

```
area = polygon_area(polygon)
print(f"Polygon Area: {area}")
```

Polyline annotations

A polyline annotation is a series of connected line segments defined by a list of (x, y) coordinates for each vertex. Polylines are often used to represent shapes with multiple line segments, such as roads or paths. Here is some Python code to work with polyline annotations:

```
# Define a polyline annotation as a list of (x, y) coordinates
polyline = [(100, 50), (200, 50), (250, 150), (150, 200)]

# Calculate the total length of the polyline
def polyline_length(vertices):
    length = 0
    for i in range(1, len(vertices)):
        x1, y1 = vertices[i - 1]
        x2, y2 = vertices[i]
        length += ((x2 - x1) ** 2 + (y2 - y1) ** 2) ** 0.5
    return length

length = polyline_length(polyline)
print(f"Polyline Length: {length}")
```

These code examples demonstrate how to work with bounding boxes, polygon annotations, and polyline annotations in Python. You can use these concepts to create rules to label images in computer vision applications.

Now, let us see the following example of how we can use contour height to classify whether an image contains a person riding a bicycle or just shows a bicycle on its own.

Example 1 – image classification – a bicycle with and without a person

Contour height, in the context of image processing and computer vision, refers to the measurement of the vertical extent or size of an object's outline or contour within an image. It is typically calculated by finding the minimum and maximum vertical positions (i.e., the topmost and bottommost points) of the object's boundary or contour.

Here's how contour height is generally determined:

1. **Contour detection**: The first step is to detect the contour of an object within an image. Contours are essentially the boundaries that separate an object from its background.

2. **A bounding rectangle**: Once the contour is detected, a bounding rectangle (often referred to as the "**bounding box**") is drawn around the contour. This rectangle encompasses the entire object.

3. **Measurement**: To calculate the contour height, the vertical extent of the bounding rectangle is measured. This is done by finding the difference between the y coordinates (the vertical positions) of the top and bottom sides of the bounding rectangle.

In summary, contour height provides information about the vertical size of an object within an image. It can be a useful feature for various computer vision tasks, such as object recognition, tracking, and dimension estimation.

Let us see how we will use Python functions to detect the following images, based on contour height.

a: A bicycle with a person   b: A bicycle without a person

Figure 5.2 – A comparison of two images with regards to the contour height

Here, the contour height of a person riding a bicycle in an image (*Figure 5.2a*) is greater than the contour height of the image of a bicycle without a person (*Figure 5.2b*).

Let us use the Python library CV2 Canny edge detector to detect the maximum contour height for the given image as, follows:

```python
# Define a function to find the contour height of an object using the
Canny edge detector
def canny_contour_height(image):
```

This function takes an image as input and returns the maximum contour height, found using the Canny edge detector:

```python
# Convert the image to grayscale
gray = cv2.cvtColor(image, cv2.COLOR_BGR2GRAY)
```

```python
# Apply the Canny edge detector with low and high threshold values
edges = cv2.Canny(gray, 100, 200)

# Find the contours of the edges
contours, _ = cv2.findContours(edges, \
    cv2.RETR_EXTERNAL, cv2.CHAIN_APPROX_SIMPLE)

# Initialize the maximum height as zero
max_height = 0

# Loop through each contour
for cnt in contours:
    # Find the bounding rectangle of the contour
    x, y, w, h = cv2.boundingRect(cnt)

    # Update the maximum height if the current height is larger
    if h > max_height:
        max_height = h

# Return the maximum height
return max_height
```

Here, Python functions are used to find the contour height of the images. As seen in the images, the results show that the contour height of the person riding a bicycle image is greater than the contour height of the bicycle image. So, we can classify these two images by using a certain threshold value for the contour height, and if that is greater than that threshold value, then we classify the images as a bicycle with a person; otherwise, if the contour height is less than that threshold value, we classify those images as just showing a bicycle.

As shown in the preceding LF, (we learned about labeling functions in *Chapter 2*) we can automate such image classification and object detection tasks using Python, and label the images as either a man riding a bicycle or just a bicycle.

The complete code to find the contour height of the preceding two images is on GitHub.

By using a diverse set of LFs that capture different aspects of the image content, we can increase the likelihood that at least some of the functions will provide a useful way to distinguish between images that depict a bicycle, a bicycle with a person, or neither. The probabilistic label generated by the majority label voter model will then reflect the combined evidence provided by all of the LFs, and it can be used to make a more accurate classification decision.

Example 2 – image classification – dog and cat images

Let us see another example of labeling images to classify dog or cat images, based on rules associated with properties.

The following are some rules to implement as LFs to detect images of dogs, based on pointy ears and snouts, the shape of the eyes, fur texture, and the shape of the body, as well as additional LFs to detect other features. The complete code for these functions is available on GitHub.

Labeling function 1: The rule is, if the image has pointy ears and a snout, label it as a dog:

```
# Define a labeling function to detect dogs based on pointy ears and
snouts
def dog_features(image):
    ....
        # If the image has pointy ears and a snout, label it as a dog
    if has_pointy_ears and has_snout:
        return 1
    else:
        return 0
```

Labeling function 2: The rule is, if the image has oval-shaped eyes, label it as a cat:

```
# Define a labeling function to detect cats based on their eyes
def cat_features(image):

    # Label images as positive if they contain cat features #such as
oval-shaped eyes

    # If the image has oval-shaped eyes, label it as a cat
    if has_oval_eyes:
        return 1
    else:
        return 0
```

Labeling function 3: The rule is, if the image has a texture with high variance, label it as a dog:

```
# Define a labeling function to detect dogs based on fur texture
def dog_fur_texture(image):
    # If the image has high variance, label it as a dog
    if variance > 100:
        return 1
    else:
        return 0
```

Labeling function 4: The rule is, if the aspect ratio is close to 1 (indicating a more circular shape), label it as a cat:

```
# Define a labeling function to detect cats based on their body shape
def cat_body_shape(image):
    ......
```

```
    # If the aspect ratio is close to 1 (indicating a more circular
shape), label it as a cat
    if abs(aspect_ratio - 1) < 0.1:
        return 1
    else:
        return 0
```

The `dog_features` LF looks for the presence of pointy ears and snouts in the image by examining specific regions of the blue channel. The `cat_features` LF looks for the presence of oval-shaped eyes in the green channel. The `dog_fur_texture` LF looks for high variance in the grayscale version of the image, which is often associated with dog fur texture. The `cat_body_shape` LF looks for a circular body shape in the image, which is often associated with cats.

These LFs could be combined with Snorkel to create a model and label the images. In the next section, let us see how we can apply labels using transfer learning.

Labeling images using transfer learning

Transfer learning is a machine learning technique where a model trained on one task is adapted for a second related task. Instead of starting the learning process from scratch, transfer learning leverages knowledge gained from solving one problem and applies it to a different but related problem. This approach has become increasingly popular in deep learning and has several advantages:

- **Faster training**: Transfer learning can significantly reduce the time and computational resources required to train a model. Instead of training a deep neural network from random initialization, you start with a pre-trained model, which already has learned features and representations.

- **Better generalization**: Models pre-trained on large datasets, such as ImageNet for image recognition, have learned general features that are useful for various related tasks. These features tend to generalize well to new tasks, leading to better performance.

- **Lower data requirements**: Transfer learning can be especially beneficial when you have a limited amount of data for your target task. Pre-trained models can provide a head start, enabling effective learning with smaller datasets.

- **Domain adaptation**: Transfer learning helps adapt models from one domain (e.g., natural images) to another (e.g., medical images). This is valuable when collecting data in the target domain is challenging.

Let us see an example of Python code to detect digits in handwritten MNIST images, using Snorkel LFs.

Example – digit classification using a pre-trained classifier

In this example, we will first load the MNIST dataset, using Keras, and then define an LF that uses a digit classification model to classify the digits in each image. We then load the MNIST images into a Snorkel dataset and apply the LF to generate labels for the specified digit. Finally, we visualize the labels using Snorkel's viewer.

Note that, in this example, we assume that you have already trained a digit classification model and saved it as a file named `digit_classifier.h5`. You can replace this with any other model of your choice. Also, make sure to provide the correct path to the model file. Finally, the labels generated by the LF will be 1 if the image has the specified digit, and -1 if it doesn't have it:

```
#Importing Libraries
import tensorflow as tf
from tensorflow.keras.datasets import mnist
from tensorflow.keras.models import load_model
```

In this block, TensorFlow is imported, along with specific modules needed to work with the MNIST dataset and pre-trained models.

The MNIST dataset is loaded into two sets – `x_test` contains the images, and `y_test` contains the corresponding labels. The training set is not used in this snippet:

```
(_, _), (x_test, y_test) = mnist.load_data()
```

A pre-trained model is loaded using the `load_model` function. Ensure to replace `mnist_model.h5` with the correct path to your pre-trained model file:

```
model = load_model('mnist_model.h5')
```

The pixel values of the images are normalized to be in the range [0, 1] by converting the data type to `float32` and dividing by 255:

```
x_test = x_test.astype('float32') / 255
```

The images are reshaped to match the input shape expected by the model, which is (`batch_size`, `height`, `width`, and `channels`):

```
x_test = x_test.reshape(x_test.shape[0], 28, 28, 1)
```

Predictions are made on the test dataset using the pre-trained model, and the predictions for the first image are printed:

```
predictions = model.predict(x_test)
print("predictions",predictions[0])
```

Class labels for the MNIST digits (0–9) are created as strings and printed:

```
class_labels = [str(i) for i in range(10)]
print("class_labels:", class_labels
```

The script iterates through the test dataset, printing the index of the maximum prediction value, the predicted digit, and the actual digit label for each image:

```
for i in range(len(x_test)):
    print("maxpredict", predictions[i].argmax())
    predicted_digit = class_labels[predictions[i].argmax()]
    actual_digit = str(y_test[i])
    print(f"Predicted: {predicted_digit}, Actual: {actual_digit}")
```

Here is the output:

```
...    313/313 [==============================] - 0s 366us/step
       predictions [1.1785620e-08 2.4082578e-09 2.0923760e-06 3.4867000e-04 2.8979172e-10
        7.4408177e-08 2.8194130e-13 9.9964345e-01 1.2078237e-07 5.4764264e-06]
       class_labels: ['0', '1', '2', '3', '4', '5', '6', '7', '8', '9']
       maxpredict 7
       Predicted: 7, Actual: 7
       maxpredict 2
       Predicted: 2, Actual: 2
       maxpredict 1
       Predicted: 1, Actual: 1
       maxpredict 0
       Predicted: 0, Actual: 0
       maxpredict 4
       Predicted: 4, Actual: 4
       maxpredict 1
       Predicted: 1, Actual: 1
       maxpredict 4
       Predicted: 4, Actual: 4
       maxpredict 9
       Predicted: 9, Actual: 9
       maxpredict 5
       Predicted: 5, Actual: 5
       maxpredict 9
       Predicted: 9, Actual: 9
       maxpredict 0
       ...
       maxpredict 5
       Predicted: 5, Actual: 5
       maxpredict 6
       Predicted: 6, Actual: 6
```

Figure 5.3 – The output of digital classification

Let us see another example of defining rules using a pre-trained classifier for image labeling. In the following example, we will use a pre-trained model, YOLO V3, to detect a person in the image, and then we will apply an LF to label the large set of image data.

Example – person image detection using the YOLO V3 pre-trained classifier

Let's get started with the code:

```
# Load an image for object detection using cv2
  image = cv2.imread('path/to/image.jpg')


# Define rules based on image properties
# Returns True if image contains a person, otherwise returns False
# Use a pre-trained person detection model, e.g. YOLOv3  , to detect
people in the image
```

The predefined YOLO model and weights are open source and can be downloaded at https://pjreddie.com/darknet/yolo:

```
def has_person(image):
# Load the YOLOv3 model with its weights and configuration files
net = cv2.dnn.readNetFromDarknet("path/to/yolov3.cfg", \
    "path/to/yolov3.weights")

# Load the COCO class names (used for labeling detected objects)
classes = []
with open("path/to/coco.names", "r") as f:
        classes = [line.strip() for line in f.readlines()]
# Create a blob from the image and set it as input to the network
blob = cv2.dnn.blobFromImage(image, 1/255.0, (416, 416), \
    swapRB=True, crop=False) net.setInput(blob)

# Run forward pass to perform object detection
detections = net.forward()
# Process and interpret the detection results
for detection in detections:

# Process detection results and draw bounding boxes if needed
# You can use classes to map class IDs to class names
if confidence > confidence_threshold and classes[class_id] ==
"person":

    if len(boxes) > 0:
        return True
    else:
        return False
```

In this code, we use OpenCV to load the YOLO V3 model, its weights, and its configuration files. Then, we provide an input image, run a forward pass through the network, and process the detection results.

You'll need to replace `"path/to/yolov3.cfg"`, `"path/to/coco.names"`, and `"path/to/image.jpg"` with the actual paths to your YOLOv3 configuration file, the class names file, and the image that you want to perform object detection on.

Remember that YOLO V3 is a complex deep learning model designed for real-time object detection, and using it effectively often requires some knowledge of computer vision and deep learning concepts.

Example – bicycle image detection using the YOLO V3 pre-trained classifier

The following is the code for this example:

```
def has_bicycle(image):
    # Returns True if image contains a bicycle, otherwise returns
False
    model = tf.saved_model.load(
        "path/to/faster_rcnn_inception_v2_coco_2018_01_28/saved_
model")
    img_resized = cv2.resize(image, (600, 600))
    input_tensor = tf.convert_to_tensor(img_resized)
    input_tensor = input_tensor[tf.newaxis, ...]
    detections = model(input_tensor)
    num_detections = int(detections.pop('num_detections'))
    detections = {key: value[0, :num_detections].numpy() \
        for key, value in detections.items()}
```

In summary, the code snippet utilizes a pre-trained Faster R-CNN model to perform object detection on an input image. It resizes the image, converts it to a tensor, and then extracts and processes the detection results. To specifically detect bicycles, you would need to filter the results based on the class labels provided by the model and check for the presence of bicycles in the detected objects.

Now, let us explore how we can apply transformations on a given image dataset to generate additional synthetic data. Additional synthetic data helps in training and achieving more accurate results, as a model will learn about different positions of images.

Labeling images using transformations

In this section, let us see the different types of transformations that can be applied to images to generate synthetic data when there is a limited amount of data. In machine learning, shearing and flipping are often used as image augmentation techniques to increase the diversity of training data. It helps improve a model's ability to recognize objects from different angles or orientations.

Shearing can be used in computer vision tasks to correct for perspective distortion in images. For example, it can be applied to rectify skewed text in scanned documents.

Image shearing is a transformation that distorts an image by moving its pixels in a specific direction. It involves shifting the pixels of an image along one of its axes while keeping the other axis unchanged. There are two primary types of shearing:

- **Horizontal shearing**: In this case, pixels are shifted horizontally, usually in a diagonal manner, causing an image to slant left or right

- **Vertical shearing**: Here, pixels are shifted vertically, causing an image to slant up or down

To perform image shearing, you typically specify the amount of shear (the extent of distortion) and the direction (horizontal or vertical). The amount of shear is usually defined as a shear angle or shear factor.

Image shearing is typically accomplished using a shear matrix. For example, in 2D computer graphics, a horizontal shear matrix might look like this:

```
| 1    shear_x |
| 0      1     |
```

Here, `shear_x` represents the amount of horizontal shearing applied.

By applying a random shearing transformation to an image, we can generate multiple versions of the image with slightly different pixel values. These variations can provide a useful way to identify visual patterns or features that are characteristic of an object.

Similarly, **image flipping** is another transformation that can be useful to identify flowers. By flipping an image horizontally or vertically, we can generate new versions of an image that may contain different visual patterns or features. For example, we could use an LF that checks whether an image is flipped along a certain axis, labeling images that are flipped as positively depicting flowers. This LF would be able to capture the fact that many flowers have bilateral symmetry, meaning that they look similar when mirrored along a particular axis.

Overall, by applying image transformations such as shearing or flipping, we can generate a larger number of labeled examples that capture different aspects of the image content. This can help to increase the accuracy of the classification model by providing more varied and robust training data.

We will further explore image transformation along with other data augmentation techniques and examples in the next chapter.

Summary

In this chapter, we embarked on an enlightening journey into the world of image labeling and classification. We began by mastering the art of creating labeling rules through manual inspection, tapping into the extensive capabilities of Python. This newfound skill empowers us to translate visual intuition into valuable data, a crucial asset in the realm of machine learning.

As we delved deeper, we explored the intricacies of size, aspect ratio, bounding boxes, and polygon and polyline annotations. We learned how to craft labeling rules based on these quantitative image characteristics, ushering in a systematic and dependable approach to data labeling.

Our exploration extended to the transformative realm of image manipulation. We harnessed the potential of image transformations such as shearing and flipping, enhancing our labeling process with dynamic versatility.

Furthermore, we applied our knowledge to real-world scenarios, classifying plant disease images using rule-based LFs. We honed our skills in predicting objects by leveraging aspect ratio and contour height, a valuable asset in scenarios such as identifying a person riding a bicycle. Additionally, we delved into the powerful domain of pre-trained models and transfer learning for image classification.

But our journey is far from over. In the upcoming chapter, we will dive even deeper into the realm of image data augmentation. We'll explore advanced techniques and learn how to perform image classification using augmented data with **support vector machines (SVMs)** and **convolutional neural networks (CNNs)**. Get ready for the next exciting chapter!

6
Labeling Image Data Using Data Augmentation

In this chapter, we will learn how to label image data using data augmentation for semi-supervised machine learning. We will use the CIFAR-10 dataset and the MNIST dataset of handwritten digits to generate labels using data augmentation. From there we will build an image classification machine learning model.

Data augmentation plays a crucial role in data labeling by enhancing the diversity, size, and quality of the dataset. Data augmentation techniques generate additional samples by applying transformations to existing data. This effectively increases the size of the dataset, providing more examples for training and improving the model's ability to generalize.

In this chapter, we will cover the following:

- How to prepare training data with image data augmentation and implement support vector machines
- How to implement convolutional neural networks with augmented image data

Technical requirements

For this chapter, we will use the CIFAR-10 dataset, which is a publicly available image dataset consisting of 60,000 32x32 color images in 10 classes (`http://www.cs.toronto.edu/~kriz/cifar.html`), along with the famous MNIST handwritten digits dataset.

Training support vector machines with augmented image data

Support Vector Machines (**SVMs**) are widely used in machine learning to solve classification problems. SVMs are known for their high accuracy and ability to handle complex datasets. One of the challenges in training SVMs is the availability of large and diverse datasets. In this section, we will discuss the importance of data augmentation in training SVMs for image classification problems. We will also provide Python code examples for each technique.

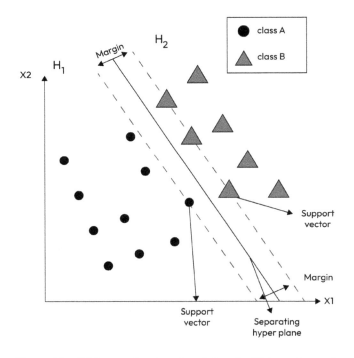

Figure 6.1 – SVM separates class A and class B with largest margin

SVMs are a type of supervised learning algorithm used for classification and regression analysis. SVMs can be used for outlier detection. SVMs were originally designed for classification tasks, but can also be adapted for anomaly or outlier detection as well.

The objective of SVMs is to find the hyperplane that maximizes the margin between two classes of data. The hyperplane is defined as the decision boundary that separates the data points of two classes. The margin is the distance between the hyperplane and the nearest data point of each class.

SVMs use something called the *kernel trick*. Let's understand what this is next.

Kernel trick

Let's say you have data points on a sheet of paper, and you want to separate them into two groups. Imagine you have a magic wand (i.e., the kernel trick) that allows you to lift the points off the paper into the air. In the air, you can easily draw a line or a curve to separate the floating points.

Now, when you're satisfied with the separation in the air, you use the magic wand again to bring everything back down to the paper. Miraculously, the separation you drew in the air translates to a more complex decision boundary on the paper that effectively separates your original data points.

In the SVM world, this "magic wand" is the kernel trick. It allows SVMs to implicitly work in a higher-dimensional space, making it possible to find more intricate decision boundaries that weren't achievable in the original space. The key is that you don't have to explicitly compute the coordinates of the higher-dimensional space; the kernel trick does this for you.

In summary, the kernel trick lifts your data into a higher-dimensional space, where SVMs can find more sophisticated ways to separate different classes. It's a powerful tool for handling complex data scenarios.

SVMs leverage the kernel trick to transform the input data into a higher-dimensional space, where a linear decision boundary can be found. The kernel function plays a crucial role in this process, mapping the input data into a feature space where the relationships between variables may be more easily separable.

The most commonly used kernel functions are the linear kernel, which represents a linear decision boundary, the polynomial kernel, which introduces non-linearity with higher-order polynomial features, and the **radial basis function** (**RBF**) kernel, which allows for a more flexible and non-linear decision boundary. The choice of the kernel function and its parameters significantly influences the SVM's ability to model complex relationships in the data.

As we now have a basic idea about SVMs, let us next understand data augmentation, image data augmentation, and the various techniques used for this.

Data augmentation

Data augmentation is the process of creating new data points from the existing data points by applying various transformations such as rotation, translation, and scaling. Data augmentation is used to increase the size of the training dataset and improve the generalizability and accuracy of the model by helping the model to learn more features and patterns in the data.

Image data augmentation

Image data augmentation is a technique of augmenting the image dataset to improve the accuracy of the model. The following is a selection of the techniques that can be used for image data augmentation.

Image rotation

Image rotation is a technique where an image is rotated by a certain angle. This technique is used to increase the size of the training dataset and improve the model's ability to recognize objects from different angles. The Python code for image rotation is as follows:

```
from PIL import Image
import numpy as np

def rotate_image(image_path, degrees):
    img = Image.open(image_path)
    rotated_image = img.rotate(degrees)
    return rotated_image

image_path = "path/to/image.jpg"
rotated_image = rotate_image(image_path, 45)
rotated_image.show()
```

In the preceding code, we load the image from the image path and rotate it by a given number of degrees. This creates a new dataset for the same image from different angles and improves model training.

Image translation

Image translation is a technique where an image is shifted horizontally or vertically by a certain amount of pixels. This technique is used to increase the size of the training dataset and improve the model's ability to recognize objects in different positions. The Python code for image translation is as follows:

```
from PIL import Image
import numpy as np

def translate_image(image_path, x_offset, y_offset):
    img = Image.open(image_path)
    translated_image = img.transform(img.size, \
        Image.AFFINE, (1, 0, x_offset, 0, 1, y_offset))
    return translated_image

image_path = "path/to/image.jpg"
translated_image = translate_image(image_path, 50, 50)
translated_image.show()
```

In the preceding code, we define a Python function that shifts the image by a certain amount of pixels.

Image scaling

Image scaling is an augmentation technique where an image is scaled up or down by a certain factor. This technique is used to increase the size of the training dataset and improve the model's ability to recognize objects at different scales. The Python code for image scaling is as follows:

```
from PIL import Image
import numpy as np

def scale_image(image_path, scale_factor):
    img = Image.open(image_path)
    scaled_image = img.resize(((int(img.size[0]*scale_factor),\
        int(img.size[1]*scale_factor)))
    return scaled_image

image_path = "path/to/image.jpg"
scaled_image = scale_image(image_path, 0.5)
scaled_image.show()
```

In the preceding code, we change the image size by multiplying the image by a scale factor in a Python function. Next, let's see how to implement an SVM with data augmentation using the CIFAR-10 dataset.

Implementing an SVM with data augmentation in Python

In this section, we will provide a step-by-step guide to implement an SVM with data augmentation in Python using the CIFAR-10 dataset. We will start by introducing the CIFAR-10 dataset and then move on to loading the dataset in Python. We will then preprocess the data for SVM training and implement an SVM with the default hyperparameters and dataset. Next, we train and evaluate the performance of the SVM with an augmented dataset, showing that the performance of the SVM improves on the augmented dataset.

Introducing the CIFAR-10 dataset

The CIFAR-10 dataset is a commonly used image classification dataset that consists of 60,000 32x32 color images in 10 classes. The classes are: airplane, automobile, bird, cat, deer, dog, frog, horse, ship, and truck. The dataset is divided into 50,000 training images and 10,000 testing images. The dataset is preprocessed in a way that the training set and test set have an equal number of images from each class.

Loading the CIFAR-10 dataset in Python

To load the CIFAR-10 dataset in Python, we will use the `cifar10` module from the Keras library. If you don't have Keras installed, you can install it using the following command:

```
pip install keras
```

Once you have installed Keras, you can load the CIFAR-10 dataset using the following code:

```
from keras.datasets import cifar10

(x_train, y_train), (x_test, y_test) = cifar10.load_data()
```

The `cifar10.load_data()` function returns two tuples: (x_train, y_train) and (x_test, y_test). The x_train and x_test tuples contain the input images, while the y_train and y_test tuples contain the corresponding class labels for the input images.

Preprocessing the data for SVM training

In this section, we will first convert the input images from 3D matrices to 2D matrices. We will also normalize the pixel values of the input images to be between 0 and 1. Finally, we will reshape the input images and convert the class labels to one-hot encoded vectors.

The `reshape()` function is used to reshape the input images from 3D matrices to 2D matrices. The -1 argument tells the function to infer the number of columns based on the number of rows and the size of each row:

```
# Reshape the input images
x_train = x_train.reshape(x_train.shape[0], -1)
x_test = x_test.reshape(x_test.shape[0], -1)
```

The pixel values of the input images are normalized to be between 0 and 1 by dividing them by 255, which is the maximum pixel value:

```
# Convert pixel values to between 0 and 1
x_train = x_train / 255
x_test = x_test / 255
```

The `to_categorical()` function is used to convert the class labels to one-hot encoded vectors. The num_classes variable is set to 10, which is the number of classes in the CIFAR-10 dataset:

```
# Convert class labels to one-hot encoded vectors
num_classes = 10
y_train = keras.utils.to_categorical(y_train, num_classes)
y_test = keras.utils.to_categorical(y_test, num_classes)
```

Implementing an SVM with the default hyperparameters

Hyperparameters in SVMs are parameters that are not learned from the data but are set prior to the training process. They control the behavior of the SVM model and can significantly impact its performance. Here are some important hyperparameters in SVM:

- **Kernel**: The kernel function determines the type of decision boundary used by the SVM. Common kernel functions include the linear, polynomial, **radial basis function** (**RBF**), and sigmoid function. The choice of kernel depends on the data and problem at hand.

- **Regularization parameter** (**C**): Regularization is a technique used to prevent overfitting or underfitting of the model. Regularization methods help to control the complexity of the model and improve its generalization on unseen data.

  For a binary classification problem, the decision boundary is a hyperplane that separates data into two classes. The margin is the distance between this hyperplane and the nearest data point from either class. The "width" of the margin is the actual numerical value of the distance or gap between the decision boundary and the nearest data point.

  A wider margin implies a larger separation between classes, providing more room for potential misclassifications without affecting the decision boundary. The regularization parameter, often denoted as C, controls the trade-off between achieving a low training error rate and maintaining a wide margin. A smaller C value allows for more misclassifications but results in a larger margin, while a larger C value tries to minimize misclassifications at the cost of a narrower margin.

- **Gamma (for RBF kernels)**: The gamma parameter influences the shape of the decision boundary for SVMs with the RBF kernel. It determines the reach of each training sample and affects the smoothness of the decision boundary. Higher gamma values tend to result in more complex decision boundaries.

- **Degree (for polynomial kernels)**: The degree parameter specifies the degree of the polynomial kernel function. It determines the nonlinearity of the decision boundary. Higher degree values allow for more complex decision boundaries but may increase the risk of overfitting.

These hyperparameters need to be carefully tuned to achieve the best performance of the SVM model. Grid search, random search, or other optimization techniques can be employed to explore different combinations of hyperparameter values and select the optimal set.

To implement an SVM with the default hyperparameters, we will use the `svm.SVC` class from the scikit-learn library. We will first create an instance of the `SVC` class and then fit the training data to the classifier.

An instance of the `SVC` class is created using `svm.SVC()`. By not specifying any hyperparameters, it uses the default values for the kernel, regularization parameter (C), and other relevant parameters:

```
from sklearn import svm
```

```
# Create an instance of the SVC class with default hyperparameters
clf = svm.SVC()
```

The `fit()` function is used to fit the training data to the classifier:

```
# Fit the training data to the classifier
clf.fit(x_train, y_train)
```

Evaluating SVM on the original dataset

We evaluate the performance of the original dataset to compare the performance with the augmented dataset.

To evaluate the performance of SVM on the original dataset, we will use the `predict()` function to predict the class labels of the test data and then use the `accuracy_score()` function from the scikit-learn library to calculate the accuracy of the classifier:

```
from sklearn.metrics import accuracy_score

# Predict the class labels of the test data
y_pred = clf.predict(x_test)

# Calculate the accuracy of the classifier
accuracy = accuracy_score(y_test, y_pred)
print("Accuracy: %.2f%%" % (accuracy * 100.0))
```

The `predict()` function is used to predict the class labels of the test data. The `accuracy_score()` function is used to calculate the accuracy of the classifier by comparing the predicted class labels to the actual class labels.

The accuracy of the SVM model on the test dataset is around `47.97%`, which is not very good. This indicates that the SVM model is not able to learn all the important features and patterns in the original dataset.

Implementing an SVM with an augmented dataset

To implement SVM with data augmentation, we will use the `ImageDataGenerator` class from the Keras library to generate new training data. We will first create an instance of the `ImageDataGenerator` class and then use the `flow()` function to generate new batches of training data:

```
from keras.preprocessing.image import ImageDataGenerator

# Create an instance of the ImageDataGenerator class
datagen = ImageDataGenerator(rotation_range=20, \
    width_shift_range=0.1, height_shift_range=0.1, \
    shear_range=0.2, zoom_range=0.2, horizontal_flip=True)
```

```
# Generate new batches of training data
gen_train = datagen.flow(x_train, y_train, batch_size=64)
```

The `ImageDataGenerator()` function creates an instance of the `ImageDataGenerator` class. The `rotation_range`, `width_shift_range`, `height_shift_range`, `shear_range`, `zoom_range`, and `horizontal_flip` arguments are used to specify the types of data augmentation to be applied to the training data.

The `flow()` function is used to generate new batches of training data from the original training data and the `ImageDataGenerator` object.

Training the SVM on augmented data

To train SVM on augmented data, we will use the `partial_fit()` function of the SVC class to train the classifier on each batch of training data generated by the `ImageDataGenerator` object:

```
# Train the classifier on each batch of training data
for i in range(100):
    x_batch, y_batch = gen_train.next()
    clf.partial_fit(x_batch, y_batch, classes=np.unique(y_train))
```

The `classes` argument is used to specify the unique classes in the training data.

Evaluating the SVM's performance on the augmented dataset

To evaluate the performance of the SVM on the augmented dataset, we will again use the `predict()` function to predict the class labels of the test data and then use the `accuracy_score()` function to calculate the accuracy of the classifier by comparing the predicted class labels to the actual class labels:

```
# Predict the class labels of the test data
y_pred_aug = clf.predict(x_test)

# Calculate the accuracy of the classifier
accuracy_aug = accuracy_score(y_test, y_pred_aug)
print("Accuracy with Data Augmentation: %.2f%%" % (accuracy_aug *
100.0))
```

The accuracy of the SVM model on the augmented test dataset is around 54.75%, which is better than the previous accuracy. This indicates that the SVM model is able to learn more important features and patterns in the augmented dataset, and is able to generalize better to new data.

To summarize, in this section, we have discussed the importance of data augmentation in training SVMs for image classification. We have used the CIFAR-10 dataset to illustrate the impact of data augmentation on the performance of the SVM model. We have also provided Python code examples for loading the CIFAR-10 dataset, training an SVM model on the original dataset, and training an SVM model on the augmented dataset.

The results show that data augmentation can improve the performance of SVM models on image classification tasks. By applying random rotations, translations, and scaling, we can generate new images that the SVM model can use to learn more features and patterns. This enables the SVM model to generalize better to new data and achieve better accuracy.

In the next section, we will see how to implement the SVM with data augmentation using the MNIST handwritten digits dataset.

Image classification using the SVM with data augmentation on the MNIST dataset

Let us see how we can apply data augmentation for image classification using an SVM with the MNIST dataset. All the steps are similar to the previous example with the CIFAR-10 dataset, except the dataset itself:

```
import tensorflow as tf
from sklearn.svm import SVC
from sklearn.model_selection import GridSearchCV
from keras.datasets import mnist
from keras.preprocessing.image import ImageDataGenerator

# load MNIST dataset
(x_train, y_train), (x_test, y_test) = mnist.load_data()

# normalize pixel values between 0 and 1
x_train = x_train / 255.0
x_test = x_test / 255.0

# convert labels to one-hot encoded vectors
y_train = tf.keras.utils.to_categorical(y_train)
y_test = tf.keras.utils.to_categorical(y_test)

# create image data generator for data augmentation
datagen = ImageDataGenerator(rotation_range=20, \
    width_shift_range=0.1, height_shift_range=0.1, zoom_range=0.2)

# fit image data generator on training dataset
datagen.fit(x_train.reshape(-1, 28, 28, 1))

# create SVM model
```

```
svm_model = SVC()

# define hyperparameters for grid search
param_grid = {'C': [0.1, 1, 10], 'kernel': ['linear', \
    'poly', 'rbf'], 'degree': [2, 3, 4]}

# perform grid search for optimal hyperparameters
svm_grid_search = GridSearchCV(svm_model, param_grid, cv=3)
svm_grid_search.fit(datagen.flow(
    x_train.reshape(-1, 28, 28, 1),y_train, batch_size=32), \
    steps_per_epoch=len(x_train) / 32)

# evaluate SVM model on test dataset
accuracy = svm_grid_search.score(x_test.reshape(-1, 28*28), y_test)
print("Accuracy with data augmentation: {:.2f}%".format(accuracy*100))
```

As stated, this code is similar to the previous example, except that we are now using the MNIST dataset and the images are grayscale and of size 28x28. We have also modified the input shape of the SVM model and the image data generator to accommodate the new image size and color channel.

The results show that data augmentation can also improve the performance of SVM models on the MNIST dataset. By applying random rotations, translations, and scaling, we can generate new images that the SVM model can use to learn more features and patterns. This enables the SVM model to generalize better to new data and achieve better accuracy.

In addition, we have used grid search to find the optimal hyperparameters for the SVM model. This is important because the performance of SVM models is highly dependent on the choice of hyperparameters. By tuning the hyperparameters using grid search, we can improve the accuracy of the SVM model even further.

Overall, this example code demonstrates the effectiveness of data augmentation in improving the performance of SVM models on image classification tasks. It also highlights the importance of hyperparameter tuning using grid search to achieve the best possible accuracy.

To summarize, data augmentation is a powerful technique for improving the performance of machine learning models on image classification tasks. By generating new images that the model can use to learn more features and patterns, we can improve the generalization ability of the model and achieve better accuracy. SVM models are particularly well suited for image classification tasks and can benefit greatly from data augmentation. With the help of Python libraries such as scikit-learn and TensorFlow, we can easily implement SVM models with data augmentation and achieve state-of-the-art performance on image classification tasks.

Next, let us see how to implement convolutional neural networks with augmented training data.

Convolutional neural networks using augmented image data

Convolutional Neural Networks (CNNs) have revolutionized the field of computer vision by demonstrating exceptional performance in various image-related tasks such as object detection, image classification, and segmentation. However, the availability of large, annotated datasets for training CNNs is often a challenge. Fortunately, one effective approach to overcome this limitation is through the use of **image data augmentation** techniques.

Let's start from scratch and explain what CNNs are and how they work. Imagine you have a picture, say a photo of a cat, and you want to teach a computer how to recognize that it's a cat. CNNs are like a special type of computer program that helps computers understand and recognize things in images, just like how you recognize objects in photos.

An image is made up of tiny dots called pixels. Each pixel has a color, and when you put them all together, you get an image. The more pixels you have, the more detailed the image is. When you look at a picture, your brain doesn't try to understand it all at once. Instead, it focuses on small parts, like the shape of an ear or the color of an eye. This is how we recognize things. We break the big picture into small pieces and understand them one by one.

CNNs work a bit like the human brain, breaking images down into small parts. These small parts are called "features" or "filters." Imagine these filters as tiny windows that move across the picture. These windows look at a small part of the image at a time and learn what's important in it.

How CNNs work

Let us understand how CNNs work for the desired output:

1. **Convolution**: This is the first step. It's like moving the small window (filter) over the picture. The filter checks the colors and shapes in the area it's looking at and learns what's important.

2. **Pooling**: After the different parts of the image have been looked at, the CNN doesn't need all the details. Pooling is like taking a summary of what it's seen. It simplifies things, but we don't lose the important parts.

3. **Fully connected layers**: After looking at the many small parts and summarizing them, everything is connected together next. It's like putting the pieces of a puzzle together to see the whole picture. This helps the CNN understand the entire image and make a final decision on what is depicted in it.

   After the convolutional layers have processed the image by extracting various features and patterns, the fully connected layers play a crucial role in bringing all the information together to make a comprehensive decision about the content of the image. This process is akin to assembling the pieces of a puzzle, where each piece corresponds to a specific feature detected by the convolutional layers. By connecting these pieces, the network gains a holistic understanding of the image.

However, as powerful as fully connected layers are, there is a risk of overfitting, a situation where the model becomes too specialized in the training data and performs poorly on new, unseen data. To mitigate this, regularization techniques are often employed.

4. **Regularization in fully connected layers**: Regularization is a set of techniques used to prevent overfitting and enhance the generalization capabilities of a model. In the context of fully connected layers, regularization methods are applied to control the complexity of the model and avoid relying too heavily on specific features present in the training data.

5. **Training a CNN**: To teach a CNN to recognize cats, you'd show it lots of cat pictures. It looks at them, learns the important features, and gets better over time at recognizing them. It also needs to see pictures of things that are not cats, so it can tell the difference.

6. **Making predictions**: Once a CNN is trained, you can show it a new picture, and it will try to find the important features just like it learned. If it finds enough cat-like features, it will say, "Hey, that's a cat!"

So, in simple terms, a CNN is like a computer program that learns to recognize things in pictures by looking at small parts of the image, finding important features, and making decisions based on those features.

As we've seen, a CNN's architecture constitutes convolution, pooling, and fully connected layers. The architecture specifies how the model is structured, including the number of layers, the size of filters, and the connections between neurons. The architecture guides how the learned weights and features are used to process images and make predictions.

So, the final model is, in essence, a combination of the architecture, the learned weights, and the learned features. Let's break down a couple of these elements:

- **Learned weights**: These are the parameters that the CNN has learned during the training process. The model adjusts these weights to make accurate predictions. These weights are essentially the "knowledge" the model gains during training. They represent how important certain features are for making decisions.

- **Learned features**: Features, in the context of a CNN, are visual patterns and characteristics of images. They are representations of important information within the image. These features are not directly visible to us but are learned by the network through the layers of convolution and pooling. Features are abstract representations of the image that help the model recognize patterns and objects.

In practice, these learned weights and features are stored in the model's parameters. When you save a trained CNN model, you are saving these parameters, which can be used to make predictions on new, unseen images. The model takes an image as input, processes it through its layers, and uses the learned weights and features to make predictions, such as classifying objects in the image or detecting specific patterns.

We will now delve into the powerful combination of CNNs and image data augmentation. By artificially augmenting the data, CNNs can be exposed to a broader range of variations during training to help them generalize better to unseen images.

Some of the benefits and considerations of using image data augmentation are reducing overfitting, enhancing model robustness, and improving generalization performance. Whether you are a beginner or an experienced practitioner, this section serves as a comprehensive guide to understanding and implementing image data augmentation in the context of CNNs, assisting you in taking your computer vision projects to new heights.

Practical example of a CNN using data augmentation

Let us see how to implement image data augmentation on a CNN. To do so, you can follow these steps:

Step 1: Start by importing the necessary libraries, including Keras and NumPy:

```
import keras
from keras.models import Sequential
from keras.layers import Conv2D, MaxPooling2D, Flatten, Dense, Dropout
from keras.preprocessing.image import ImageDataGenerator
import numpy as np
```

Step 2: Create an `ImageDataGenerator` object and specify the desired data augmentation techniques:

```
datagen = ImageDataGenerator(
    rotation_range=20,
    width_shift_range=0.2,
    height_shift_range=0.2,
    horizontal_flip=True,
    validation_split=0.2
)
```

The `ImageDataGenerator` object will generate batches of augmented data using the specified data augmentation techniques. In this example, we are using rotation, width and height shifts, and horizontal flipping.

Step 3: Load the original dataset and split it into training and validation sets:

```
train_generator = datagen.flow_from_directory(
    '/path/to/dataset',
    target_size=(224, 224),
    batch_size=32,
    class_mode='categorical',
    subset='training'
)
```

```
val_generator = datagen.flow_from_directory(
    '/path/to/dataset',
    target_size=(224, 224),
    batch_size=32,
    class_mode='categorical',
    subset='validation'
)
```

Here, we are using the `flow_from_directory()` function to load the original dataset from the specified directory. We also specify the target size of the images, the batch size, and the class mode (categorical in this case). We split the data into training and validation sets using the `subset` parameter.

In the provided code snippet, the `flow_from_directory` function is used to generate a data generator to load images from a directory. Let's break down the parameters:

- `'/path/to/dataset'`: This is the path to the directory containing the dataset. The function will look for subdirectories inside this directory, where each subdirectory represents a different class or category.

- `target_size=(224, 224)`: `target_size` is the size to which all images will be resized during loading. In this case, each image will be resized as a square with dimensions of 224x224 pixels. Standardizing the image size is important for consistency and compatibility with neural network models, especially when using pre-trained models that expect a specific input size.

- `batch_size=32`: `batch_size` determines the number of images loaded and processed in each iteration during training or validation. A larger batch size can lead to faster training but may require more memory. Smaller batch sizes are often used when memory is limited or for fine-tuning models. It also affects the gradient update during training, impacting the stability and convergence of the training process.

- `class_mode='categorical'`: `class_mode` specifies how the target classes are represented. In this case, it is set to `categorical`, indicating that the labels are one-hot encoded (a binary matrix representation of class membership). Other possible values include `binary` for binary classification, `sparse` for integer-encoded class labels, and `None` for no labels (used for test datasets).

- `subset='validation'`: Subset is used to specify whether the generator is for the training set or the validation set. In this case, it is set to `validation`, indicating that the generator is for the validation set. When using subset, make sure the dataset directory contains subdirectories like `train` and `validation` to facilitate the split.

In summary, these parameters help configure the data generator to load and preprocess images from a directory. The choices made for target size, batch size, and class mode are often determined by the requirements of the machine learning model being used, the available computing resources, and the characteristics of the dataset.

Step 4: Create a CNN model:

```
model = Sequential()
model.add(Conv2D(32, (3, 3), activation='relu', input_shape=(224, 224, 3)))
model.add(MaxPooling2D((2, 2)))
model.add(Conv2D(64, (3, 3), activation='relu'))
model.add(MaxPooling2D((2, 2)))
model.add(Conv2D(128, (3, 3), activation='relu'))
model.add(MaxPooling2D((2, 2)))
model.add(Conv2D(256, (3, 3), activation='relu'))
model.add(MaxPooling2D((2, 2)))
model.add(Flatten())
model.add(Dense(512, activation='relu'))
model.add(Dropout(0.5))
model.add(Dense(2, activation='softmax'))

model.compile(loss='categorical_crossentropy', \
    optimizer='adam', metrics=['accuracy'])
```

Here, we are creating a simple CNN model with four convolutional layers and one fully connected layer. We are using ReLU activation for the convolutional layers and softmax activation for the output layer. We also compile the model with the categorical cross-entropy loss function, the Adam optimizer, and the accuracy metric.

In the preceding code snippet, a CNN model is being created using the Keras library. Let's break down the components:

- **Rectified Linear Unit (ReLU) Activation**: `activation='relu'` is used for the convolutional and dense layers. ReLU is an activation function that introduces non-linearity to the model. It outputs the input directly if it is positive; otherwise, it outputs zero. ReLU is preferred for CNNs because it helps the model learn complex patterns and relationships in data. It is computationally efficient and mitigates the vanishing gradient problem.

  The effect of ReLU: ReLU introduces non-linearity, enabling the model to learn complex features and relationships in the data. It helps address the vanishing gradient problem, promoting more efficient training by allowing the model to propagate gradients during backpropagation.

- **Softmax activation**: `activation='softmax'` is used for the output layer. Softmax is a function that converts raw scores (logits) into probabilities. It is often used in the output layer of a multi-class classification model. In this binary classification case (two classes), the softmax activation function normalizes the output scores for each class, assigning a probability to each class. The class with the highest probability is considered the model's prediction. Softmax is useful for producing probability distributions over multiple classes, making it suitable for classification problems.

The effect of Softmax: Softmax converts raw model outputs into probability distributions over classes. It ensures that the predicted probabilities sum to 1, facilitating a meaningful interpretation of the model's confidence in each class. In binary classification, it is often used in conjunction with categorical cross-entropy loss.

Why should we use them? ReLU is chosen for its simplicity, computational efficiency, and effectiveness in training deep neural networks. Softmax is selected for the output layer to obtain class probabilities, which are valuable for interpreting and evaluating the model's predictions.

In summary, ReLU and softmax activations contribute to the effectiveness of the CNN model by introducing non-linearity, promoting efficient training, and producing meaningful probability distributions for classification. They are widely used in CNNs for image classification tasks.

In the provided code snippet, the model is compiled with three important components – categorical cross-entropy loss, the Adam optimizer, and the accuracy metric. Let's delve into each of them:

- **Categorical cross-entropy loss** (`loss='categorical_crossentropy'`):

  - Categorical cross-entropy is a loss function commonly used for multi-class classification problems.

  - In this context, the model is designed for binary classification (two classes), but it uses categorical cross-entropy to handle a case where there are more than two classes. The target labels are expected to be one-hot-encoded.

  - The loss function measures the dissimilarity between the predicted probabilities (obtained from the softmax activation in the output layer) and the true class labels.

  - The goal during training is to minimize this loss, effectively improving the model's ability to make accurate class predictions.

- **Adam optimizer** (`optimizer='adam'`):

  - **Adaptive Moment Estimation** (**Adam**) is an optimization algorithm widely used to train neural networks.

  - It combines ideas from two other optimization algorithms – **Root Mean Square Propagation** (**RMSprop**) and Momentum.

  - Adam adapts the learning rates of each parameter individually, making it well-suited for a variety of optimization problems.

  - It is known for its efficiency and effectiveness in training deep neural networks and is often a default choice for many applications.

- **Accuracy metric** (`metrics=['accuracy']`):

  - Accuracy is a metric used to evaluate the performance of a classification model.

  - In the context of binary classification, accuracy measures the proportion of correctly classified instances (both true positives and true negatives) among all instances.

- The accuracy metric is essential for assessing how well the model performs on the training and validation datasets.

- While accuracy is a commonly used metric, it might not be sufficient for imbalanced datasets, where one class is much more prevalent than the other. In such cases, additional metrics such as precision, recall, or F1 score may be considered.

In summary, the choice of categorical cross-entropy loss, the Adam optimizer, and the accuracy metric during compilation reflects the best practices for training a binary classification model. These choices are based on their effectiveness in optimizing the model parameters, handling multi-class scenarios, and providing a straightforward evaluation of classification accuracy.

Step 5: Train the model using the augmented dataset:

```
model.fit(
    train_generator,
    steps_per_epoch=train_generator.samples // 32,
    validation_data=val_generator,
    validation_steps=val_generator.samples // 32,
    epochs=10
)
```

We use the `fit()` function to train the model on the augmented dataset. We specify the training and validation generators, the number of steps per epoch, the validation steps, and the number of epochs.

In this code snippet, the `fit()` function is used to train the model on an augmented dataset. Let's break down the key components:

- **Training generator** (`train_generator`):The training generator is an instance of a data generator that generates batches of training data with augmentation on the fly in *Step 3*. A data generator is a way to efficiently load and preprocess data in chunks during training rather than loading the entire dataset into memory. `train_generator` is responsible for providing the model with batches of augmented training data.

- **Validation generator** (`val_generator`): Similar to the training generator, the validation generator is an instance of a data generator that generates batches of validation data. The validation generator provides a separate set of data that the model has not seen during training. It helps assess the model's generalization to unseen examples and prevents overfitting.

- **Number of steps per epoch** (`steps_per_epoch=train_generator.samples //  32`): `steps_per_epoch` specifies the number of batches of data to process in each epoch of training. It is calculated as the total number of samples in the training dataset divided by the batch size (`32` in this case). Each step involves a forward pass (prediction) and a backward pass (gradient computation and parameter updates) on a batch of data. A smaller `steps_per_epoch` value means that the model will see fewer batches in each epoch, potentially leading to faster training but with less exposure to the entire dataset.

- **Validation steps** (`validation_steps=val_generator.samples // 32`): `validation_steps` is similar to `steps_per_epoch` but for the validation dataset. It determines the number of batches processed during each validation epoch. Like `steps_per_epoch`, it is calculated based on the total number of samples in the validation dataset divided by the batch size.

- **Number of epochs** (`epochs=10`): Epoch specifies the number of times the entire dataset is processed during training. Training for more epochs allows the model to learn from the data over multiple passes, potentially improving performance. However, training for too many epochs may lead to overfitting, where the model memorizes the training data but fails to generalize to new data.

Adjusting the batch size, steps per epoch, and validation steps can impact the training speed and memory requirements. A larger batch size and more steps per epoch may lead to slower training but can be more memory-efficient. The number of epochs should be chosen carefully to balance model training and prevent overfitting.

In summary, the settings provided to `fit()` control how the model is trained, the data it sees in each epoch, and the evaluation of the validation set. Properly tuning these settings is crucial to achieving good model performance and preventing issues such as overfitting.

By following these steps, you can implement supervised CNNs using image data augmentation in Keras. This can help improve the performance of your model and make it more robust to variations in the input data.

CNN using image data augmentation with the CIFAR-10 dataset

Let us see some example Python code for a supervised CNN using image data augmentation with the CIFAR-10 dataset:

```python
import tensorflow as tf
from tensorflow.keras.datasets import cifar10
from tensorflow.keras.models import Sequential
from tensorflow.keras.layers import Conv2D, MaxPooling2D, Flatten,
Dense, Dropout
from tensorflow.keras.preprocessing.image import ImageDataGenerator

# Load the CIFAR-10 dataset
(x_train, y_train), (x_test, y_test) = cifar10.load_data()

# Normalize the input data
x_train = x_train.astype('float32') / 255.0
x_test = x_test.astype('float32') / 255.0

# Convert the labels to one-hot encoding
```

```
y_train = tf.keras.utils.to_categorical(y_train)
y_test = tf.keras.utils.to_categorical(y_test)


# Define the CNN architecture
```

The preceding code defines the architecture of a CNN using the Keras library. Let's go through each line to understand the purpose and functionality of each component.

The following line creates a sequential model, which allows us to stack layers on top of each other sequentially:

```
model = Sequential()
```

The following code snippet adds a 2D convolutional layer to the model. It has 32 filters, a filter size of (3, 3), the ReLU activation function, and the 'same' padding. The input_shape parameter is set to the shape of the input data (x_train) without the batch dimension:

Let's break down the following CNN code snippet to understand it more in depth:

```
model.add(Conv2D(32, (3, 3), activation='relu', \
    padding='same', input_shape=x_train.shape[1:]))
```

2D convolutional layer addition: In deep learning for image processing, convolutional layers are crucial to learning hierarchical features from input images. Convolutional layers are used to detect local patterns in the input data. Each filter in the convolutional layer learns to recognize different features or patterns. The code adds a layer to the neural network model, and specifically, it's a 2D convolutional layer.

The convolutional layer has the following configurations:

- **Filters**: There are 32 filters. Filters are small grids that slide over the input data to detect patterns or features.

- **Filter size**: Each filter has a size of (3, 3). This means it considers a 3x3 grid of pixels at some point during the convolution operation capturing local information.

- **Activation function**: The ReLU activation function is applied element-wise to the output of each convolutional operation. ReLU introduces non-linearity, allowing the model to learn complex patterns.

- **Padding**: The Same padding is used. Padding is a technique to preserve spatial dimensions after convolution preventing information loss at the edges of the image. Same padding pads the input so that the output has the same spatial dimensions as the it.

- **Input shape parameter**: The input_shape parameter is set to the shape of the input data (x_train) without the batch dimension. The input shape determines the size of the input data that the layer will process. In this case, it is set to the shape of the training data x_train without considering the batch dimension.

In summary, this code snippet adds a convolutional layer to the neural network model, configuring it with specific parameters for filter size, number of filters, activation function, and padding. The convolutional layer plays a crucial role in learning hierarchical features from input images.

The following line adds another 2D convolutional layer with the same specifications as the previous one, but without specifying the input shape. The model will infer the input shape based on the previous layer:

```
model.add(Conv2D(32, (3, 3), activation='relu'))
```

The following line adds a max-pooling layer with a pool size of (2, 2), which reduces the spatial dimensions of the input by taking the maximum value within each pool:

```
model.add(MaxPooling2D(pool_size=(2, 2)))
```

The following line adds a dropout layer with a rate of 0.25, which randomly sets 25% of the input units to 0 during training. Dropout helps prevent overfitting by introducing randomness and reducing the reliance on specific features:

```
model.add(Dropout(0.25))
```

The code continues adding more convolutional layers, max-pooling layers, and dropout layers, and finally ends with fully connected (dense) layers:

```
model.add(Conv2D(64, (3, 3), activation='relu', padding='same'))
model.add(Conv2D(64, (3, 3), activation='relu'))
model.add(MaxPooling2D(pool_size=(2, 2)))
model.add(Dropout(0.25))
```

The following line flattens the previous layer's output to a 1D tensor, preparing it to be connected to a dense layer:

```
model.add(Flatten())
```

The following line adds a dense layer with 512 units and ReLU activation:

```
model.add(Dense(512, activation='relu'))
```

The following line adds a dropout layer with a rate of 0.5:

```
model.add(Dropout(0.5))
```

The following line adds a final dense layer with 10 units and softmax activation, which produces a probability distribution over the 10 classes for classification:

```
model.add(Dense(10, activation='softmax'))
```

The following code initializes an instance of the `ImageDataGenerator` class from Keras, which is used for data augmentation in image datasets:

```
# Define the data augmentation parameters
datagen = ImageDataGenerator(
    rotation_range=15,
    width_shift_range=0.1,
    height_shift_range=0.1,
    horizontal_flip=True
)
# Compile the model
model.compile(optimizer='adam', loss='categorical_crossentropy',\
    metrics=['accuracy'])


# Train the model with data augmentation
history = model.fit(datagen.flow(x_train, y_train, \
    batch_size=64), epochs=100, \
    validation_data=(x_test, y_test))


# Evaluate the model on the test set
score = model.evaluate(x_test, y_test, verbose=0)
print('Test loss:', score[0])
print('Test accuracy:', score[1])
```

This code defines a CNN with two convolutional layers, two max-pooling layers, and three fully connected layers. Data augmentation is performed using the `ImageDataGenerator` class, which randomly applies various transformations to the training images to generate more training data. The model is trained for 100 epochs using the `fit` method with the data generator as the input. Finally, the model is evaluated on the test set using the `evaluate` method.

Summary

In this chapter, we covered a variety of image data augmentation techniques. We learned how to implement an SVM with data augmentation in Python using the scikit-learn and Keras libraries. We first implemented SVM with the default hyperparameters and evaluated the performance of the classifier on the original dataset. We then implemented an SVM with data augmentation and trained the classifier on each batch of training data generated by the `ImageDataGenerator` object. Finally, we evaluated the performance of the classifier on the augmented dataset.

We also saw how to implement a CNN using augmentation with the CIFAR-10 dataset. Using data augmentation, we were able to improve the accuracy of the classifier on the augmented dataset. This demonstrates the effectiveness of data augmentation in improving the performance of machine learning models, especially in cases where the available dataset is limited.

Data augmentation can reduce the need for manual annotation by creating variations of existing labeled data. Instead of labeling each transformed image separately, augmentation techniques allow for the generation of additional labeled samples without the need for additional human annotation efforts.

In the next chapter, we will explore how to label text data using generative models.

Part 3:
Labeling Text,
Audio, and Video Data

In this part of the book, you will explore how to read text, audio, and video data using Python, analyze the data, and extract features. The content delves into various methods for programmatically labeling text, video, and audio data in Python, leveraging OpenAI's large language models, as well as semi-supervised and unsupervised techniques such as K-means clustering. Additionally, this section aids in understanding different open source data annotation tools such as Label Studio, CVAT, pyOpenAnnotate, and Azure Machine Learning for image, video, audio, and text data, providing a comprehensive comparison between them.

This part comprises the following chapters:

- *Chapter 7, Labeling Text Data*
- *Chapter 8, Exploring Video Data*
- *Chapter 9, Labeling Video Data*
- *Chapter 10, Exploring Audio Data*
- *Chapter 11, Labeling Audio Data*
- *Chapter 12, Hands-On Exploring Data Labeling Tools*

7
Labeling Text Data

In this chapter, we will explore techniques for labeling text data for classification in cases where an insufficient amount of labeled data is available. We are going to use Generative AI to label the text data, in addition to Snorkel and k-means clustering. The chapter focuses on the essential process of annotating textual data for NLP and text analysis. It aims to provide readers with practical knowledge and insights into various labeling techniques. The chapter will specifically cover automatic labeling using OpenAI, rule-based labeling using Snorkel labeling functions, and unsupervised learning using k-means clustering. By understanding these techniques, readers will be equipped to effectively label text data and extract meaningful insights from unstructured textual information.

We will cover the following sections in this chapter:

- Real-world applications of text data labeling
- Tools and frameworks for text data labeling
- Exploratory data analysis of text
- Generative AI and OpenAI for labeling text data
- Labeling text data using Snorkel
- Labeling text data using logistic regression
- Labeling text data using K-means clustering
- Labeling customer reviews (sentiment analysis) using neural networks

Technical requirements

The code files used in this chapter are located at https://github.com/PacktPublishing/Data-Labeling-in-Machine-Learning-with-Python/tree/main/code/Ch07.

The Gutenberg Corpus and movie review dataset can be found here:

- `https://pypi.org/project/Gutenberg/`

- `https://www.nltk.org/api/nltk.sentiment.util.html?highlight=movie#nltk.sentiment.util.demo_movie_reviews`

You also need to create an Azure account and add the OpenAI resource for working with Generative AI. To sign up for a free Azure subscription, visit `https://azure.microsoft.com/free`. To request access to the Azure OpenAI service, visit `https://aka.ms/oaiapply`.

Once you have provisioned the Azure OpenAI service, set up the following environment variables:

```
os.environ['AZURE_OPENAI_KEY'] = 'your_api_key'
os.environ['AZURE_OPENAI_ENDPOINT") ='your_azure_openai_endpoint'
```

Your endpoint should look like `https://YOUR_RESOURCE_NAME.openai.azure.com/`.

Real-world applications of text data labeling

Text data labeling or classification is widely used across various industries and applications to extract valuable information, automate processes, and improve decision-making. Here are some real-world examples across different use cases:

- Customer support ticket classification:

  - Use case: Companies receive a large volume of customer support tickets.

  - Application: Automated classification of support tickets into categories such as Billing, Technical Support, and Product Inquiry. This helps prioritize and route tickets to the right teams.

- Spam email filtering:

  - Use case: Sorting emails into spam and non-spam categories.

  - Application: Email providers use text classification to identify and filter out unwanted emails, providing users with a cleaner inbox and reducing the risk of phishing attacks.

- Sentiment analysis in social media:

  - Use case: Analyzing social media comments and posts.

  - Application: Brands use sentiment analysis to gauge public opinion, track brand sentiment, and respond to customer feedback. It helps with reputation management and understanding customer preferences.

- News categorization:

  - Use case: Sorting news articles into categories.

  - Application: News websites use text classification to automatically categorize articles into sections such as Politics, Technology, and Entertainment, making it easier for readers to find relevant content.

- Resume screening:

  - Use case: Sorting job applications.

  - Application: Human resources departments use text classification to quickly identify resumes that match specific job requirements. This accelerates the hiring process and ensures a more efficient candidate screening.

- Medical document classification:

  - Use case: Sorting medical records and documents.

  - Application: Healthcare organizations use text classification to categorize and organize medical records, lab reports, and patient notes. This aids in efficient data retrieval and analysis.

- Legal document classification:

  - Use case: Sorting legal documents.

  - Application: Law firms use text classification to categorize and manage legal documents, contracts, and case-related information, streamlining legal research and case management.

- Fraud detection in financial transactions:

  - Use case: Identifying fraudulent activity.

  - Application: Financial institutions use text classification to analyze transaction descriptions and identify potential cases of fraud or suspicious activities, enhancing security measures.

- Product review analysis:

  - Use case: Analyzing customer reviews.

  - Application: E-commerce platforms use sentiment analysis to categorize and understand product reviews. This helps in improving products, addressing customer concerns, and enhancing overall customer satisfaction.

- Language identification:

  - Use case: Determining the language of a given text.

  - Application: Social media platforms and translation services use text classification to automatically identify the language of a user's post or content, enabling accurate language-specific interactions.

These examples highlight the versatility of text classification across different domains, showcasing its significance in automating tasks, improving efficiency, and gaining valuable insights from textual data.

Tools and frameworks for text data labeling

There are several open source tools and frameworks available for text data analysis and labeling. Here are some popular ones, along with their pros and cons:

Tools and frameworks	Pros	Cons
Natural Language Toolkit (NLTK)	Comprehensive library for NLP tasks. Rich set of tools for tokenization, stemming, tagging, parsing, and more. Active community support. Suitable for educational purposes and research projects.	Some components may not be as efficient for large-scale industrial applications. Steep learning curve for beginners.
spaCy	Fast and efficient, designed for production use. Pre-trained models for various languages. Provides robust support for tokenization, named entity recognition, and dependency parsing. Easy-to-use API.	Less emphasis on educational resources compared to NLTK. Limited support for some languages.
scikit-learn	General-purpose machine learning library with excellent text processing capabilities. Easy integration with other scikit-learn modules for feature extraction and model training. Well-documented and widely used in the machine learning community.	May not have specialized tools for certain NLP tasks. Limited support for deep learning-based models.

TextBlob	Simple API for common NLP tasks such as part-of-speech tagging, noun phrase extraction, and sentiment analysis. Built on NLTK and provides an easy entry point for beginners. Useful for quick prototyping and small projects.	Limited customization options compared to lower-level libraries. May not be as performant for large-scale applications.
Gensim	Focus on topic modeling, document similarity, and vector space modeling. Efficient implementation of algorithms such as Word2Vec. Suitable for large text corpora and document similarity tasks.	Less versatile for general-purpose NLP tasks. Limited support for some advanced NLP functionalities.
Transformers (Hugging Face)	Provides pre-trained models for a wide range of NLP tasks (BERT, GPT, etc.). Easy-to-use interfaces for integrating state-of-the-art models. Excellent community support.	Heavy computational requirements for fine-tuning large models. May not be as straightforward for beginners.
Stanford NLP	Comprehensive suite of NLP tools, including tokenization, part-of-speech tagging, and named entity recognition. Java-based, making it suitable for Java projects.	Heavier resource usage compared to Python-based libraries. May have a steeper learning curve for certain tasks.
Flair	Focus on state-of-the-art NLP models and embeddings. Provides embeddings for a variety of languages. Easy-to-use API.	May not have as many pre-built models as other libraries. May not be as established as some older frameworks.

Table 7.1 – Popular tools with their pros and cons

In addition to this list is OpenAI's **Generative Pre-trained Transformer** (**GPT**), which is a state-of-the-art language model that utilizes transformer architecture. It's pre-trained on a massive amount of diverse data and can be fine-tuned for specific tasks. GPT is known for its ability to generate coherent and contextually relevant text, making it a powerful tool for various **natural language processing** (**NLP**) applications.

The transformer architecture, introduced by Vaswani et al. in the paper *Attention is All You Need*, revolutionized NLP. It relies on self-attention mechanisms to capture contextual relationships between words in a sequence, enabling parallelization and scalability. Transformers have become the foundation of numerous advanced language models, including GPT and BERT, due to their ability to capture long-range dependencies in sequential data efficiently. Its pros include versatility and the ability to understand context in text which is why it is used for various natural language understanding tasks. Its cons are that it is resource-intensive, requiring substantial computing power, and fine-tuning requires access to significant computational resources.

Each of these tools has strengths and weaknesses, and the choice depends on project requirements, available resources, and the desired level of customization. It's common to see a combination of these tools being used together in more complex NLP pipelines. When selecting a tool, it's important to consider factors such as ease of use, community support, and compatibility with the specific tasks at hand.

Exploratory data analysis of text

Exploratory Data Analysis (**EDA**) is a crucial step in any data science project. When it comes to text data, EDA can help us understand the structure and characteristics of the data, identify potential issues or inconsistencies, and inform our choice of data preprocessing and modeling techniques. In this section, we will walk through the steps involved in performing EDA on text data.

Loading the data

The first step in EDA is to load the text data into our environment. Text data can come in many formats, including plain text files, CSV files, or database tables. Once we have the data loaded, we can begin to explore its structure and content.

Understanding the data

The next step in EDA is to gain an understanding of the data. For text data, this may involve examining the size of the dataset, the number of documents or samples, and the overall structure of the text (e.g., whether it is structured or unstructured). We can use descriptive statistics to gain insights into the data, such as the distribution of text lengths or the frequency of certain words or phrases.

Cleaning and preprocessing the data

After understanding the data, the next step in EDA is to clean and preprocess the text data. This can involve a number of steps, such as removing punctuation and stop words, stemming or lemmatizing words, and converting text to lowercase. Cleaning and preprocessing the data is important for preparing the data for modeling and ensuring that we are working with high-quality data.

Exploring the text's content

Once we have cleaned and preprocessed the data, we can begin to explore the content of the text itself. This can involve examining the most frequent words or phrases, identifying patterns or themes in the text, and visualizing the data using techniques such as word clouds or frequency histograms. We can also use NLP techniques to extract features from the text, such as named entities, part-of-speech tags, or sentiment scores.

Analyzing relationships between text and other variables

In some cases, we may want to explore the relationships between the text data and other variables, such as demographic or behavioral data. For example, we may want to examine whether the sentiment of movie reviews varies by genre, or whether the topics discussed in social media posts differ by user age or location. This type of analysis can help us gain deeper insights into the text data and inform our modeling approach.

Visualizing the results

Finally, we can visualize the results of our EDA using a variety of techniques, such as word clouds, bar charts, scatterplots, or heat maps. Visualization is an important tool for communicating insights and findings to stakeholders, and can help us identify patterns and relationships in the data that might not be immediately apparent from the raw text.

In conclusion, exploratory data analysis is a critical step in any text data project. By understanding the structure and content of the data, cleaning and preprocessing it, exploring the text's content, analyzing relationships between text and other variables, and visualizing the results, we can gain deep insights into the textual data and inform our modeling approach. With the right tools and techniques, EDA can help us uncover hidden patterns and insights in text data that can be used to drive business decisions and improve outcomes.

Exploratory data analysis of sample text data set

Here's an example Python code for performing EDA on a text dataset. We will be using the Gutenberg corpus (`https://pypi.org/project/Gutenberg/`), which is a publicly available collection of over 60,000 electronic books.

The NLTK corpus is a collection of publicly available datasets for NLP research and development. The Gutenberg corpus (`https://www.nltk.org/book/ch02.html`), which is one of the datasets included in NLTK, specifically contains a selection of public domain texts from Project Gutenberg. Project Gutenberg is a digital library that offers free access to books and other texts that are no longer protected by copyright.

Therefore, the Gutenberg corpus within the NLTK is based on public domain texts, making it a publicly available dataset. It can be used for various NLP tasks, such as text classification, language modeling, and information retrieval, without any commercial restrictions or licensing requirements:

```
import nltk
from nltk.corpus import gutenberg
import string
import pandas as pd
import numpy as np
import matplotlib.pyplot as plt
import seaborn as sns
```

Let's download the Gutenberg corpus using the NLTK library:

```
# Download the Gutenberg corpus
nltk.download('gutenberg')
```

Let's load the text data into a Pandas DataFrame by iterating the fields from Gutenberg and appending documents to the list data. Then we'll convert the list data to dataframe, df, with a single column, text, to store the document:

```
# Load the data
data = []
for file_id in gutenberg.fileids():
    document = ' '.join(gutenberg.words(file_id))
    data.append(document)
df = pd.DataFrame(data, columns=['text'])


# View the first few rows of the data
print(df.head())
```

Let's check the dataframe's size by calling the shape function:

```
# Check the size of the dataset
print("Dataset size:", df.shape)
```

Here's the output:

```
                                                    text
0   [ Emma by Jane Austen 1816 ] VOLUME I CHAPTER ...
1   [ Persuasion by Jane Austen 1818 ] Chapter 1 S...
2   [ Sense and Sensibility by Jane Austen 1811 ] ...
3   [ The King James Bible ] The Old Testament of ...
4   [ Poems by William Blake 1789 ] SONGS OF INNOC...
Dataset size: (18, 1)
```

Figure 7.1 – The first few rows of data

Let's check the length of each document by calling the `apply` function:

```
# Check the length of each document
df['text_length'] = df['text'].apply(len)
  Let us plot the histogram plot of the 'text_length' column using
seaborn library sns.
# Visualize the distribution of document lengths
plt.figure(figsize=(8, 6))
sns.distplot(df['text_length'], bins=50, kde=False, color='blue')
plt.title('Distribution of Text Lengths')
plt.xlabel('Text Length')
plt.ylabel('Count')
plt.show()
```

Here's the output:

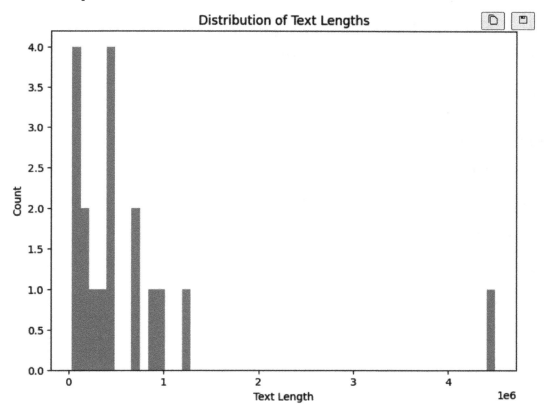

Figure 7.2 – Distribution of document length

In text analysis, removing stopwords and punctuation is one of the most common tasks because stopwords do not tell us anything about the text:

```
# Remove punctuation and stop words
def remove_punctuation(text):
    return text.translate(str.maketrans('', '', string.punctuation))
```

We will use the stopwords list from the NLTK corpus:

```
def remove_stopwords(text):
    stopwords_list = nltk.corpus.stopwords.words('english')
    return " ".join([word for word in text.split() if \
        word.lower() not in stopwords_list])

df['text_clean'] = df['text'].apply(remove_punctuation)
df['text_clean'] = df['text_clean'].apply(remove_stopwords)
```

Now let's count the frequency of words in the clean text using the `value_counts` function:

```
# Count the frequency of each word
word_freq = pd.Series(np.concatenate([x.split() for x in \
    df['text_clean']])).value_counts()
```

Finally, plot a bar chart to visualize the most frequent words:

```
# Visualize the most frequent words
plt.figure(figsize=(12, 8))
word_freq[:20].plot(kind='bar', color='blue')
plt.title('Most Frequent Words')
plt.xlabel('Word')
plt.ylabel('Frequency')
plt.show()
```

Here's the output:

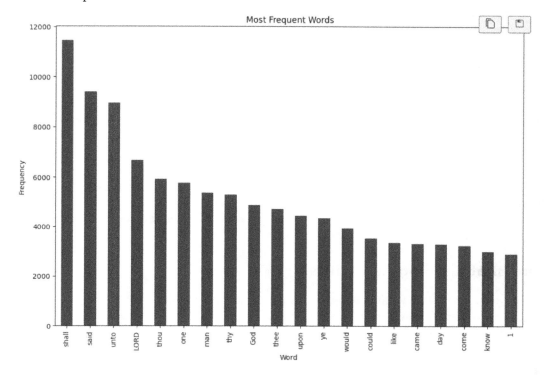

Figure 7.3 – Most frequent words

In this code, we first downloaded the Gutenberg corpus using the NLTK library. We then loaded the text data into a Pandas DataFrame and performed some initial checks on the size and structure of the dataset.

Next, we calculated the length of each document and visualized the distribution of document lengths using a histogram. We then removed punctuation and stop words from the text data and calculated the frequency of each word. We visualized the most frequent words using a bar chart.

Note that this code is just a basic example of EDA on text data, and you may need to modify it to suit your specific dataset and research question. Now we have clean text data.

Let's see how to use Generative AI to label text data in the following section.

Exploring Generative AI and OpenAI for labeling text data

Generative AI refers to a category of artificial intelligence that involves training models to generate new content or data based on patterns and information present in the training data. OpenAI is a prominent organization that has developed and released powerful generative models for various NLP tasks. One of the notable models is GPT, such as GPT-3, GPT-3.5, and GPT-4. These models have been influential in the fields of text data labeling and classification.

Generative AI focuses on training models to generate new data instances that resemble existing examples. It is often used for tasks such as text generation, image synthesis, and more. Generative models are trained on large datasets to learn underlying patterns, allowing them to generate coherent and contextually relevant content. In text-related tasks, generative AI can be applied to text completion, summarization, question answering, and even creative writing. Let's take a look at some key concepts that will help us with labeling text data.

GPT models by OpenAI

OpenAI has developed a series of sophisticated language models, with GPT-4 being among the most advanced. These models undergo pre-training on diverse datasets, enabling them to excel in various natural language understanding and generation tasks.

Zero-shot learning capabilities

GPT models are renowned for their zero-shot learning capabilities, enabling them to make predictions or generate content for tasks they were not explicitly trained on. This versatility enhances their applicability across diverse domains.

Text classification with OpenAI models

Leveraging the language understanding and generation capabilities of OpenAI models, they can be effectively utilized for text classification tasks. This includes sentiment analysis, topic categorization, and other classification-based applications.

Data labeling assistance

Although GPT models are not specifically designed for traditional data labeling tasks, they can offer assistance in generating labeled data. This can be achieved through natural language instructions or by providing context that aids in making labeling decisions.

OpenAI API overview

The OpenAI API is a service provided by OpenAI that allows users to access their advanced language models through an API. It serves as a gateway for integrating OpenAI's language capabilities into various applications.

Let's see the pros and cons of OpenAI's GPT models:

- Pros:

  - Versatility: OpenAI's GPT models are versatile and can be adapted for various text-related tasks, including data labeling and classification

  - Large scale: These models are trained on massive amounts of data, enabling them to capture intricate patterns and nuances present in natural language

- Cons:

  - Interpretability: The generated content might lack interpretability, making it challenging to understand the model's decision-making process

  - Resource intensive: Training and using large generative models such as GPT-4 can be computationally expensive

In summary, OpenAI's generative models, particularly GPT-3 , GPT-3.5, and GPT-4, have made significant contributions to the field of text data processing, and they can be used creatively for tasks such as data labeling and classification by utilizing their language-understanding capabilities. However, careful consideration and evaluation are needed, especially regarding ethical concerns and potential bias in generated content.

In the realm of language processing, text classification serves to categorize documents based on their content. Traditionally, this task relied on labeled training data; however, advanced models such as OpenAI's GPT have revolutionized the process by autonomously generating labels with the assistance of explicit instructions or **prompts**.

Exploring text data labeling with **Azure OpenAI**, a collaborative initiative within Microsoft Azure's cloud, unlocks the potential of powerful language models. This section acts as a guide, facilitating efficient text data labeling by harnessing the capabilities of Generative AI and OpenAI models, and providing users with custom tools for typical tasks in text data analysis.

Let's take a look at some use cases with Python and Azure OpenAI for text data labeling.

Use case 1 – summarizing the text

Summarization is a crucial NLP task that involves condensing a piece of text while retaining its essential information and main ideas. In the context of Azure OpenAI, the following code exemplifies the application of summarization using the GPT-3.5-turbo model deployed on the Azure platform.

The following code example begins by setting the necessary environment variables for the Azure OpenAI API, including the API key and endpoint. The OpenAI API is then configured with the deployment name of the model, allowing the code to interact with the specific GPT-3.5-turbo instance.

The input text, which is a detailed description of Dachepalli, a town in Andhra Pradesh, India, is provided for summarization. The code utilizes the Azure OpenAI Completion API to generate a summary, employing parameters such as temperature, max tokens, and penalties for frequency and presence.

The output of the code includes the generated summary, showcasing the main ideas extracted from the input text. The summarized content emphasizes key aspects such as the author's connection to Dachepalli, the town's features, and notable historical events. This example demonstrates how Azure OpenAI can effectively summarize information, providing concise and informative outputs.

Let's start by importing the required libraries and getting the configuration values (the Azure OpenAI key and endpoint, API version, and the GPT model deployment name) that we have set already:

```
import os
openai.api.key=os.getenv("AZURE_OPENAI_KEY")
Openai.api_base=os.getenv("AZURE_OPENAI_ENDPOINT")
Openai.api_type='azure'
Openai.api_version='2023-5-15' # this might change in the future
#this will correspond to the custom name you choose for your
deployment when you deployed a model.
model_deployment_name = 'your_azure_openai_model_name'
# Set the input text
text = "create a summary of below text and provide main idea.\n\n
Dachepalli is popular town in palnadu district in Andhra pradesh,
India.I love dachepalli because i born and brought up at Dachepalli.
I studied at Dachepalli zph school and got school first and my name
was written on school toppers board at high school.My father worked in
the same high school as hindi pandit for 20 years.The famous palnadu
battle has took place near Naguleru river of Karempudi which flows
across Dachepalli.It has lime mines and number of cement factories
around Dachepalli.The Nadikudi railway junction connect Dachepalli
to Hyderbad and Guntur. being born in Dachepalli and studied at
Dachepalli high school, I love Dachepalli."

response = openai.Completion.create(
    engine=model_deployment_name,
    prompt=text,
    temperature=0,
    max_tokens=118,
    top_p=1,
    frequency_penalty=0,
    presence_penalty=0,
    stop=None)
```

Let's understand the parameters used in this OpenAI completion API.

OpenAI's parameters control the behavior of the language model during text generation. Here's a brief description of the provided parameters:

- Temperature (`temperature=0`): It determines the randomness of the model's output. A high value (e.g., `0.8`) makes the output more diverse, while a low value (e.g., `0.2`) makes it more deterministic.

- Max tokens (`max_tokens=118`): This specifies the maximum number of tokens (words or characters) to generate in the output. It's useful for limiting response length.

- Top P (`top_p=1`): Also known as nucleus sampling, it controls the diversity of the generated output. Setting it to `1` ensures that only the top probability tokens are considered during sampling.

- Frequency penalty (`frequency_penalty=0`): This discourages the repetition of specific tokens in the output. A non-zero value penalizes the model for choosing frequently occurring tokens.

- Presence Penalty (`presence_penalty=0`): Similar to frequency penalty, presence penalty discourages the repetition of entire phrases or concepts, promoting more diverse responses.

- Stop (`stop=None`): This allows users to specify a custom stopping criterion for generation. When the model encounters the specified token, it stops generating further content.

These parameters provide users with fine-grained control over the generation process, allowing customization of the model's output based on factors such as randomness, length, diversity, and repetition. Adjusting these parameters enables users to tailor the language model's behavior to meet specific requirements in various applications, such as chatbots, content generation, and more:

```
# Print the generated summary
print("Generated summary:", summary.choices[0].text.strip())
```

Running this code will output the following summary:

```
Generated summary: Main Idea: The author loves Dachepalli because he
was born and brought up there and studied at Dachepalli high school.
The town is located in Palnadu district in Andhra Pradesh, India and
is known for its lime mines and cement factories. The Nadikudi railway
junction connects Dachepalli to Hyderabad and Guntur. The famous
Palnadu battle took place near Naguleru river of Karempudi which flows
across Dachepalli. The author's father worked in the same high school
as a Hindi pandit for 20 years.
```

We have seen how to generate a summary using the OpenAI GPT-3.5 model. Now let's see how to generate the topic for news articles using OpenAI's GPT model.

Use case 2 – topic generation for news articles

Let's explore generating topic names for news articles using a generative model, specifically, Azure OpenAI.

Topic generation is a powerful application of NLP that involves creating relevant and coherent content based on a given prompt. In the context of Azure OpenAI prompts, the ability to generate topics is demonstrated using a news headline classification example.

In this code snippet, the task is to categorize a news headline into one of the predefined categories, which are Business, Tech, Politics, Sport, and Entertainment. The news headline, provided as input, is *Trump is ready to contest in Nov 2024 elections.* The code uses the Azure OpenAI API to generate a response that predicts the most appropriate category for the given headline.

The completion engine is configured with specific parameters, such as temperature, max tokens, and penalties for frequency and presence. After generating the response, the code extracts and prints the predicted category from the output.

This example showcases how Azure OpenAI prompts can be utilized for the automatic categorization of news headlines, demonstrating the versatility and effectiveness of NLP in topic-generation tasks:

```
news_headline="Label the following news headline into 1 of the
following categories: Business, Tech, Politics, Sport, Entertainment\
n\n Headline 1: Trump is ready to contest in nov 2024 elections\
nCategory:",
response = openai.Completion.create(
    engine=model_deployment_name,
    prompt= news_headline,
    temperature=0,
    max_tokens=118,
    top_p=1,
    frequency_penalty=0,
    presence_penalty=0,
    stop=None)
index_of_newline=response.choice[0].text.find('\n')
print('category:',response.choices[0].text[:index_of_newline])
```

Here's the output:

```
category: Politics
```

Use case 3 – classification of customer queries using the user-defined categories and sub-categories

Let's see how to classify the customer queries into user-defined categories and sub-categories using **Azure OpenAI**.

Text classification is a fundamental NLP task that involves assigning predefined categories to textual input. In the provided code, a customer support system utilizes text classification to categorize customer queries related to their orders. The system employs user-defined primary and secondary categories, each with specific sub-categories.

The system message serves as a guide for the classification task, outlining the primary categories (Order Status, Product Inquiries, Shipping and Delivery, and Payment Assistance) and their corresponding secondary categories. The primary and secondary categories are structured to capture various aspects of customer queries, such as tracking information, product availability, and payment confirmation.

For example, when a user submits a query to cancel an order, the code uses the OpenAI ChatCompletion API to generate a response. The output includes a JSON-formatted response indicating the primary and secondary categories assigned to the user's query. In this case, the primary category is Order Status, and the secondary category is Order Modification or Cancellation.

This example demonstrates how text classification can be applied in a customer support context, allowing for the efficient handling and categorization of customer queries based on predefined categories. The system provides a structured approach to address diverse aspects of order-related inquiries, enhancing the overall customer support experience:

```
system_message = f"""
Welcome to Customer Order Support!

You will receive customer queries related to their orders, each
delimited by {delimiter} characters.
Your task is to classify each query into a primary and secondary
category.

Provide your response in JSON format with the keys: "primary" and
"secondary."

Primary Categories:
1. Order Status
2. Product Inquiries
3. Shipping and Delivery
4. Payment Assistance

Order Status Secondary Categories:
- Tracking Information
- Order Confirmation
- Order Modification or Cancellation
- Refund Status

Product Inquiries Secondary Categories:
- Product Availability
```

```
- Size and Color Options
- Product Specifications
- Return and Exchange Policies

Shipping and Delivery Secondary Categories:
- Delivery Timeframe
- Shipping Methods
- Address Changes
- Lost or Delayed Shipments

Payment Assistance Secondary Categories:
- Payment Confirmation
- Refund Process
- Payment Errors
- Billing Inquiries

Please review each query and provide the appropriate primary and
secondary category in your response.
Thank you for assisting our customers with their orders!"""

user_message=f"""\
 I want to cancel my order """
response = openai.ChatCompletion.create(
    engine=deployment_name, # engine = "deployment_name".
    messages=[
        {"role": "system", "content": system_message},
        {"role": "user", "content": f"{delimiter}{user_message}
        {delimiter}"},],
    temperature=0,
    max_tokens=60,
    top_p=1,
    frequency_penalty=0,
    presence_penalty=0,
    stop=None
)

print(response)
print(response['choices'][0]['message']['content'])
```

Here's the output:

```
{ "id": "chatcmpl-8eEc86GxAO4BePuRepvve9XhTQZfa", "object": "chat.
completion", "created": 1704599988, "model": "gpt-35-turbo",
"choices": [ { "finish_reason": "stop", "index": 0, "message": {
"role": "assistant", "content": "{\n \"primary\": \"Order Status\",\n
```

```
\"secondary\": \"Order Modification or Cancellation\"\n}" } } ],
"usage": { "prompt_tokens": 232, "completion_tokens": 21, "total_
tokens": 253 } } { "primary": "Order Status", "secondary": "Order
Modification or Cancellation" }
```

Use case 4 – information retrieval using entity extraction

Let us see how to extract the entity names from the text data using Azure OpenAI.

Entity extraction is a vital aspect of NLP, involving the identification and extraction of specific entities, such as names, organizations, locations, and contact numbers, from a given text. In the presented code snippet, the task is to identify and extract people's names, organization names, geographical locations, and contact numbers from various text passages.

The prompt provides clear instructions for the entity extraction task, specifying the entities of interest and their corresponding categories. It includes examples that illustrate how to extract information from different texts, showcasing the versatility of the entity extraction process.

The code utilizes the OpenAI API to generate responses that include extracted entities, such as people's names, organization names, locations, and contact numbers, from the given text passages. The output is structured in a JSON format, making it easy to parse and integrate the extracted entities into further processing or analysis.

This example demonstrates the practical application of entity extraction for extracting relevant information from diverse textual data, showcasing its potential in various domains, such as customer relationship management, information retrieval, and data analysis:

```
response = openai.Completion.create(
    engine="gpt3.5 deployment name",
    prompt = "Identify the individual's name, organization,
geographical location, and contact number in the following text.\n\
nHello. I'm Sarah Johnson, and I'm reaching out on behalf of XYZ
Tech Solutions based in Austin, Texas. Our team believes that our
innovative products could greatly benefit your business. Please feel
free to contact me at (555) 123-4567 at your convenience, and we can
discuss how our solutions align with your needs.",
    temperature=0.2,
    max_tokens=150,
    top_p=1,
    frequency_penalty=0,
    presence_penalty=0,
    stop=None)

print(response['choices'])
```

Here's the output:

```
[<OpenAIObject at 0x215d2c40770> JSON: {
    "text": " Thank you for your time, and I look forward to hearing
from you soon. \n\nName: Sarah Johnson\nOrganization: XYZ Tech
Solutions\nGeographical location: Austin, Texas\nContact number: (555)
123-4567",
    "index": 0,
    "finish_reason": "stop",
    "logprobs": null,
    "content_filter_results": {
    "hate": {
        "filtered": false,
        "severity": "safe"
    },
    "self_harm": {
        "filtered": false,
        "severity": "safe"
    },
    "sexual": {
        "filtered": false,
        "severity": "safe"
    },
    "violence": {
        "filtered": false,
        "severity": "safe"
    }
}
}]
```

Now let's extract the required information name, organization, location, and contact information from the output JSON, as follows:

```python
import json
# Parse JSON
json_data = response['choices']

# Extract information

# Extracting information from the JSON object
for entry in json_data:
    text = entry.get("text", "")

    # Extracting information using string manipulation or regular
expressions
```

```
    name = text.split("Name:")[1].split("\n")[0].strip()
    organization = text.split("Organization:")[1].split("\n")[0].
strip()
    location = text.split("Geographical location:")[1].split("\n")[0].
strip()
    contact_number = text.split("Contact number:")[1].split("\n")[0].
strip()

    # Print the extracted information
    print("Name:", name)
    print("Organization:", organization)
    print("Location:", location)
    print("Contact Number:", contact_number)
```

Here's the output:

```
Name: Sarah Johnson Organization: XYZ Tech Solutions Location: Austin,
Texas Contact Number: (555) 123-4567
```

Use case 5 – aspect-based sentiment analysis

Sentiment aspect analysis is a sophisticated NLP task that involves evaluating the sentiment expressed towards specific aspects or features within a given text. In the provided code snippet, aspect-based sentiment analysis is conducted on product reviews, aiming to assess both the overall sentiment of the reviews and the sentiment polarity associated with individual aspects mentioned.

The prompt outlines the objectives of the sentiment analysis task, which include providing an overall sentiment score for each review on a scale from 0 to 5, assigning sentiment polarity scores between 0 and 5 for each aspect, and identifying the top positive and negative aspects.

The code processes multiple product reviews, extracting sentiments associated with aspects such as camera quality, battery life, design, speaker quality, performance, keyboard, display, trackpad responsiveness, sound quality, touch controls, graphics, load times, online community, subscription fee, and controller.

The output includes comprehensive sentiment scores, polarity scores, and the identification of the most positively and negatively rated aspects in each review. This example illustrates how aspect-based sentiment analysis can provide detailed insights into the nuanced opinions expressed in diverse reviews, assisting businesses in understanding customer sentiments towards specific product features.

Let's see the code example for aspect-based sentiment analysis:

```
response = openai.Completion.create(
    engine="gpt3.5 deployment name",
prompt = "Conduct aspect-based sentiment analysis on the following
product reviews:\n Provide an overall sentiment score between 0 and 5
for each review.\n Assign a sentiment polarity score between 0 and 5
```

```
for each aspect mentioned. \n Identify the top positive and negative
aspects, if any. \n Review 1: \n I recently purchased this smartphone,
and it has exceeded my expectations! The camera quality is superb,
capturing vivid and detailed photos. The battery life is impressive,
easily lasting a full day with regular use. The sleek design adds
a premium feel to the device. However, the speaker quality could
be improved. Overall sentiment score: 4.8 \nAspects with sentiment
polarity score: \n - Camera: 5 \n - Battery Life: 5 \n - Design: 5 \n
- Speaker: 3 \n \n Top positive aspect: Camera \n Top negative aspect:
Speaker \n \n Review 2: \n This laptop offers powerful performance
and a sleek design. The keyboard is comfortable for extended typing
sessions, and the display is vibrant with accurate colors. However,
the trackpad responsiveness can be inconsistent at times.",
    temperature=0,
    max_tokens=100,
    top_p=1,
    frequency_penalty=0,
    presence_penalty=0,
    stop=None)
print(response.choices[0].text.strip())
```

Here's the output:

```
Overall sentiment score: 4.5
Aspects with sentiment polarity score:
 - Performance: 5
 - Design: 5
 - Keyboard: 5
 - Display: 5
 - Trackpad: 3

 Top positive aspects: Performance, Design, Keyboard, Display
 Top negative aspect: Trackpad
```

Next, let's use the Snorkel API to classify this text data and generate labels by creating rule-based labeling functions.

Hands-on labeling of text data using the Snorkel API

In this section, we are going to learn how to label text data using the Snorkel API.

Snorkel provides an API for programmatically labeling text data using a small set of ground truth labels that are created by domain experts. Snorkel, an open source data labeling and training platform, is used by various companies and organizations across different industries, such as Google, Apple, Facebook, IBM, and SAP.

It has unique features that differentiate it from other competitors, especially in the context of weak supervision and programmatically generating labeled data. Here's a comparison with some of the other tools:

- **Weak supervision**: Snorkel excels in scenarios where labeled data is scarce, and manual labeling is expensive. It allows users to programmatically label large amounts of data using heuristics, patterns, and external resources.

- **Flexible labeling functions**: Snorkel enables the creation of labeling functions, which are essentially heuristic functions that assign labels to data. This provides a flexible and scalable way to generate labeled data.

- **Probabilistic labeling**: Snorkel generates probabilistic labels, acknowledging that labeling functions may have varying levels of accuracy. This probabilistic framework is useful in downstream tasks.

There can be a learning curve with Snorkel, especially for users who are new to weak supervision concepts. Other tools, such as Prodigy and Labelbox, are commercial tools and may involve licensing costs.

When choosing between these tools, the specific requirements of the project, the available budget, and the expertise of the users play crucial roles. Snorkel stands out when weak supervision and programmatically generated labels are essential for the task at hand. It's particularly well suited for scenarios where manual labeling is impractical or cost-prohibitive. Other tools may be more appropriate based on different use cases, interface preferences, and integration requirements.

We will create rule-based labeling functions using Snorkel and then apply these labeling functions to classify and label text.

We have seen what a labeling function is and how to create labeling functions in *Chapter 2*. Let's recap. In Snorkel, a labeling function is a Python function that heuristically generates labels for a dataset. These functions are used in the process of weak supervision, where instead of relying solely on manually labeled data, a machine learning model is trained using noisy, imperfect, or weakly labeled data.

Here is an example Python code that uses the Snorkel API to label text data using rule-based labeling functions.

Let's install Snorkel using pip and import the required Python libraries for labeling as follows:

```
!pip install snorkel
```

Let's break down the code into four steps and explain each one.

Step 1: Data preparation and labeling function definition. This step prepares the data and defines the labeling functions. It first imports the Pandas library and defines some constants for the labels. It then creates a DataFrame with movie reviews and splits it into a training set and a test set. The true labels for the test set are defined and converted to a NumPy array. Finally, it defines three labeling functions that label a review as positive, negative, or abstain based on the presence of certain words:

```python
import pandas as pd

# Define the constants
ABSTAIN = -1
POS = 0
NEG = 1

# Create a DataFrame with more data
df = pd.DataFrame({
    'id': [1, 2, 3, 4, 5, 6, 7, 8],
    'review': [
        "This movie was absolutely wonderful!",
        "The film was terrible and boring.",
        "I have mixed feelings about the movie.",
        "I have no opinion about the movie.",
        "The movie was fantastic and exciting!",
        "I didn't like the movie, it was too slow.",
        "The movie was okay, not great but not bad either.",
        "The movie was confusing and dull."
    ]
})

# Split the DataFrame into a training set and a test set
df_train = df.iloc[:6]  # First 6 records for training
df_test = df.iloc[6:]   # Remaining records for testing

# Define the true labels for the test set
Y_test = [ABSTAIN, NEG]  # Replace this with the actual labels

# Convert Y_test to a NumPy array
Y_test = np.array(Y_test)
```

Now let's define the labeling functions, one for positive reviews, one for negative reviews, and one for neutral reviews, using regular expressions as follows:

```
# Define rule-based labeling functions using regular expressions

@labeling_function()
def lf_positive_review(x):
    return POS if 'wonderful' in x.review or 'fantastic' in x.review
else ABSTAIN

@labeling_function()
def lf_negative_review(x):
    return NEG if 'terrible' in x.review or 'boring' in \
        x.review or 'slow' in x.review or 'dull' in \
        x.review else ABSTAIN

@labeling_function()
def lf_neutral_review(x):
    return ABSTAIN if 'mixed feelings' in x.review or \
        'no opinion' in x.review or 'okay' in x.review \
        else ABSTAIN
```

Step 2: Applying labeling functions and majority voting. This chunk of code applies the labeling functions to the training and test sets, and then uses a majority vote model to predict the labels. It first creates a list of the labeling functions and applies them to the training and test sets using `PandasLFApplier`. It then prints the resulting label matrices and their shapes. It imports the `MajorityLabelVoter` and `LabelModel` classes from Snorkel, creates a majority vote mode, and uses it to predict the labels for the training set:

```
# Apply the labeling functions to the training set and the test set
lfs = [lf_positive_review, lf_negative_review, lf_neutral_review]
applier = PandasLFApplier(lfs=lfs)
L_train = applier.apply(df=df_train)
L_test = applier.apply(df=df_test)

print(L_train)
print(L_test)
print(L_test.shape)
print(Y_test.shape)
```

Here's the output:

```
100%|████████| 6/6 [00:00<00:00, 2516.58it/s]
100%|████████| 2/2 [00:00<00:00, 3269.14it/s]
[[ 0 -1 -1]
 [-1  1 -1]
 [-1 -1 -1]
 [-1 -1 -1]
 [ 0 -1 -1]
 [-1  1 -1]]
[[-1 -1 -1]
 [-1  1 -1]]
(2, 3)
(2,)
```

Figure 7.4 – Label matrices

Let's calculate the accuracy of the model using `MajorityLabelVoter` model on the test set and print it:

```
from snorkel.labeling.model import MajorityLabelVoter, LabelModel
majority_model = MajorityLabelVoter()
majority_model.predict(L=L_train)
majority_acc = majority_model.score(L=L_test, Y=Y_test, \
    tie_break_policy="random")["accuracy"]
print( majority_acc)
```

Here's the output:

```
1.0
```

Finally, it predicts the labels for the training set and prints them:

```
preds_train = majority_model.predict(L=L_train)
print(preds_train)
```

Here's the output:

```
[ 0  1 -1 -1  0  1]
```

Step 3: Training a label model and predicting labels. This chunk of code trains a label model and uses it to predict the labels. It creates a `LabelModel` with a `cardinality` of 2 (for the two labels, positive and negative), fits it to the training set, and calculates its accuracy on the test set:

```
label_model = LabelModel(cardinality=2, verbose=True)
label_model.fit(L_train=L_train, n_epochs=500, \
    log_freq=100, seed=123)
label_model_acc = label_model.score(L=L_test, Y=Y_test, \
```

```
        tie_break_policy="random")[
        "accuracy"
    ]
    print(label_model_acc)
```

Here's the output:

```
INFO:root:Computing O...
INFO:root:Estimating \mu...
  0%|            | 0/500 [00:00<?, ?epoch/s]INFO:root:[0 epochs]: TRAIN:[loss=0.058]
INFO:root:[100 epochs]: TRAIN:[loss=0.000]
INFO:root:[200 epochs]: TRAIN:[loss=0.000]
 46%|████    | 231/500 [00:00<00:00, 2306.08epoch/s]INFO:root:[300 epochs]: TRAIN:[loss=0.000]
INFO:root:[400 epochs]: TRAIN:[loss=0.000]
100%|████████| 500/500 [00:00<00:00, 2896.35epoch/s]
INFO:root:Finished Training
1.0
```

Figure 7.5 – Training a LabelModel

It then predicts the labels for the training set and prints them:

```
# Predict the labels for the training data
Y_train_pred = label_model.predict(L=L_train)
# Print the predicted labels
print(Y_train_pred)
```

Here's the output:

```
[ 0  1 -1 -1  0  1]
```

Step 4: Analyzing labeling functions and creating a DataFrame with predicted labels. We can use the LFAnalysis class to analyze the labeling functions by passing the labels (L) and the list of labeling functions (lfs). The lf_summary() method provides an overview of the labeling functions and their coverage:

```
# Analyze the labeled data
LFAnalysis(L=L_train, lfs=lfs).lf_summary()
```

Here's the output:

	j	Polarity	Coverage	Overlaps	Conflicts
lf_positive_review	0	[0]	0.333333	0.0	0.0
lf_negative_review	1	[1]	0.333333	0.0	0.0
lf_neutral_review	2	[]	0.000000	0.0	0.0

Figure 7.6 – LFAnalysis summary

The table is a summary of the results from LFAnalysis, specifically for three labeling functions: `lf_positive_review`, `lf_negative_review`, and `if_neutral_review`.

Let's break down the columns:

- `j`: The index of the labeling function in the list of labeling functions. Here, `j` = 0 corresponds to `lf_positive_review`, and `j` = 1 corresponds to `lf_negative_review`.

- `Polarity`: The polarity assigned to the labeling function, representing the label value assigned by the function. In this case, `lf_positive_review` has a polarity of `[0, 1]`, meaning it assigns both label 0 and label 1. On the other hand, `lf_negative_review` has a polarity of `[0]`, indicating it only assigns label 0.

- `Coverage`: The set of labels predicted by the labeling function. For `lf_positive_review`, it predicts both label 0 and label 1 (`[0, 1]`), indicating it provides a non-abstain output for all examples. However, `lf_negative_review` predicts only label 0 (`[0]`), meaning it provides a non-abstain output for only 55.25% of the examples.

- `Overlaps`: The percentage of examples for which the labeling function provides a non-abstain output. It represents the extent to which the labeling function is applicable. In this case, both `lf_positive_review` and `lf_negative_review` have a coverage of 0.5525, indicating that they provide a non-abstain label for 55.25% of the examples.

- `Conflicts`: The percentage of examples for which the labeling function disagrees with at least one other labeling function. It measures the level of conflict between the labeling function and other functions. Both `lf_positive_review` and `lf_negative_review` have a conflict value of 0.2105, indicating they have conflicts with other labeling functions in approximately 21.05% of the examples.

This summary provides insights into the performance, coverage, and conflicts of the labeling functions, allowing you to assess their effectiveness and identify areas of improvement in your labeling process.

Lastly, the following chunk of code analyzes the labeling functions and creates a DataFrame with the predicted labels. It uses the `LFAnalysis` class from Snorkel to analyze the labeling functions and print a summary. It then creates a DataFrame with the predicted labels:

```
# Create a DataFrame with the predicted labels
df_train_pred = df_train.copy()
df_train_pred['predicted_label'] = Y_train_pred

# Display the DataFrame
print(df_train_pred)
```

Here's the output:

```
     id                                          review  predicted_label
  0   1          This movie was absolutely wonderful!                 0
  1   2              The film was terrible and boring.                 1
  2   3        I have mixed feelings about the movie.                -1
  3   4          I have no opinion about the movie.                  -1
  4   5          The movie was fantastic and exciting!                0
  5   6  I didn't like the movie, it was too slow.                    1
```

Figure 7.7 – Predicted labels

In this example, we first created the `Movie Reviews` DataFrame. We then defined three rule-based labeling functions using regular expressions to label reviews as positive, negative, or neutral based on the presence of certain keywords. We applied these labeling functions to the text data using the `PandasLFApplier` provided by the Snorkel API. Finally, we analyzed the labeled data using `LFAnalysis` and printed a summary of the results.

Note that this is a simple example and you may need to adjust the code depending on the specific requirements of your use case. Also, you can add more labeling functions depending on your task, and these functions should be carefully designed and tested to ensure high-quality labels.

Now, let's look into labeling the data using logistic regression.

Hands-on text labeling using Logistic Regression

Text labeling is a crucial task in NLP, enabling the categorization of textual data into predefined classes or sentiments. Logistic Regression, a popular machine learning algorithm, proves effective in text classification scenarios. In the following code, we walk through the process of using Logistic Regression to classify movie reviews into positive or negative sentiments. Here's a breakdown of the code.

Step 1. Import necessary libraries and modules.

The code begins by importing the necessary libraries and modules. These include NLTK for NLP, scikit-learn for machine learning, and specific modules for sentiment analysis, text preprocessing, and classification:

```
from nltk.corpus import stopwords
from nltk.stem import WordNetLemmatizer
from sklearn.feature_extraction.text import TfidfVectorizer
from sklearn.model_selection import train_test_split
from sklearn.linear_model import LogisticRegression
import nltk
from nltk.corpus import movie_reviews
from nltk.sentiment import SentimentAnalyzer
from nltk.classify import NaiveBayesClassifier
```

Step 2. Download the necessary NLTK data. The code downloads the movie reviews dataset and other necessary NLTK data, such as the WordNet lemmatizer and the Punkt tokenizer:

```
nltk.download('movie_reviews')
nltk.download('wordnet')
nltk.download('omw-1.4')
nltk.download('punkt')
```

Step 3. Initialize the sentiment analyzer and get movie review IDs. The code initializes a sentiment analyzer and gets the IDs of the movie reviews:

```
sentiment_analyzer = SentimentAnalyzer()
ids = movie_reviews.fileids()
```

Step 4. Preprocessing setup. The code sets up the preprocessing tools, including a lemmatizer and a list of English stopwords. It also defines a preprocessing function that tokenizes the text, removes stop words, and lemmatizes the words:

```
lemmatizer = WordNetLemmatizer()
stop_words = set(stopwords.words('english'))
def preprocess(document):
    words = word_tokenize(document)
    words = [lemmatizer.lemmatize(word) for word in \
        words if word not in stop_words]
    return ' '.join(words)
```

Step 5. Feature extraction. The code sets up a TF-IDF vectorizer with the preprocessing function and uses it to transform the movie reviews into a feature matrix:

```
vectorizer = TfidfVectorizer(preprocessor=preprocess, ngram_
range=(1, 2))
    X = vectorizer.fit_transform( \
        [movie_reviews.raw(fileid) for fileid in ids])
```

Step 6. Create a target vector. The code creates a target vector with the categories of the movie reviews:

```
y = [movie_reviews.categories([f])[0] for f in ids]
```

Step 7. Split the data. The code splits the data into training and test sets:

```
X_train, X_test, y_train, y_test = train_test_split( \
    X, y, test_size=0.2, random_state=42)
```

Step 8. Model training. The code initializes a Logistic Regression classifier and trains it on the training data:

```
model = LogisticRegression()
model.fit(X_train, y_train)
```

Step 9. Model evaluation. The code evaluates the model on the test data and prints the accuracy:

```
accuracy = model.score(X_test, y_test)
print(f"Accuracy: {accuracy:.2%}")
```

Here's the output:

```
[nltk_data] Downloading package movie_reviews to
[nltk_data]     /Users/sudachk/nltk_data...
[nltk_data]     Unzipping corpora/movie_reviews.zip.
[nltk_data] Downloading package wordnet to /Users/sudachk/nltk_data...
[nltk_data]     Package wordnet is already up-to-date!
[nltk_data] Downloading package omw-1.4 to /Users/sudachk/nltk_data...
[nltk_data]     Package omw-1.4 is already up-to-date!
[nltk_data] Downloading package punkt to /Users/sudachk/nltk_data...
[nltk_data]     Package punkt is already up-to-date!
Accuracy: 81.75%
```

Figure 7.8 – Accuracy of logistic regression

Step 10. Testing with custom sentences. The code tests the model with custom sentences. It preprocesses the sentences, transforms them into features, predicts their sentiment, and prints the results:

```
custom_sentences = [
    "I loved the movie and it was amazing. Best movie I have seen
this year.",
    "The movie was terrible. The plot was non-existent and the
acting was subpar.",
    "I have mixed feelings about the movie. Some parts were good,
but some were not.",
]

for sentence in custom_sentences:
    preprocessed_sentence = preprocess(sentence)
    features = vectorizer.transform([preprocessed_sentence])
    sentiment = model.predict(features)
    print(f"Sentence: {sentence}\nSentiment: {sentiment[0]}\n")
```

Here's the output:

```
Sentence: I loved the movie and it was amazing. Best movie I have seen this year.
Sentiment: pos

Sentence: The movie was terrible. The plot was non-existent and the acting was subpar.
Sentiment: neg

Sentence: I have mixed feelings about the movie. Some parts were good, but some were not.
Sentiment: neg
```

Figure 7.9 – Predicted labels

This code serves as a comprehensive guide to text labeling using logistic regression, encompassing data preprocessing, model training, evaluation, and application to custom sentences.

Now, let's look into the second method, K-means clustering, to label the text data by grouping similar text together and creating labels for that group or cluster.

Hands-on label prediction using K-means clustering

K-means clustering is a powerful unsupervised machine learning technique used for grouping similar data points into clusters. In the context of text data, K-means clustering can be employed to predict labels or categories for the given text based on their similarity. The provided code showcases how to utilize K-Means clustering to predict labels for movie reviews, breaking down the process into several key steps.

Step 1: Importing libraries and downloading data.

The following code begins by importing essential libraries such as scikit-learn and NLTK. It then downloads the necessary NLTK data, including the movie reviews dataset:

```
from sklearn.feature_extraction.text import TfidfVectorizer
from sklearn.cluster import KMeans
from nltk.corpus import movie_reviews
from nltk.corpus import stopwords
from nltk.stem import WordNetLemmatizer
import nltk
import re

# Download the necessary NLTK data
nltk.download('movie_reviews')
nltk.download('stopwords')
nltk.download('wordnet')
```

Step 2: Retrieving and preprocessing movie reviews.

Retrieve movie reviews from the NLTK dataset and preprocess them. This involves lemmatization, removal of stop words, and converting text to lowercase:

```
# Get the reviews
reviews = [movie_reviews.raw(fileid) for fileid in movie_reviews.
fileids()]

# Preprocess the text
stop_words = set(stopwords.words('english'))
lemmatizer = WordNetLemmatizer()
reviews = [' '.join(lemmatizer.lemmatize(word) for word in
re.sub('[^a-zA-Z]', ' ', review).lower().split() if word not in stop_
words) for review in reviews]
```

Step 3: Creating the TF-IDF vectorizer and transforming data.

Create a TF-IDF vectorizer to convert the preprocessed reviews into numerical features. This step is crucial for preparing the data for clustering:

```
# Create a TF-IDF vectorizer
vectorizer = TfidfVectorizer()

# Transform the reviews into TF-IDF features
X_tfidf = vectorizer.fit_transform(reviews)
```

Step 4: Applying K-means clustering.

Apply K-means clustering to the TF-IDF features, specifying the number of clusters. In this case, the code sets n_clusters=3:

```
# Cluster the reviews using K-means
kmeans = KMeans(n_clusters=3).fit(X_tfidf)
```

Step 5: Labeling and testing with custom sentences.

Define labels for the clusters and test the K-means classifier with custom sentences. The code preprocesses the sentences, transforms them into TF-IDF features, predicts the cluster, and assigns a label based on the predefined cluster labels:

```
# Define the labels for the clusters
cluster_labels = {0: "positive", 1: "negative", 2: "neutral"}
# Test the classifier with custom sentences
custom_sentences = ["I loved the movie and Best movie I have seen this
year.",
"The movie was terrible. The plot was non-existent and the acting was
subpar.",
```

```
"I have mixed feelings about the movie.it is partly good and partly
not good."]

for sentence in custom_sentences:
    # Preprocess the sentence
    sentence = ' '.join(lemmatizer.lemmatize(word) for word in
re.sub('[^a-zA-Z]', ' ', sentence).lower().split() if word not in
stop_words)
    # Transform the sentence into TF-IDF features
    features = vectorizer.transform([sentence])
    # Predict the cluster of the sentence
    cluster = kmeans.predict(features)
    # Get the label for the cluster
    label = cluster_labels[cluster[0]]
    print(f"Sentence: {sentence}\nLabel: {label}\n")
```

Here's the output:

```
[nltk_data] Downloading package movie_reviews to
[nltk_data]     /Users/sudachk/nltk_data...
[nltk_data]   Unzipping corpora/movie_reviews.zip.
[nltk_data] Downloading package stopwords to
[nltk_data]     /Users/sudachk/nltk_data...
[nltk_data]   Package stopwords is already up-to-date!
[nltk_data] Downloading package wordnet to /Users/sudachk/nltk_data...
[nltk_data]   Package wordnet is already up-to-date!
Sentence: loved movie best movie seen year
Label: positive

Sentence: movie terrible plot non existent acting subpar
Label: neutral

Sentence: mixed feeling movie partly good partly good
Label: neutral
```

Figure 7.10 – K-means clustering for text

This code demonstrates a comprehensive process of utilizing K-means clustering for text label prediction, covering data preprocessing, feature extraction, clustering, and testing with custom sentences.

Generating labels for customer reviews (sentiment analysis)

Customer reviews are a goldmine of information for businesses. Analyzing sentiment in customer reviews helps in understanding customer satisfaction, identifying areas for improvement, and making data-driven business decisions.

In the following example, we delve into sentiment analysis using a neural network model. The code utilizes TensorFlow and Keras to create a simple neural network architecture with an embedding layer, a flatten layer, and a dense layer. The model is trained on a small labeled dataset for sentiment classification, distinguishing between positive and negative sentiments. Following training, the model is employed to classify new sentences. The provided Python code demonstrates each step, from tokenizing and padding sequences to compiling, training, and making predictions.

The following dataset is used for training on sentiment analysis:

```
sentences = ["I love this movie", "This movie is terrible", "The
acting was amazing", "The plot was confusing"]
labels = [1, 0, 1, 0]  # 1 for positive, 0 for negative
```

We then use a tokenizer to convert the text into sequences of numbers, and then pad the sequences so that they have the same length. We then define a generative AI model with an embedding layer, a flatten layer, and a dense layer. Then, we compile and train the model on the training data. Finally, we use the trained model to classify a new sentence as either positive or negative.

Here is a complete Python code example with a dataset of four sentences labeled as positive or negative. We begin by importing libraries:

```
import numpy as np
from tensorflow import keras
from tensorflow.keras.preprocessing.text import Tokenizer
from tensorflow.keras.preprocessing.sequence import pad_sequences
```

The NumPy library is imported as np for numerical computations. The necessary modules from the TensorFlow library are imported for text preprocessing and model creation. Then we define the labeled dataset:

```
sentences = ["I love this movie", "This movie is terrible", "The
acting was amazing", "The plot was confusing"]
labels = [1, 0, 1, 0]
```

The `sentences` list contains textual sentences. The `labels` list contains corresponding labels where 1 represents a positive sentiment and 0 represents a negative sentiment. Next, we tokenize the text and convert it to sequences:

```
tokenizer = Tokenizer()
tokenizer.fit_on_texts(sentences)
sequences = tokenizer.texts_to_sequences(sentences)
tokenizer = Tokenizer()
tokenizer.fit_on_texts(sentences)
sequences = tokenizer.texts_to_sequences(sentences)
```

A `Tokenizer` object is created to tokenize the text. The `fit_on_texts` method is used to fit the tokenizer on the provided sentences. The `texts_to_sequences` method is used to convert the sentences into sequences of tokens. Now we need to pad the sequences so they are the same length:

```
max_sequence_length = max([len(seq) for seq in sequences])
padded_sequences = pad_sequences(sequences, maxlen=max_sequence_
length)
```

The maximum sequence length is determined by finding the length of the longest sequence. The `pad_sequences` function is used to pad the sequences to the maximum length. Next, we define the model architecture:

```
model = keras.Sequential([
    keras.layers.Embedding(len(tokenizer.word_index) + 1, \
        16, input_length=max_sequence_length),
    keras.layers.Flatten(),
    keras.layers.Dense(1, activation='sigmoid')
])
```

A sequential model is created using the `Sequential` class from Keras. The model consists of an embedding layer, a flatten layer, and a dense layer. The embedding layer converts the tokens into dense vectors. The flatten layer flattens the input for the subsequent dense layer. The dense layer is used for binary classification with sigmoid activation. Now, we need to compile the model:

```
model.compile(optimizer='adam', loss='binary_crossentropy', \
    metrics=['accuracy'])
```

The model is compiled with the Adam optimizer, binary cross-entropy loss, and accuracy as the metric. Now, we train the model:

```
model.fit(padded_sequences, np.array(labels), epochs=10)
```

The model is trained on the padded sequences and corresponding labels for a specified number of epochs. Next, we classify a new sentence:

```
new_sentence = ["This movie is good"]
new_sequence = tokenizer.texts_to_sequences(new_sentence)
padded_new_sequence = pad_sequences(new_sequence, \
    maxlen=max_sequence_length)

raw_prediction = model.predict(padded_new_sequence)
print("raw_prediction:",raw_prediction)

prediction = (raw_prediction > 0.5).astype('int32')
print("prediction:",prediction)
```

A new sentence is provided for classification. The sentence is converted to a sequence of tokens using the tokenizer. The sequence is padded to match the maximum sequence length used during training. The model predicts the sentiment class for the new sentence. Finally, we print the predicted label:

```
if prediction[0][0] == 1:
    print("Positive")
else:
    print("Negative")
```

Here's the output:

```
Epoch 1/10
1/1 [==============================] - 0s 210ms/step - loss: 0.7102 - accuracy: 0.0000e+00
Epoch 2/10
1/1 [==============================] - 0s 2ms/step - loss: 0.7066 - accuracy: 0.2500
Epoch 3/10
1/1 [==============================] - 0s 2ms/step - loss: 0.7030 - accuracy: 0.2500
Epoch 4/10
1/1 [==============================] - 0s 2ms/step - loss: 0.6994 - accuracy: 0.5000
Epoch 5/10
1/1 [==============================] - 0s 3ms/step - loss: 0.6959 - accuracy: 0.7500
Epoch 6/10
1/1 [==============================] - 0s 2ms/step - loss: 0.6924 - accuracy: 0.7500
Epoch 7/10
1/1 [==============================] - 0s 2ms/step - loss: 0.6889 - accuracy: 0.7500
Epoch 8/10
1/1 [==============================] - 0s 3ms/step - loss: 0.6855 - accuracy: 0.7500
Epoch 9/10
1/1 [==============================] - 0s 3ms/step - loss: 0.6820 - accuracy: 0.7500
Epoch 10/10
1/1 [==============================] - 0s 2ms/step - loss: 0.6786 - accuracy: 0.7500
1/1 [==============================] - 0s 25ms/step
raw_prediction: [[0.50196236]]
prediction: [[1]]
Positive
```

Figure 7.11 – Prediction with a neural network model

The predicted label is printed based on the prediction output. If the predicted label is 1, it is considered a positive sentiment, and if it is 0, it is considered a negative sentiment. In summary, the provided code demonstrates a sentiment analysis task using a neural network model.

Summary

In this chapter, we delved into the realm of text data exploration using Python, gaining a comprehensive understanding of harnessing Generative AI and OpenAI models for effective text data labeling. Through code examples, we explored diverse text data labeling tasks, including classification, summarization, and sentiment analysis.

We then extended our knowledge by exploring Snorkel labeling functions, allowing us to label text data with enhanced flexibility. Additionally, we delved into the application of K-means clustering for labeling text data and concluded by discovering how to label customer reviews using neural networks.

With these acquired skills, you now possess the tools to unlock the full potential of your text data, extracting valuable insights for various applications. The next chapter awaits, where we will shift our focus to video data exploration, exploring different methods to gain insights from this dynamic data type.

8

Exploring Video Data

In today's data-driven world, videos have become a significant source of information and insights. Analyzing video data can provide valuable knowledge about human actions, scene understanding, and various real-world phenomena. In this chapter, we will embark on an exciting journey to explore and understand video data using the powerful combination of Python, Matplotlib, and cv2.

We will start by learning how to use the cv2 library, a popular computer vision library in Python, to read in video data. With cv2, we can effortlessly load video files, access individual frames, and perform various operations on them. These fundamental skills set the stage for our exploration and analysis.

Next, we will dive into the process of extracting frames from video data. Video frames are the individual images that make up a video sequence. Extracting frames allows us to work with individual snapshots, enabling us to analyze, manipulate, and extract useful insights from video data. We will discuss different strategies to extract frames efficiently and explore the possibilities of working with specific time intervals or frame rates.

Once we have our frames extracted, we will explore the properties of image frames in videos. This includes analyzing characteristics such as color distribution, texture patterns, object motion, and spatial relationships. By leveraging the power of Python's Matplotlib library, we can create captivating visualizations that provide a deeper understanding of video data.

In this chapter, we will learn how to explore video data in Python using Matplotlib and OpenCV (cv2). Specifically, we will be delving into the kinetics human actions dataset. In the upcoming chapter, we will focus on labeling this video dataset. The current chapter serves as a foundational introduction to video data, providing essential knowledge necessary for the subsequent labeling process.

We are going to learn about the following:

- Loading video data using cv2
- Extracting frames from video data for analysis
- Extracting features from video frames
- Visualizing video data using Matplotlib

- Labeling video data using k-means clustering
- Advanced concepts in video data analysis

By the end of this chapter, you will have gained invaluable skills in exploring and analyzing video data. You will be equipped with the knowledge and tools to unlock the hidden potential of videos, enabling you to extract meaningful insights and make informed decisions. So, let's embark on this thrilling journey of exploring video data and unraveling the captivating stories it holds.

Technical requirements

In this section, we are going to use the dataset at the following GitHub link: `https://github.com/PacktPublishing/Data-Labeling-in-Machine-Learning-with-Python./datasets/Ch08`.

Let's start with how to read video data into your application using Python.

Loading video data using cv2

Exploratory Data Analysis (**EDA**) is an important step in any data analysis process. It helps you understand your data, identify patterns and relationships, and prepare your data for further analysis. Video data is a complex type of data that requires specific tools and techniques to be analyzed. In this section, we will explore how to perform EDA on video data using Python.

The first step in any EDA process is to load and inspect the data. In the case of video data, we will use the OpenCV library to load video files. OpenCV is a popular library for computer vision and image processing, and it includes many functions that make it easy to work with video data.

OpenCV and cv2 often refer to the same computer vision library – they are used interchangeably, with a slight difference in naming conventions:

- **OpenCV** (short for **Open Source Computer Vision Library**): This is the official name of the library. It is an open source computer vision and machine learning software library containing various functions for image and video processing. OpenCV is written in C++ and provides bindings for Python, Java, and other languages.

- **cv2** (standing for **OpenCV for Python**): In Python, the OpenCV library is typically imported using the name cv2. This naming convention comes from the fact that the Python bindings for OpenCV are provided under the cv2 module. So, when you see `import cv2` in Python code, it means the code is utilizing the OpenCV library.

To load a video file using OpenCV, we can use the `cv2.VideoCapture` function. This function takes the path to the video file as input and returns a `VideoCapture` object that we can use to access the frames of the video. Here is example code that loads a video file and prints some information about it:

```
import cv2

video_path = "path/to/video.mp4"
cap = cv2.VideoCapture(video_path)

fps = cap.get(cv2.CAP_PROP_FPS)
num_frames = int(cap.get(cv2.CAP_PROP_FRAME_COUNT))
frame_size = (int(cap.get(cv2.CAP_PROP_FRAME_WIDTH)), \
    int(cap.get(cv2.CAP_PROP_FRAME_HEIGHT)))

print("FPS: ", fps)
print("Number of frames: ", num_frames)
print("Frame size: ", frame_size)
```

Here's the output:

```
FPS:  10.0
Number of frames:  102
Frame size:  (128, 128)
```

Figure 8.1 – Information for the video file

This code loads a video file from the specified path and prints its **frames per second** (**FPS**), number of frames, and frame size. This information can be useful for understanding the properties of the video data.

Extracting frames from video data for analysis

Once we have loaded the video data, we can start exploring it. One common technique for the EDA of video data is to visualize some frames of the video. This can help us identify patterns and anomalies in the data. Here is example code that displays the first 10 frames of the video:

```
import cv2

video_path = "path/to/video.mp4"
cap = cv2.VideoCapture(video_path)

for i in range(10):
    ret, frame = cap.read()
    if not ret:
```

```
        break
    cv2.imshow("Frame", frame)
    cv2.waitKey(0)

cap.release()
cv2.destroyAllWindows()
```

This code reads the first 10 frames of the video from the given path and displays them using the `cv2.imshow` function. The `cv2.waitKey(0)` function waits for a key press before displaying the next frame. This allows us to inspect each frame before moving on to the next one.

Extracting features from video frames

Another useful technique for the EDA of video data is to extract features from each frame and analyze them. Features are measurements or descriptors that capture some aspect of the image, such as color, texture, or shape. By analyzing these features, we can identify patterns and relationships in the data.

To extract features from each frame, we can use the OpenCV functions that compute various types of features, such as color histograms, texture descriptors, and shape measurements. Choosing the best feature extraction method depends on the characteristics of your data and the nature of the clustering task.

Let us see the **color histogram** feature extraction method.

Color histogram

A color histogram is a representation of the distribution of colors in an image. It shows the number of pixels that have different colors in each range of the color space. For example, a color histogram can show how many pixels are red, green, or blue in an image. Here is example code that extracts the color histogram from each frame and plots it:

```
import cv2
import matplotlib.pyplot as plt

video_path = "path/to/video.mp4"
cap = cv2.VideoCapture(video_path)

histograms = []
```

Here is a detailed explanation of each line in the code:

- The first line imports the `cv2` library, which we will use to read and process video data.
- The second line imports the `matplotlib` library, which we will use to plot the histograms.

- The third line sets the path to the video file. Replace `"path/to/video.mp4"` with the actual path to your video file.

- The fourth line creates a `VideoCapture` object using the `cv2.VideoCapture` function. This object allows us to read frames from the video.

- The fifth line creates an empty list called `histograms`. We will store the histograms of each frame in this list.

Then, we add a `while` loop. The `while` loop reads frames from the video one by one until there are no more frames:

```
while True:
    ret, frame = cap.read()
    if not ret:
        break
    histogram = cv2.calcHist([frame], [0, 1, 2], \
        None, [8, 8, 8], [0, 256, 0, 256, 0, 256])
    histogram = cv2.normalize(histogram, None).flatten()
    histograms.append(histogram)
cap.release()
```

Here is what each line inside the loop does:

- `ret, frame = cap.read()`: This line reads the next frame from the video using the `cap.read()` function. The `ret` variable is a Boolean value that indicates whether the frame was successfully read, and the `frame` variable is a NumPy array that contains the pixel values of the frame.

- `if not ret: break`: If `ret` is `False`, it means there are no more frames in the video, so we break out of the loop.

- `histogram = cv2.calcHist([frame], [0, 1, 2], None, [8, 8, 8], [0, 256, 0, 256, 0, 256])`: This line calculates the color histogram of the frame using the `cv2.calcHist` function. The first argument is the frame, the second argument specifies which channels to include in the histogram (in this case, all three RGB channels), the third argument is a mask (which we set to `None`), the fourth argument is the size of the histogram (8 bins per channel), and the fifth argument is the range of values to include in the histogram (0 to 256 for each channel).

- `histogram = cv2.normalize(histogram, None).flatten()`: This line normalizes the histogram using the `cv2.normalize` function and flattens it into a 1D array using the `flatten` method of the NumPy array. Normalizing the histogram ensures that it is scale-invariant and can be compared with histograms from other frames or videos.

- `histograms.append(histogram)`: This line appends the histogram to the `histograms` list.

The final line releases the `VideoCapture` object using the `cap.release()` function. This frees up the resources used by the object and allows us to open another video file if we need to.

Optical flow features

We will extract features based on the optical flow between consecutive frames. Optical flow captures the movement of objects in video. Libraries such as OpenCV provide functions to compute optical flow.

Let's look at example code for optical flow features:

```
# Example of optical flow calculation
prev_frame = cv2.cvtColor(frame1, cv2.COLOR_BGR2GRAY)
next_frame = cv2.cvtColor(frame2, cv2.COLOR_BGR2GRAY)
flow = cv2.calcOpticalFlowFarneback(prev_frame, \
    next_frame, None, 0.5, 3, 15, 3, 5, 1.2, 0)
```

Motion vectors

Motion vectors play a crucial role in understanding the dynamic aspects of video data. They represent the trajectory of key points or regions across frames, providing insights into the movement patterns within a video sequence. A common technique to calculate these motion vectors involves the use of Shi-Tomasi corner detection combined with Lucas-Kanade optical flow:

- **Shi-Tomasi Corner Detection**: In the following code, Shi-Tomasi corner detection is utilized to identify distinctive feature points in the initial frame (`prev_frame`). These feature points act as anchor points for tracking across subsequent frames.

- **Lucas-Kanade Optical Flow**: The Lucas-Kanade optical flow algorithm is then applied using `cv2.calcOpticalFlowPyrLK`. This algorithm estimates the motion vectors by calculating the flow of these feature points from the previous frame (`prev_frame`) to the current frame (`next_frame`).

We calculate motion vectors by tracking key points or regions across frames. These vectors represent the movement patterns in the video. Let's see the example code for motion vectors:

```
# Example of feature tracking using Shi-Tomasi corner detection and
Lucas-Kanade optical flow
corners = cv2.goodFeaturesToTrack(prev_frame, \
    maxCorners=100, qualityLevel=0.01, minDistance=10)
next_corners, status, err = cv2.calcOpticalFlowPyrLK(\
    prev_frame, next_frame, corners, None)
```

This code snippet demonstrates the initialization of feature points using Shi-Tomasi corner detection and subsequently calculating the optical flow to obtain the motion vectors. Understanding these concepts is fundamental for tasks such as object tracking and motion analysis in computer vision.

Deep learning features

Use features from pre-trained models other than VGG16, such as ResNet, Inception, or MobileNet. Experiment with models that are well-suited for image and video analysis. Implementation of these methods is beyond the scope of this book. You can find details in various deep learning documentation.

When working with pre-trained models such as ResNet, Inception, or MobileNet, you will find comprehensive documentation and examples from the respective deep learning frameworks. Here are some suggestions based on popular frameworks:

- **TensorFlow documentation**: TensorFlow provides detailed documentation and examples for using pre-trained models. You can explore TensorFlow Hub, which offers a repository of pre-trained models, including various architectures, such as ResNet, Inception, and MobileNet.

- **Keras documentation**: If you're using Keras as part of TensorFlow, you can refer to the Keras Applications module. It includes pre-trained models such as ResNet50, InceptionV3, and MobileNet.

- **PyTorch documentation**: PyTorch provides documentation for using pre-trained models through the torchvision library. You can find ResNet, Inception, and MobileNet models, among others.

- **Hugging Face Transformers library**: For a broader range of pre-trained models, including those for natural language processing and computer vision, you can explore the Hugging Face Transformers library. It covers various architectures and allows easy integration into your projects.

- **OpenCV deep neural networks (DNN) module**: If you are working with OpenCV, the DNN module supports loading pre-trained models from frameworks such as TensorFlow, Caffe, and others. You can find examples and documentation on how to use these models.

By consulting these resources, you'll find ample documentation, code examples, and guidelines for integrating pre-trained models into your image and video analysis tasks. Remember to check the documentation for the framework you are using in your project.

Appearance and shape descriptors

Extract features based on object appearance and shape characteristics. Examples include Hu Moments, Zernike Moments, and Haralick texture features.

Appearance and shape descriptors are methods used in computer vision and image processing to quantify the visual characteristics of objects. Here are details about three commonly used descriptors:

- **Hu Moments**: Hu Moments is a set of seven moments invariant to translation, rotation, and scale changes. They are derived from the image's central moments and are used to describe the shape of an object.

  Application: Hu Moments are particularly useful in shape recognition and object matching, where robustness to transformations is crucial.

- **Zernike Moments**: Zernike Moments are a set of orthogonal moments defined on a circular domain. They are used to represent the shape of an object and are invariant to rotation.

  Application: Zernike Moments find applications in pattern recognition, image analysis, and **optical character recognition (OCR)**.

- **Haralick texture features**: Haralick texture features are a set of statistical measures used to describe the texture patterns in an image. They are based on the co-occurrence matrix, which represents the spatial relationships between pixel intensities.

  Application: Haralick texture features are applied in texture analysis tasks, such as identifying regions with different textures in medical images or material inspection.

Feature extraction methods involve extracting specific numerical values or vectors from an image to represent its appearance or shape characteristics. Invariance to transformations such as translation, rotation, and scale make these descriptors robust for object recognition tasks.

They provide a quantifiable representation of the visual features of an object, enabling efficient comparison and analysis. Many of these descriptors can be implemented using the OpenCV library, which provides functions for calculating moments, texture features, and other descriptors. These descriptors are valuable in applications where understanding the shape and texture of objects is essential, such as in image recognition, content-based image retrieval, and medical image analysis. By utilizing these appearance and shape descriptors, computer vision systems can gain insights into the distinctive features of objects, enabling effective analysis and recognition in various domains.

Experimenting with different feature extraction methods and observing their impact on clustering performance is often necessary. You may also consider combining multiple types of features to capture various aspects of the data.

Remember to preprocess the features appropriately (scaling, normalization) before applying clustering algorithms. Additionally, the choice of the number of clusters in K-means may also impact the results, and tuning this parameter may be required.

Visualizing video data using Matplotlib

Let's see the visualization examples for exploring and analyzing video data. We will generate some sample data and demonstrate different visualizations using the Matplotlib library in Python. We'll import libraries first. Then we'll generate some sample data. `frame_indices` represents the frame indices and `frame_intensities` represents the intensity values for each frame:

```
import matplotlib.pyplot as plt
import numpy as np

# Generate sample data
frame_indices = np.arange(0, 100)
frame_intensities = np.random.randint(0, 255, size=100)
```

Frame visualization

We create a line plot to visualize the frame intensities over the frame indices. This helps us understand the variations in intensity across frames:

```
# Frame Visualization
plt.figure(figsize=(10, 6))
plt.title("Frame Visualization")
plt.xlabel("Frame Index")
plt.ylabel("Intensity")
plt.plot(frame_indices, frame_intensities)
plt.show()
```

We get the following result:

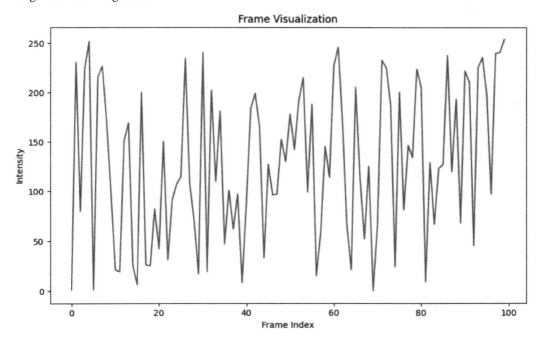

Figure 8.2 – Frame visualization plot

Temporal visualization

Here, we plot the frame intensities against the timestamps. This allows us to observe how the intensity changes over time, providing insights into temporal patterns:

```
# Temporal Visualization
timestamps = np.linspace(0, 10, 100)
```

```
plt.figure(figsize=(10, 6))
plt.title("Temporal Visualization")
plt.xlabel("Time (s)")
plt.ylabel("Intensity")
plt.plot(timestamps, frame_intensities)
plt.show()
```

We get the following graph:

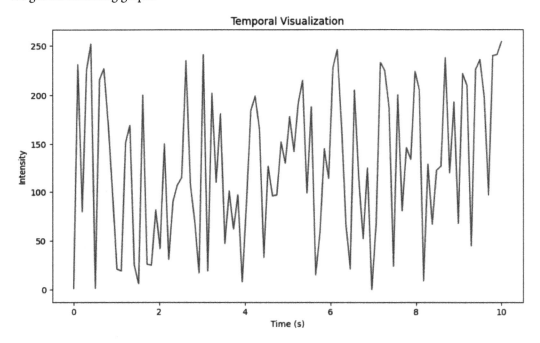

Figure 8.3 – Temporal visualization plot

Motion visualization

To visualize motion, we generate random displacement values dx and dy representing the motion in the x and y directions, respectively. Using the quiver function, we plot arrows at each frame index, indicating the motion direction and magnitude:

```
# Motion Visualization
dx = np.random.randn(100)
dy = np.random.randn(100)
plt.figure(figsize=(6, 6))
plt.title("Motion Visualization")
plt.quiver(frame_indices, frame_indices, dx, dy)
```

```
plt.xlabel("X")
plt.ylabel("Y")
plt.show()
```

We get the following result:

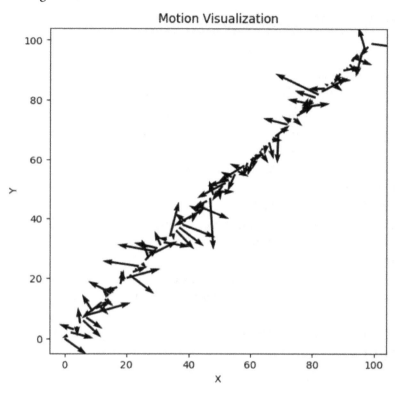

Figure 8.4 – Motion visualization plot

By utilizing these visualizations, we can gain a better understanding of video data, explore temporal patterns, and analyze motion characteristics.

It's important to note that these are just a few examples of the visualizations you can create when exploring video data. Depending on the specific characteristics and goals of your dataset, you can employ a wide range of visualization techniques to gain deeper insights into the data.

Labeling video data using k-means clustering

Data labeling is an essential step in machine learning, and it involves assigning class labels or categories to data points in a dataset. For video data, labeling can be a challenging task, as it involves analyzing a large number of frames and identifying the objects or events depicted in each frame.

One way to automate the labeling process is to use unsupervised learning techniques such as clustering. **k-means clustering** is a popular method for clustering data based on its similarity. In the case of video data, we can use k-means clustering to group frames that contain similar objects or events together and assign a label to each cluster.

Overview of data labeling using k-means clustering

Here is a step-by-step guide on how to perform data labeling for video data using k-means clustering:

1. Load the video data and extract features from each frame. The features could be color histograms, edge histograms, or optical flow features, depending on the type of video data.

2. Apply k-means clustering to the features to group similar frames together. The number of clusters k can be set based on domain knowledge or by using the elbow method to determine the optimal number of clusters.

3. Assign a label to each cluster based on the objects or events depicted in the frames. This can be done manually by analyzing the frames in each cluster or using an automated approach such as object detection or scene recognition.

4. Apply the assigned labels to the frames in each cluster. This can be done by either adding a new column to the dataset containing the cluster labels or by creating a mapping between the cluster labels and the frame indices.

5. Train a machine learning model on the labeled data. The labeled video data can be used to train a model for various tasks such as action recognition, event detection, or video summarization.

Example of video data labeling using k-means clustering with a color histogram

Let us see example code for performing k-means clustering on video data using the open source scikit-learn Python package and the *Kinetics human action* dataset. This dataset is available at GitHub path specified in the *Technical requirements* section.

This code performs K-means clustering on video data using color histogram features. The steps include loading video frames from a directory, extracting color histogram features, standardizing the features, and clustering them into two groups using K-means.

Let's see the implementation of the steps with the corresponding code snippet:

1. **Load videos and preprocess frames**: Load video frames from a specified directory. Resize frames to (64, 64), normalize pixel values, and create a structured video dataset:

    ```
    input_video_dir = "<your_path>/PacktPublishing/DataLabeling/
    ch08/kmeans/kmeans_input"
    input_video, _ = load_videos_from_directory(input_video_dir)
    ```

2. **Extract color histogram features**: Convert each frame to the HSV color space. Calculate histograms for each channel (hue, saturation, value). Concatenate the histograms into a single feature vector:

```
hist_features = extract_histogram_features( \
    input_video.reshape(-1, 64, 64, 3))
```

3. **Standardize features**: Standardize the extracted histogram features using `StandardScaler` to have zero mean and unit variance:

```
scaler = StandardScaler()
scaled_features = scaler.fit_transform(hist_features)
```

4. **Apply K-means clustering**: Use K-means clustering with two clusters on the standardized features. Print the predicted labels assigned to each video frame:

```
kmeans = KMeans(n_clusters=2, random_state=42)
predicted_labels = kmeans.fit_predict(scaled_features)
print("Predicted Labels:", predicted_labels)
```

This code performs video frame clustering based on color histogram features, similar to the previous version. The clustering is done for the specified input video directory, and the predicted cluster labels are printed at the end.

We get the following output:

```
Predicted Labels: [1 1 1 1 1 1 1 1 1 1 1 1 1 1 1 1 1 1 1 1 1 1 1 1 1 1 1 1 1 1 1 1 1 1
 1 1 1 1 1 1 1 1 1 1 1 1 1 1 1 1 1 1 1 1 1 1 1 1 1 1 1 1 1 1 1 1 1 1 1
 1 1 1 1 1 1 1 1 1 1 1 1 1 1 1 1 1 1 1 1 1 1 1 1 1 0 0 0 0 0 0 0 0 0 0
 0 0 0 0 0 0 0 0 0 0 0 0 0 0 0 0 0 0 0 0 0 0 0 0 0 0 0 0 0 0 0 0 0 0 0
 0 0 0 0 0 0 0 0 0 0 0 0 0 0 0 0 0 0 0 0 0 0 0 0 0 0 0 0 0 0 0 0 0 0 0
 0 0 0 0 0 0 0 0 0 0 0 0 0]
```

Figure 8.5 – Output of the k-means predicted labeling

Now write these predicted label frames to the corresponding output cluster directory.

The following code flattens a video data array to iterate through individual frames. It then creates two output directories for clusters (`Cluster_0` and `Cluster_1`). Each frame is saved in the corresponding cluster folder based on the predicted label obtained from k-means clustering. The frames are written as PNG images in the specified output directories:

```
# Flatten the video_data array to iterate through frames
flattened_video_data = input_video.reshape(-1, \
    input_video.shape[-3], input_video.shape[-2], \
    input_video.shape[-1])
```

```
# Create two separate output directories for clusters
output_directory_0 = "/<your_path>/kmeans_output/Cluster_0"
output_directory_1 = "/<your_path>/kmeans_output/Cluster_1"
os.makedirs(output_directory_0, exist_ok=True)
os.makedirs(output_directory_1, exist_ok=True)

# Iterate through each frame, save frames in the corresponding cluster
folder
for idx, (frame, predicted_label) in enumerate( \
    zip(flattened_video_data, predicted_labels)):
    cluster_folder = output_directory_0 if predicted_label == 0 else
output_directory_1

    frame_filename = f"video_frame_{idx}.png"
    frame_path = os.path.join(cluster_folder, frame_filename)
    cv2.imwrite(frame_path, (frame * 255).astype(np.uint8))
```

Now let's plot to visualize the frames in each cluster. The following code visualizes a few frames from each cluster created by K-means clustering. It iterates through the `Cluster_0` and `Cluster_1` folders, selects a specified number of frames from each cluster, and displays them using Matplotlib. The resulting images show frames from each cluster with corresponding cluster labels:

```
# Visualize a few frames from each cluster
num_frames_to_visualize = 2
for cluster_label in range(2):
    cluster_folder = os.path.join("./kmeans/kmeans_output", \
        f"Cluster_{cluster_label}")
    frame_files = os.listdir(cluster_folder)[:num_frames_to_visualize]

    for frame_file in frame_files:
        frame_path = os.path.join(cluster_folder, frame_file)
        frame = cv2.imread(frame_path)
        frame = cv2.cvtColor(frame, cv2.COLOR_BGR2RGB)

        plt.imshow(frame)
        plt.title(f"Cluster {cluster_label}")
        plt.axis("off")
        plt.show()
```

We get the output for cluster 0 as follows:

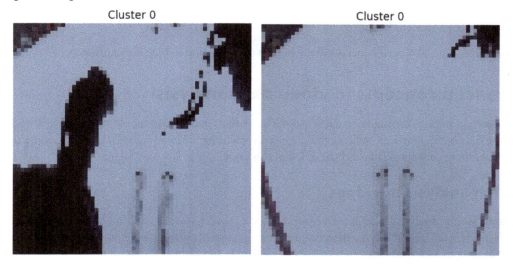

Figure 8.6 – Snow skating (Cluster 0)

And we get the following output for cluster 1:

Figure 8.7 – Child play (Cluster 1)

In this section, we have seen how to label the video data using k-means clustering and clustered videos into two classes. One cluster (`Label: Cluster 0`) contains frames of a skating video, and the second cluster (`Label: Cluster 1`) contains the child play video.

Now let's see some advanced concepts in video data analysis used in real-world projects.

Advanced concepts in video data analysis

The following concepts are fundamental in video data analysis and are commonly applied in real-world machine learning applications. Let's see those concepts briefly here. Please note that the implementation of some of these concepts is beyond the scope of this book.

Motion analysis in videos

Concept: Motion analysis involves extracting and understanding information about the movement of objects in a video. This can include detecting and tracking moving objects, estimating their trajectories, and analyzing motion patterns.

Tools: OpenCV (for computer vision tasks) and optical flow algorithms (e.g., the Lucas-Kanade method).

Let's see the overview of the code for motion analysis in video data.

Initialization: Open a video file and set up parameters for Lucas-Kanade optical flow:

```
import cv2
import numpy as np

# Read a video file
cap = cv2.VideoCapture('/<your_path>/CricketBowling.mp4')
# Initialize Lucas-Kanade optical flow
lk_params = dict(winSize=(15, 15), maxLevel=2, \
    criteria=(cv2.TERM_CRITERIA_EPS |
    cv2.TERM_CRITERIA_COUNT, 10, 0.03))
```

Feature detection: Detect good feature points in the first frame using the Shi-Tomasi corner detection algorithm:

```
ret, frame1 = cap.read()
prvs = cv2.cvtColor(frame1, cv2.COLOR_BGR2GRAY)
prvs_points = cv2.goodFeaturesToTrack(prvs, maxCorners=100, \
    qualityLevel=0.3, minDistance=7)
```

Motion analysis loop: Iterate through video frames, calculating optical flow and drawing motion vectors on each frame:

```
while True:
    ret, frame2 = cap.read()
    if not ret:
        break

    next_frame = cv2.cvtColor(frame2, cv2.COLOR_BGR2GRAY)

    # Calculate optical flow
    next_points, status, err = cv2.calcOpticalFlowPyrLK( \
        prvs, next_frame, prvs_points, None, **lk_params)
```

Visualization: Display the original frame overlaid with motion vectors in real time:

```
    # Draw motion vectors on the frame
    mask = np.zeros_like(frame2)
    for i, (new, old) in enumerate(zip(next_points, prvs_points)):
        a, b = new.ravel().astype(int)
        c, d = old.ravel().astype(int)
        mask = cv2.line(mask, (a, b), (c, d), (0, 255, 0), 2)
        frame2 = cv2.circle(frame2, (a, b), 5, (0, 0, 255), -1)

    result = cv2.add(frame2, mask)
    cv2.imshow('Motion Analysis', result)
```

Exit condition: Break the loop upon pressing the *Esc* key:

```
    # Break the loop on 'Esc' key
    if cv2.waitKey(30) & 0xFF == 27:
        break
```

Cleanup: Release the video capture object and close all OpenCV windows:

```
cap.release()
cv2.destroyAllWindows()
```

This code provides a simple yet effective demonstration of motion analysis using optical flow, visualizing the movement of feature points in a video.

We get the following output:

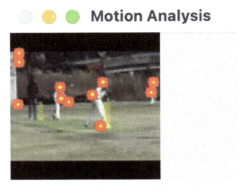

Figure 8.8 – Motion analysis in video

Object tracking in videos

Concept: Object tracking involves locating and following objects across consecutive video frames. It is essential for applications such as surveillance, human-computer interaction, and autonomous vehicles.

Tools: OpenCV (for tracking algorithms such as KLT and MedianFlow).

Here's a brief overview of the steps in the object tracker code:

Tracker initialization: Create a **Kernelized Correlation Filters** (**KCF**) object tracker using OpenCV's `cv2.TrackerKCF_create()`:

```
import cv2

# Create a KCF tracker
tracker = cv2.TrackerKCF_create()
```

Video capture: Open a video file (`sample_video.mp4`) using `cv2.VideoCapture`:

```
# Read a video file
cap = cv2.VideoCapture('./PacktPublishing/DataLabeling/ch08/video_
dataset/CricketBowling.mp4')
```

Select object to track: Read the first frame and use `cv2.selectROI` to interactively select the object to be tracked:

```
# Read the first frame
ret, frame = cap.read()
bbox = cv2.selectROI('Select Object to Track', frame, False)
```

We get the following result:

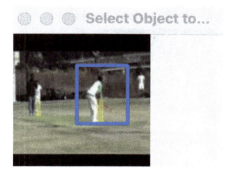

Figure 8.9 – Select object to track

Initialize tracker: Initialize the KCF tracker with the selected bounding box (bbox) in the first frame:

```
tracker.init(frame, bbox)
```

Object tracking loop: Iterate through subsequent frames in the video:

```
while True:
    ret, frame = cap.read()
    if not ret:
        break
```

Update tracker: Update the tracker with the current frame to obtain the new bounding box of the tracked object:

```
    # Update the tracker
    success, bbox = tracker.update(frame)
```

Draw bounding box: If the tracking is successful, draw a green bounding box around the tracked object in the frame.

```
    if success:
        p1 = (int(bbox[0]), int(bbox[1]))
        p2 = (int(bbox[0] + bbox[2]), int(bbox[1] + bbox[3]))
        cv2.rectangle(frame, p1, p2, (0, 255, 0), 2)
```

Display tracking result: Show the frame with the bounding box in a window named 'Object Tracking' using cv2.imshow:

```
    cv2.imshow('Object Tracking', frame)
```

We see the following result:

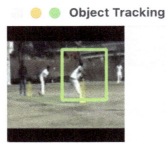

Figure 8.10 – Object tracking

Exit condition: Break the loop upon pressing the *Esc* key (`cv2.waitKey`):

```
# Break the loop on 'Esc' key
if cv2.waitKey(30) & 0xFF == 27:
    break
```

Cleanup: Release the video capture object and close all OpenCV windows:

```
cap.release()
cv2.destroyAllWindows()
```

This code demonstrates a basic object-tracking scenario where a user selects an object in the first frame, and the KCF tracker is used to follow and draw a bounding box around that object in subsequent frames of the video.

Facial recognition in videos

Concept: Facial recognition involves identifying and verifying faces in videos. It's used in security systems, user authentication, and various human-computer interaction applications.

Tools: OpenCV (for face detection), Dlib (for facial landmark detection), and face recognition libraries (e.g., `face_recognition`)

Here's a brief overview of the steps in the facial recognition code:

1. **Load face detector and landmark predictor**: Load a pre-trained face detector (`dlib.get_frontal_face_detector()`) and a facial landmark predictor (`dlib.shape_predictor('shape_predictor_68_face_landmarks.dat')`).

2. **Video capture**: Open a video file (`sample_video.mp4`) using `cv2.VideoCapture`.

3. **Face detection loop**: Iterate through frames in the video.

4. **Detect faces**: Use the face detector to identify faces in each frame.

5. **Facial landmark detection**: For each detected face, use the facial landmark predictor to locate facial landmarks.

6. **Draw facial landmarks**: Draw circles in the positions of the detected facial landmarks on the frame.

7. **Draw bounding box**: Draw a green bounding box around each detected face on the frame.

8. **Display facial recognition result**: Show the frame with facial landmarks and bounding boxes in a window named **Facial Recognition** using `cv2.imshow`.

9. **Exit condition**: Break the loop upon pressing the *Esc* key (`cv2.waitKey`).

10. **Cleanup**: Release the video capture object and close all OpenCV windows.

This code showcases a basic facial recognition application where faces are detected in each frame, and facial landmarks are drawn for each detected face. The bounding box outlines the face, and circles highlight specific facial features:

```
from deepface import DeepFace
import cv2

# Load a sample image
img_path1 = './PacktPublishing/DataLabeling/ch08/data/pic1.jpeg'
img_path2 = './PacktPublishing/DataLabeling/ch08/data/pic2.jpeg'
img = cv2.imread(img_path)

# Perform facial recognition
result = DeepFace.verify(img1_path=img_path1, img2_path=img_path2)

# Display the result
print("Are these faces the same person? ", result["verified"])

# Additional information
print("Facial recognition result:", result)
```

We get the output that follows:

```
Are these faces the same person? True
Facial recognition result: {'verified': True, 'distance':
0.20667349278322178, 'threshold': 0.4, 'model': 'VGG-Face', 'detector_
backend': 'opencv', 'similarity_metric': 'cosine', 'facial_areas':
{'img1': {'x': 74, 'y': 50, 'w': 713, 'h': 713}, 'img2': {'x': 63,
'y': 8, 'w': 386, 'h': 386}}, 'time': 0.48}
```

Video compression techniques

Video compression reduces the file size of videos, making them more manageable for storage, transmission, and processing.

Some common techniques are as follows:

- **Lossy compression**: Sacrifices some quality for reduced file size (e.g., H.264, H.265)

  Video streaming platforms such as YouTube utilize lossy compression (H.264) to efficiently transmit videos over the internet. The sacrifice in quality ensures smoother streaming experiences, faster loading times, and reduced data usage for users.

- **Lossless compression**: Maintains original quality but with less compression (e.g., Apple ProRes, FFV1)

  In professional video editing workflows, where preserving the highest possible quality is crucial, lossless compression is employed. Formats such as Apple ProRes or FFV1 are used for storing and processing video files without compromising quality. This is common in film production, video editing studios, and for archival purposes.

Real-time video processing

Real-time video processing involves analyzing and manipulating video data with minimal latency, often crucial for applications such as surveillance, robotics, and live streaming.

Its challenges are as follows:

- **Computational efficiency**: Algorithms need to be optimized for quick execution
- **Hardware acceleration**: The use of GPUs or specialized hardware for parallel processing
- **Streaming infrastructure**: k-means clustering data transfer and processing in real-time scenarios

Here are some common techniques for real-time video data capturing and processing:

- **Video streaming**:

  - **Technique**: Real-time video streaming involves the continuous transmission of video data over a network
  - **Applications**: Live broadcasts, surveillance systems, video conferencing
  - **Tools**:
    - **RTMP** (short for **Real-Time Messaging Protocol**): Used for streaming video over the internet
    - **WebRTC** (short for **Web Real-Time Communication**): Enables real-time communication in web browsers

- **IP cameras and CCTV**:

  - **Technique**: IP cameras and **Closed-Circuit Television** (**CCTV**) systems capture and transmit video data

- **Applications**: Surveillance and security monitoring
- **Tools**:
  - **Axis Communications**: Provides IP cameras and surveillance solutions
  - **Hikvision**: Offers a range of CCTV and IP camera products

- **Depth-sensing cameras**:
  - **Technique**: Cameras with depth-sensing capabilities capture 3D information in addition to 2D images
  - **Applications**: Gesture recognition, object tracking, augmented reality
  - **Tools**:
    - **Intel RealSense**: Depth-sensing cameras for various applications
    - **Microsoft Azure Kinect**: Features a depth camera for computer vision tasks

- **Frame grabbers**:
  - **Technique**: Frame grabbers capture video frames from analog or digital sources
  - **Applications**: Industrial automation and medical imaging
  - **Tools**:
    - **Matrox Imaging**: Offers frame grabbers for machine vision applications
    - **Euresys**: Provides video acquisition and image processing solutions

- **Temporal Convolutional Networks (TCNs)**:
  - **Overview**: TCNs extend CNNs to handle temporal sequences and are beneficial for video data
  - **Applications**:
    - Recognizing patterns and events over time in videos
    - Temporal feature extraction for action recognition

- **Action recognition**
  - **Overview**: Identify and classify actions or activities in a video sequence
  - **Techniques**:
    - **3D CNNs**: Capture spatial and temporal features for action recognition
    - **Two-stream networks**: Separate streams for spatial and motion information

- **Deepfake detection**:

  - **Overview**: Detect and mitigate the use of deep learning techniques to create realistic but fake videos

  - **Techniques**:

    - **Forensic analysis**: Analyze inconsistencies, artifacts, or anomalies in deepfake videos

    - **Deepfake datasets**: Train models on diverse datasets to improve detection accuracy.

Let us also discuss a few important ethical considerations:

- **Informed consent**: Ensure individuals are aware of video recording and its potential analysis.

  Actions: Clearly communicate the purpose of video data collection. Obtain explicit consent for sensitive applications.

- **Transparency**: Promote transparency in how video data is collected, processed, and used.

  Actions: Clearly communicate data processing practices to stakeholders. Provide accessible information about the algorithms used.

- **Bias mitigation**: Address and mitigate bias that may be present in video data analysis.

  Actions: Regularly assess and audit models for bias. Implement fairness-aware algorithms and strategies.

- **Data security**: Safeguard video data against unauthorized access and use.

  Actions: Implement strong encryption for stored and transmitted video data. Establish strict access controls and permissions.

- **Accountability**: Ensure accountability for the consequences of video data analysis.

  Actions: Establish clear lines of responsibility for data handling. Have mechanisms in place for addressing and correcting errors.

As video data analysis and processing technologies advance, ethical considerations become increasingly important to ensure the responsible and fair use of video data. Adhering to ethical principles helps build trust with stakeholders and contributes to the positive impact of video-based AI applications.

Video data formats and quality in machine learning

- **Video formats**:

  Common formats: Videos can be stored in various formats, such as MP4, AVI, MKV, MOV, and so on.

  Container versus codec: The container (format) holds video and audio streams, while the codec (compression) determines how data is encoded.

- **Video quality**:

  Resolution: Varies from **standard definition (SD)** to **high definition (HD)** and beyond

  Frame rate: The number of frames per second can vary, affecting the smoothness of motion

  Bitrate: A higher bitrate generally means better quality but larger file sizes

Common issues in handling video data for ML models

- **Inconsistent frame rates**
- **Issue**: Videos with varying frame rates can disrupt model training

  Solution: Standardize frame rates during preprocessing or use techniques such as interpolation
- **Variable resolutions**
- **Issue**: Differing resolutions can complicate model input requirements

  Solution: Resize or crop frames to a consistent resolution, balancing quality and computation
- **Large file sizes**
- **Issue**: High-quality videos may lead to large datasets, impacting storage and processing

  Solution: Compress videos if possible, and consider working with subsets during development
- **Lack of standardization**
- **Issue**: Non-uniform encoding and compression may lead to compatibility issues

  Solution: Convert videos to a standard format, ensuring consistency across the dataset
- **Limited metadata**
- **Issue**: Insufficient metadata (e.g., timestamps, labels) can hinder model understanding

  Solution: Enhance videos with relevant metadata to aid model learning and evaluation

Troubleshooting steps

- **Preprocessing and standardization**:

  Action: Normalize video properties (e.g., frame rate, resolution) during preprocessing

  Benefit: Ensures uniformity and compatibility across the dataset
- **Data augmentation**:

  Action: Apply data augmentation techniques to artificially increase the dataset size

  Benefit: Helps address limited data concerns and improves model generalization

- **Quality versus computational trade-off**:

  Action: Balance video quality and computational resources based on project requirements

  Benefit: Optimizes model training and deployment for specific use cases

- **Metadata enhancement**:

  Action: Include relevant metadata (e.g., timestamps, labels) for better model context

  Benefit: Improves model understanding and facilitates accurate predictions

- **Collaborative debugging**:

  Action: Collaborate with domain experts and fellow researchers to troubleshoot specific challenges

  Benefit: Gain diverse insights and accelerate problem-solving

- **Model performance monitoring**:

  Action: Regularly monitor model performance on diverse video samples

  Benefit: Identifies drifts or performance degradation, prompting timely adjustments

Handling video data in machine learning requires a combination of technical expertise, thoughtful preprocessing, and continuous monitoring to address challenges and optimize model performance. Regularly assessing and refining the approach based on project-specific requirements ensures effective integration of video data into AI models.

Summary

In this chapter, we have embarked on a journey to explore video data and unlock its insights. By leveraging the cv2 library, we have learned how to read video data, extract frames for analysis, analyze the features of the frames, and visualize them using the powerful Matplotlib library. Armed with these skills, you will be well-equipped to tackle video datasets, delve into their unique characteristics, and gain a deeper understanding of the data they contain. Exploring video data opens doors to a range of possibilities, from identifying human actions to understanding scene dynamics, and this chapter lays the foundation for further exploration and analysis in the realm of video data labeling.

Finally, you learned how to label video data using unsupervised machine learning k-means clustering. In the next chapter, we will see how to label video data using a CNNs, an autoencoder, and the watershed algorithm.

9
Labeling Video Data

The era of big data has ushered in an exponential growth of multimedia content, including videos, which are becoming increasingly prevalent in various domains, such as entertainment, surveillance, healthcare, and autonomous systems. Videos contain a wealth of information, but to unlock their full potential, it is crucial to accurately label and annotate the data they contain. Video data labeling plays a pivotal role in enabling machine learning algorithms to understand and analyze videos, leading to a wide range of applications such as video classification, object detection, action recognition, and video summarization.

In this chapter, we will explore the fascinating world of video data classification. Video classification involves the task of assigning labels or categories to videos based on their content, enabling us to organize, search, and analyze video data efficiently. We will explore different use cases where video classification plays a crucial role and learn how to label video data, using Python and a public dataset.

We will learn how to use supervised and unsupervised machine learning models to label video data. We will use the *Kinetics Human Action Video* dataset to train machine learning models on the labeled data for action detection.

We will delve into the intricacies of building supervised **convolutional neural network** (**CNN**) models tailored for video data classification. Additionally, we will explore the application of autoencoders to efficiently compress video data, extracting crucial features. The chapter extends its scope to include the Watershed algorithm, providing insights into its utilization for video data segmentation and labeling. Real-world examples and advancements in video data labeling techniques further enrich this comprehensive exploration of video data analysis and annotation.

In the real world, companies use a combination of software, tools, and technologies for video data labeling. While the specific tools used may vary, some common ones are as follows:

- **TensorFlow and Keras**: These frameworks are popular for deep learning and provide pre-trained models for video classification and object detection tasks.

- **PyTorch**: PyTorch offers tools and libraries for video data analysis, including pre-trained models and modules designed for handling video data.

- **MATLAB**: MATLAB provides a range of functions and toolboxes for video processing, computer vision, and machine learning. It is commonly used in research and development for video data analysis.

- **OpenCV**: OpenCV is widely used for video data processing, extraction, and analysis. It provides functions and algorithms for image and video manipulation, feature extraction, and object detection.

- **Custom-built solutions**: Some companies develop their own proprietary software or tools tailored to their specific video data analysis needs.

These are just a few examples of tools used by companies for their use cases in different industries. The choice of tools and technologies depends on the specific requirements, data volume, and desired outcomes of each company.

In this chapter, we're going to cover the following main topics:

- Capturing real-time video data using Python CV2

- Building supervised CNN models with video data

- Using autoencoders to compress the data to reduce dimensional space and then extracting the important features of the video data

- Using the Watershed algorithm for the segmentation of the video data

- Real-world examples and advances in video data labeling

Technical requirements

In this section, we are going to use the video dataset from the following GitHub link: `https://github.com/PacktPublishing/Data-Labeling-in-Machine-Learning-with-Python/datasets/Ch9`.

You can find the Kinetics Human Action Video Dataset on its official website: `https://paperswithcode.com/dataset/kinetics-400-1`.

Capturing real-time video

Real-time video capture finds applications in various domains. One prominent use case is security and surveillance.

In large public spaces, such as airports, train stations, or shopping malls, real-time video capture is utilized for security monitoring and threat detection. Surveillance cameras strategically placed throughout the area continuously capture video feeds, allowing security personnel to monitor and analyze live footage.

Key components and features

Cameras with advanced capabilities: High-quality cameras equipped with features such as pan-tilt-zoom, night vision, and wide-angle lenses are deployed to capture detailed and clear footage.

Real-time streaming: Video feeds are streamed in real time to a centralized monitoring station, enabling security personnel to have immediate visibility of various locations.

Object detection and recognition: Advanced video analytics, including object detection and facial recognition, are applied to identify and track individuals, vehicles, or specific objects of interest.

Anomaly detection: Machine learning algorithms analyze video streams to detect unusual patterns or behaviors, triggering alerts for potential security threats or abnormal activities.

Integration with access control systems: Video surveillance systems are often integrated with access control systems. For example, if an unauthorized person is detected, the system can trigger alarms and automatically lock down certain areas.

Historical video analysis: Recorded video footage is stored for a certain duration, allowing security teams to review historical data if there are incidents, investigations, or audits.

These use cases demonstrate how real-time video capture plays a crucial role in enhancing security measures, ensuring the safety of public spaces, and providing a rapid response to potential threats.

A hands-on example to capture real-time video using a webcam

This following Python code opens a connection to your webcam, captures frames continuously, and displays them in a window. You can press Q to exit the video capture. This basic setup can serve as a starting point for collecting video data to train a classifier:

```
import cv2

# Open a connection to the webcam (default camera index is usually 0)
cap = cv2.VideoCapture(0)

# Check if the webcam is opened successfully
if not cap.isOpened():
    print("Error: Could not open webcam.")
    exit()

# Set the window name
window_name = 'Video Capture'

# Create a window to display the captured video
cv2.namedWindow(window_name, cv2.WINDOW_NORMAL)
```

```
# Define the codec and create a VideoWriter object
fourcc = cv2.VideoWriter_fourcc(*'XVID')
out = cv2.VideoWriter('captured_video.avi', fourcc, 20.0, (640, 480))

while True:
    # Read a frame from the webcam
    ret, frame = cap.read()

    # If the frame is not read successfully, exit the loop
    if not ret:
        print("Error: Could not read frame.")
        break

    # Display the captured frame
    cv2.imshow(window_name, frame)

    # Write the frame to the video file
    out.write(frame)

    # Break the loop when 'q' key is pressed
    if cv2.waitKey(1) & 0xFF == ord('q'):
            break

    # Release the webcam, release the video writer, and close the
window
cap.release()
out.release()
cv2.destroyAllWindows()
```

Now, let's build a CNN model for the classification of video data.

Building a CNN model for labeling video data

In this section, we will explore the process of building CNN models to label video data. We learned the basic concepts of CNN in *Chapter 6*. Now, we will delve into the CNN architecture, training, and evaluation techniques required to create effective models for video data analysis and labeling. By understanding the key concepts and techniques, you will be equipped to leverage CNNs to automatically label video data, enabling efficient and accurate analysis in various applications.

A typical CNN contains convolutional layers, pooling layers, and fully connected layers. These layers extract and learn spatial features from video frames, allowing the model to understand patterns and structures. Additionally, the concept of parameter sharing contributes to the efficiency of CNNs in handling large-scale video datasets.

Let's see an example of how to build a supervised CNN model for video data using Python and the TensorFlow library. We will use this trained CNN model to predict either "dance" or "brushing" labels for the videos in the Kinetics dataset. Remember to replace the path to the dataset with the actual path on your system. We'll explain each step in detail along with the code:

1. **Import the libraries**: First, we need to import the necessary libraries – TensorFlow, Keras, and any additional libraries required for data preprocessing and model evaluation:

```
import tensorflow as tf
from tensorflow import keras
from tensorflow.keras import layers
import os
import numpy as np
import cv2
from sklearn.model_selection import train_test_split
```

2. **Data preprocessing**: Next, we need to preprocess the video data before feeding it into the CNN model. The preprocessing steps may vary, depending on the specific requirements of your dataset. Here, we'll provide a general outline of the steps involved:

   I.   **Load the video data**: Load the video data from a publicly available dataset or your own dataset. You can use libraries such as OpenCV or scikit-video to read the video files.

   II. **Extract the frames**: Extract individual frames from the video data. Each frame will be treated as image input to the CNN model.

   III. **Resize the frames**: Resize the frames to a consistent size suitable for the CNN model. This step ensures that all frames have the same dimensions, which is a requirement for CNN models.

   Let's create a Python function to load videos from a directory path:

```
# Function to load videos from a directory
def load_videos_from_directory(directory, max_frames=100):
    video_data = []
    labels = []
    # Extract label from directory name
    label = os.path.basename(directory)
    for filename in os.listdir(directory):
        if filename.endswith('.mp4'):
            file_path = os.path.join(directory, filename)
            # Read video frames
            cap = cv2.VideoCapture(file_path)
            frames = []
            frame_count = 0
            while True:
                ret, frame = cap.read()
                if not ret or frame_count >= max_frames:
```

```
                        break
                        # Preprocess frame (resize, normalize, etc.)
                        frame = cv2.resize(frame, (64, 64))
                        frame = frame.astype("float32") / 255.0
                        frames.append(frame)
                        frame_count += 1
                cap.release()
                # Pad or truncate frames to max_frames
                frames = frames + [np.zeros_like(frames[0])] * /
                    (max_frames - len(frames))
                video_data.append(frames)
                labels.append(label)
        return np.array(video_data), np.array(labels)
```

Assuming you have already downloaded and extracted the Kinetics dataset from GitHub, let's proceed further:

```
# Define the path to the Kinetics Human action dataset
# Specify the directories
dance = "<your_path>/datasets/Ch9/Kinetics/dance"
brush = "<your_path>/datasets/Ch9/Kinetics/brushing"

new_video_data = "<your_path>/datasets/Ch9/Kinetics/test"

# Load video data and get the maximum number of frames

dance_video, _ = load_videos_from_directory(dance)
brushing_video, _ = load_videos_from_directory(brush)
test_video, _ = load_videos_from_directory(new_video_data)

# Calculate the overall maximum number of frames
max_frames = max(dance_video.shape[1], brushing_video.shape[1])

# Truncate or pad frames to max_frames for both classes
dance_video = dance_video[:, :max_frames, :, :, :]
brushing_video = brushing_video[:, :max_frames, :, :, :]

# Combine data from both classes
video_data = np.concatenate([dance_video, brushing_video])
```

IV.   **One-hot encoding**: Create labels and perform one-hot encoding:

```
labels = np.array([0] * len(dance_video) + [1] * \
    len(brushing_video))
```

```
# Check the size of the dataset
print("Total samples:", len(video_data))
```

V.   **Split the video frames into training and test sets**: The training set will be used to train the model, while the test set will be used to evaluate the model's performance:

```
# Split the data into training and testing sets
X_train, X_test, y_train, y_test = train_test_split(video_data, \
    labels_one_hot, test_size=0.2, random_state=42)
```

In machine learning, the `random_state` parameter is used to ensure reproducibility of the results. When you set a specific `random_state` value, the data splitting process becomes deterministic, meaning that every time you run the code with the same `random_state`, you will get the same split. This is particularly important for experimentation, sharing code, or comparing results between different models or algorithms.

By setting a specific value for `random_state` (in this case, 42), the train–test split will be the same every time the code is executed. This is crucial for reproducibility, as it ensures that others who run the code will obtain the same training and test sets, making results comparable.

3.   **Define the CNN model**: Now, we'll define the architecture of the CNN model using the Keras API. The architecture can vary, depending on the specific requirements of your task. Here's a basic example:

```
model = keras.Sequential(
[
layers.Conv3D(32, kernel_size=(3, 3, 3), activation="relu",
input_shape=(max_frames, 64, 64, 3)),
layers.MaxPooling3D(pool_size=(2, 2, 2)),
layers.Conv3D(64, kernel_size=(3, 3, 3), activation="relu"),
layers.MaxPooling3D(pool_size=(2, 2, 2)),
layers.Flatten(),
layers.Dense(128, activation="relu"),
layers.Dense(2, activation="softmax") # Two output nodes for
binary classification with softmax activation
]
)
```

In this example, we define a simple CNN architecture with two pairs of convolutional and max-pooling layers, followed by a flattening layer and a dense layer with `softmax` activation for classification. Adjust the number of filters, kernel sizes, and other parameters based on your specific task requirements.

4.   **Compile the model**: Before training the model, we need to compile it by specifying loss function, optimizer, and metrics to evaluate during training:

```
model.compile(loss="categorical_crossentropy", optimizer="adam", /
    metrics=["accuracy"])
```

In this example, we're using categorical cross-entropy as the loss function, the Adam optimizer, and accuracy as the evaluation metric. Adjust these settings based on your specific problem.

5. **Train the model**: Now, let's proceed to train the CNN model using the preprocessed video frames. The `fit` method is utilized for this purpose:

```
model.fit(X_train, y_train, epochs=10, batch_size=32, \
    validation_data=(X_test, y_test))
```

In this code snippet, `x_train` and `y_train` represent the training data (the preprocessed video frames and their corresponding labels). The `batch_size` parameter determines the number of samples processed in each training iteration, and epochs specify the number of complete passes through the training dataset. Additionally, `validation_data` is provided to evaluate the model on the test dataset during training.

6. **Evaluate the model**: After training the model, we need to evaluate its performance on the test set to assess its accuracy and generalization capability:

```
test_loss, test_accuracy = model.evaluate(x_test, y_test)
print("Test Loss:", test_loss)
print("Test Accuracy:", test_accuracy)
```

Here is the output:

```
Total samples: 5
Epoch 1/10
1/1 [==============================] - 3s 3s/step - loss: 0.6650 - accuracy: 0.5000 - val_loss: 3.0426 - val_accuracy: 0.0000e+00
Epoch 2/10
1/1 [==============================] - 2s 2s/step - loss: 2.9802e-08 - accuracy: 1.0000 - val_loss: 0.0790 - val_accuracy: 1.0000
Epoch 3/10
1/1 [==============================] - 2s 2s/step - loss: 2.9802e-08 - accuracy: 1.0000 - val_loss: 7.7486e-06 - val_accuracy: 1.0000
Epoch 4/10
1/1 [==============================] - 2s 2s/step - loss: 1.3172e-05 - accuracy: 1.0000 - val_loss: 0.0000e+00 - val_accuracy: 1.0000
Epoch 5/10
1/1 [==============================] - 2s 2s/step - loss: 0.0011 - accuracy: 1.0000 - val_loss: 20.9112 - val_accuracy: 0.0000e+00
Epoch 6/10
1/1 [==============================] - 2s 2s/step - loss: 0.0000e+00 - accuracy: 1.0000 - val_loss: 60.4221 - val_accuracy: 0.0000e+00
Epoch 7/10
1/1 [==============================] - 2s 2s/step - loss: 2.9802e-08 - accuracy: 1.0000 - val_loss: 99.0033 - val_accuracy: 0.0000e+00
Epoch 8/10
1/1 [==============================] - 2s 2s/step - loss: 6.8645 - accuracy: 0.7500 - val_loss: 0.0000e+00 - val_accuracy: 1.0000
Epoch 9/10
1/1 [==============================] - 2s 2s/step - loss: 0.0000e+00 - accuracy: 1.0000 - val_loss: 0.0000e+00 - val_accuracy: 1.0000
Epoch 10/10
1/1 [==============================] - 2s 2s/step - loss: 60.9730 - accuracy: 0.5000 - val_loss: 0.0000e+00 - val_accuracy: 1.0000
1/1 [==============================] - 0s 77ms/step - loss: 0.0000e+00 - accuracy: 1.0000
Test Loss: 0.0
Test Accuracy: 1.0
```

Figure 9.1 – CNN model loss and accuracy

This code snippet calculates the test loss and accuracy of the model on the test set, using the `evaluate` function. The results will provide insights into how well the model performs on unseen video data.

7. **Make predictions**: Once the model is trained and evaluated, we can use it to make predictions on new video data:

```
# Predictions on new video data
# Assuming 'test_video' is loaded and preprocessed similarly to
the training data
predictions = loaded_model.predict(test_video)
# Define the label mapping
label_mapping = {0: 'Dance', 1: 'Brushing'}
# Print class probabilities for each video in the test set
for i, pred in enumerate(predictions):
    print(f"Video {i + 1} - Class Probabilities: \
        Dance={pred[0]:.4f}, Brushing={pred[1]:.4f}")
# Convert predictions to labels using the mapping
predicted_labels = np.vectorize(label_mapping.get) \
    (np.argmax(predictions, axis=1))
print(predicted_labels)
```

Here is the output:

```
1/1 [==============================] - 0s 82ms/step
Video 1 - Class Probabilities: Dance=1.0000, Brushing=0.0000
['Dance']
```

Figure 9.2 – The CNN model's predicted label

In this code snippet, `test_video` represents new video frames or sequences that the model hasn't seen before. The `predict` function generates predictions for each input sample, which can be used for further analysis or decision-making. In the provided code, after making predictions, you convert the predictions to labels and print them.

8. **Save and load the model**: If you want to reuse the trained model later without retraining, you can save it to disk and load it when needed:

```
# Save the model
model.save("video_classification_model.h5")
# Load the model
loaded_model = keras.models.load_model( \
    "video_classification_model.h5")
```

The `save` function saves the entire model architecture, weights, and optimizer state to a file. The `load_model` function allows you to load the saved model and use it for predictions or further training.

9. **Fine-tuning and hyperparameter optimization**: To improve the performance of your video classification model, you can explore techniques such as fine-tuning and hyperparameter optimization. Fine-tuning involves training the model on a smaller, task-specific dataset to adapt it to your specific video classification problem. Hyperparameter optimization involves systematically searching for the best combination of hyperparameters (e.g., the learning rate, batch size, and number of layers) to maximize the model's performance.

These steps can help you build a supervised CNN model for video data classification. You can customize the steps according to your specific dataset and requirements. Experimentation, iteration, and tuning are key to achieving the best performance for your video classification task.

This code demonstrates the steps of loading, preprocessing, training, evaluating, and saving the model using the Kinetics Human Action Video dataset. Modify and customize the code based on your specific dataset and requirements.

Building CNN models for labeling video data has become essential for extracting valuable insights from the vast amount of visual information available in videos. In this section, we introduced the concept of CNNs, discussed architectures suitable for video data labeling, and covered essential steps in the modeling process, including data preparation, training, and evaluation. By understanding the principles and techniques discussed in this section, you will be empowered to develop your own CNN models for video data labeling, facilitating the analysis and understanding of video content in diverse applications.

In the next section, let's see how to classify videos using autoencoders

Using autoencoders for video data labeling

Autoencoders are a powerful class of neural networks widely used for **unsupervised learning** tasks, particularly in the field of deep learning. They are a fundamental tool in data representation and compression, and they have gained significant attention in various domains, including image and video data analysis. In this section, we will explore the concept of autoencoders, their architecture, and their applications in video data analysis and labeling.

The basic idea behind autoencoders is to learn an efficient representation of data by encoding it into a lower-dimensional latent space and then reconstructing it from this representation. The encoder and decoder components of autoencoders work together to achieve this data compression and reconstruction process. The key components of an autoencoder include the activation functions, loss functions, and optimization algorithms used during training.

An autoencoder is an unsupervised learning model that learns to encode and decode data. It consists of two main components – an encoder and a decoder.

The encoder takes an input data sample, such as an image, and maps it to a lower-dimensional representation, also called a latent space or encoding. The purpose of the encoder is to capture the most important features or patterns in the input data. It compresses the data by reducing its dimensionality, typically to a lower-dimensional space.

Conversely, the decoder takes the encoded representation from the encoder and aims to reconstruct the original input data from this compressed representation. It learns to generate an output that closely resembles the original input. The objective of the decoder is to reverse the encoding process and recreate the input data as faithfully as possible.

The autoencoder is trained by comparing the reconstructed output with the original input, measuring the reconstruction error. The goal is to minimize this reconstruction error during training, which encourages the autoencoder to learn a compact and informative representation of the data.

The idea behind autoencoders is that by training the model to compress and then reconstruct the input data, it forces the model to learn a compressed representation that captures the most salient and important features of the data. In other words, it learns a compressed version of the data that retains the most relevant information. This can be useful for tasks such as data compression, denoising, and anomaly detection.

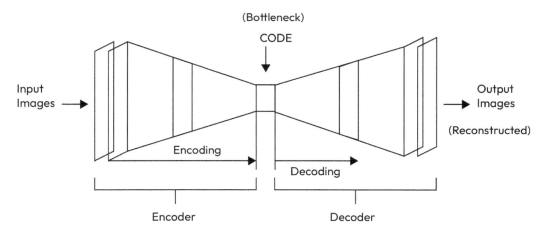

Figure 9.3 – An autoencoder network

Autoencoders can be used to label video data by first training the autoencoder to reconstruct the original input frames, and then using the learned representations to perform **classification** or **clustering** on the encoded frames.

Here are the steps you can follow to use autoencoders to label video data:

1. **Collect and preprocess the video data**: This involves converting the videos into frames, resizing them, and normalizing pixel values to a common scale.

2. **Train the autoencoder**: You can use a convolutional autoencoder to learn the underlying patterns in the video frames. The encoder network takes in a frame as input and produces a

compressed representation of the frame, while the decoder network takes in the compressed representation and produces a reconstructed version of the original frame. The autoencoder is trained to minimize the difference between the original and reconstructed frames using a loss function, such as mean squared error.

3. **Encode the frames**: Once the autoencoder is trained, you can use the encoder network to encode each frame in the video into a compressed representation.

4. **Perform classification or clustering**: The encoded frames can now be used as input to a classification or clustering algorithm. For example, you can use a classifier such as a neural network to predict the label of the video, based on the encoded frames. Alternatively, you can use clustering algorithms such as k-means or hierarchical clustering to group similar frames together.

5. **Label the video**: Once you have predicted the label or cluster for each frame in the video, you can assign a label to the entire video based on the majority label or cluster.

It's important to note that autoencoders can be computationally expensive to train, especially on large datasets. It's also important to choose the appropriate architecture and hyperparameters for your autoencoder based on your specific video data and labeling task.

A hands-on example to label video data using autoencoders

Let's see some example Python code to label the video data, using a sample dataset:

1. **Load and preprocess video data** To begin, we will read the video files from a directory and extract the frames for each video. Then, when we have a dataset of labeled video frames. We will split the data into training and testing sets for evaluation purposes.

    Let's import the libraries and define the functions:

    ```
    import cv2
    import numpy as np
    import cv2
    import os
    from tensorflow import keras
    ```

    Let us write a function to load all video data from a directory:

    ```
    # Function to load all video data from a directory
    def load_videos_from_directory(directory, max_frames=100
    ):
        video_data = []
        # List all files in the directory
        files = os.listdir(directory)
        for file in files:
            if file.endswith(".mp4"):
                video_path = os.path.join(directory, file)
                frames = load_video(video_path, max_frames)
    ```

```
        video_data.append(frames)
    return np.concatenate(video_data)
```

Let us write a function to load each video data from a path:

```
# Function to load video data from file path
def load_video(file_path, max_frames=100, frame_shape=(64, 64)):
    cap = cv2.VideoCapture(file_path)
    frames = []
    frame_count = 0

    while True:
        ret, frame = cap.read()
        if not ret or frame_count >= max_frames:
            break
        frame = cv2.cvtColor(frame, cv2.COLOR_BGR2GRAY)
        frame = cv2.resize(frame, frame_shape)
        frame = np.expand_dims(frame, axis=-1)
        frames.append(frame / 255.0)
        frame_count += 1

    cap.release()
    # Pad or truncate frames to max_frames
    frames = frames + [np.zeros_like(frames[0])] * (max_frames -
len(frames))
    return np.array(frames)
```

Now, let's specify the directories and load the video data:

```
# Specify the directories
brushing_directory = "<your_path>/datasets/Ch9/Kinetics/
autoencode/brushing"
dancing_directory = "<your_path>/datasets/Ch9/Kinetics/
autoencode/dance"

# Load video data for "brushing"
brushing_data = load_videos_from_directory(brushing_directory)

# Load video data for "dancing"
dancing_data = load_videos_from_directory(dancing_directory)

# Find the minimum number of frames among all videos
min_frames = min(min(len(video) for video in brushing_data),
min(len(video) for video in dancing_data))

# Ensure all videos have the same number of frames
```

```
brushing_data = [video[:min_frames] for video in brushing_data]
dancing_data = [video[:min_frames] for video in dancing_data]
# Reshape the data to have the correct input shape
# Selecting the first instance from brushing_data for training
and dancing_data for testing
train_data = brushing_data[0]
test_data = dancing_data[0]

# Define the input shape based on the actual dimensions of the
loaded video frames
input_shape= train_data.shape[1:]
print("Input shape:", input_shape)
```

2. **Build the autoencoder model**: In this step, we construct the architecture of the autoencoder model using TensorFlow and the Keras library. The autoencoder consists of an encoder and a decoder. The encoder part gradually reduces the spatial dimensions of the input frames through convolutional and max-pooling layers, capturing important features:

```
# Define the encoder part of the autoencoder
encoder_input = keras.Input(shape=input_shape)
encoder = keras.layers.Conv2D(filters=16, kernel_size=3, \
    activation="relu", padding="same")(encoder_input)
encoder = keras.layers.MaxPooling2D(pool_size=2)(encoder)
encoder = keras.layers.Conv2D(filters=8, kernel_size=3, \
    activation="relu", padding="same")(encoder)
encoder = keras.layers.MaxPooling2D(pool_size=2)(encoder)

# Define the decoder part of the autoencoder
decoder = keras.layers.Conv2D(filters=8, kernel_size=3, \
    activation="relu", padding="same")(encoder)
decoder = keras.layers.UpSampling2D(size=2)(decoder)
decoder = keras.layers.Conv2D(filters=16, kernel_size=3, \
    activation="relu", padding="same")(decoder)
decoder = keras.layers.UpSampling2D(size=2)(decoder)

# Modify the last layer to have 1 filter (matching the number of
channels in the input)
decoder_output = keras.layers.Conv2D(filters=1, kernel_size=3, \
    activation="sigmoid", padding="same")(decoder)

# Create the autoencoder model
autoencoder = keras.Model(encoder_input, decoder_output)
autoencoder.summary()
```

Here is the output:

```
Input shape: (64, 64, 1)
Model: "model"
```

Layer (type)	Output Shape	Param #
input_1 (InputLayer)	[(None, 64, 64, 1)]	0
conv2d (Conv2D)	(None, 64, 64, 16)	160
max_pooling2d (MaxPooling2 D)	(None, 32, 32, 16)	0
conv2d_1 (Conv2D)	(None, 32, 32, 8)	1160
max_pooling2d_1 (MaxPoolin g2D)	(None, 16, 16, 8)	0
conv2d_2 (Conv2D)	(None, 16, 16, 8)	584
up_sampling2d (UpSampling2 D)	(None, 32, 32, 8)	0
conv2d_3 (Conv2D)	(None, 32, 32, 16)	1168
up_sampling2d_1 (UpSamplin	(None, 64, 64, 16)	0

Figure 9.4 – The model summary

3. **Compile and train the autoencoder model**: Once the autoencoder model is constructed, we need to compile it with appropriate loss and optimizer functions before training. In this case, we will use the Adam optimizer, which is a popular choice for gradient-based optimization. The `binary_crossentropy` loss function is suitable for the binary classification task of reconstructing the input frames accurately. Finally, we will train the autoencoder on the training data for a specified number of epochs and a batch size of 32:

```
# Compile the model
autoencoder.compile(optimizer="adam", loss="binary_crossentropy")
```

The choice of loss function, whether it's **binary cross-entropy** (**BCE**) or **mean squared error** (**MSE**), depends on the nature of the problem you're trying to solve with an autoencoder.

BCE is commonly used when the output of the autoencoder is a binary representation, especially in scenarios where each pixel or feature can be considered as a binary outcome (activated or not activated). For example, if you're working with grayscale images and the goal is to have pixel values close to 0 or 1 (representing black or white), BCE might be suitable.

In the context of your specific autoencoder application, if the input frames are not binary, and you're looking for a reconstruction that resembles the original input closely in a continuous space, you might want to experiment with using MSE as the loss function. It's always a good idea to try different loss functions and evaluate their impact on the model's performance, choosing the one that aligns best with your specific problem and data characteristics:

```
# Train the model
autoencoder.fit(train_data, train_data, epochs=10, \
    batch_size=32, validation_data=(test_data, test_data))
# Save the trained autoencoder model to a file
autoencoder.save('autoencoder_model.h5')
```

In an autoencoder, during training, you typically use the same data for both the input and target (also known as self-supervised learning). The autoencoder is trained to reconstruct its input, so you provide the same data for training and evaluate the reconstruction loss.

Here's why the parameters are the same in your code.

In the fit method, you pass `train_data` as both the input data (x) and target data (y). This is a common practice in autoencoder training.

Note that you will need to adjust the code according to your specific video data, including the input shape, number of filters, kernel sizes, and the number of epochs for training. Additionally, you can explore different architectures and experiment with different hyperparameters to improve the performance of your autoencoder model for video data labeling.

Using the same dataset for validation allows you to directly compare the input frames with the reconstructed frames to evaluate the performance of the autoencoder.

4.   **Generate predictions and evaluate the model**: Once the autoencoder model is trained, you can generate predictions on the testing data and evaluate its performance. This step allows you to assess how well the model can reconstruct the input frames and determine its effectiveness in labeling video data:

```
# Generate predictions on testing data
decoded_frames = autoencoder.predict(test_data)
# Evaluate the model
loss = autoencoder.evaluate( decoded_frames, test_data)
print("Reconstruction loss:", loss)
```

Here is the output:

```
...
4/4 [==============================] - 0s 36ms/step - loss: 0.6215 - val_loss: 0.3862
4/4 [==============================] - 0s 6ms/step
4/4 [==============================] - 0s 6ms/step - loss: 0.4193
Reconstruction loss: 0.419280081987381
```

Figure 9.5 – Calculating reconstruction loss

If loss is low, it indicates that the autoencoder has successfully learned to encode and decode the input data.

By generating predictions on the testing data, you obtain the reconstructed frames using the trained autoencoder model. You can then evaluate the model's performance by calculating the reconstruction loss, which measures the dissimilarity between the original frames and the reconstructed frames. A lower reconstruction loss indicates better performance.

5. **Apply thresholding for labeling**: To label the video data based on the reconstructed frames, you can apply a thresholding technique. By setting a threshold value, you can classify each pixel in the frame as either the foreground or background. This allows you to distinguish objects or regions of interest in the video:

```
# Apply thresholding
threshold = 0.50
binary_frames = (decoded_frames > threshold).astype('uint8')
```

In this example, a threshold value of 0.5 is used. Pixels with values greater than the threshold are considered part of the foreground, while those below the threshold are considered part of the background. The resulting binary frames provide a labeled representation of the video data.

6. **Visualize the labeled video data**: To gain insights into the labeled video data, you can visualize the original frames alongside the corresponding binary frames obtained from thresholding. This visualization helps you understand the effectiveness of the labeling process and the identified objects or regions:

```
import matplotlib.pyplot as plt

# Visualize original frames and binary frames
# Let's visualize the first 2 frames.
num_frames =2;
fig, axes = plt.subplots(2, num_frames, figsize=(15, 6))
for i in range(num_frames):
    axes[0, i].imshow(test_data[i], cmap='gray')
    axes[0, i].axis('off')
    axes[0, i].set_title("Original")ocess
    axes[1, i].imshow(binary_frames[i], cmap='gray')
    axes[1, i].axis('off')
    axes[1, i].set_title("Binary")
plt.tight_layout()
plt.show()
```

The `plt.subplots(2, num_frames, figsize=(15, 6))` function is from the Matplotlib library and is used to create a grid of subplots. It takes three parameters – the number of rows (two), the number of columns (two), and `figsize`, which specifies the size of the figure (width and height) in inches. In this case, the width is set to 15 inches, and the height is set to 6 inches.

By plotting the original frames and the binary frames obtained after the encoding and decoding process side by side, you can visually compare the labeling results. The original frames are displayed in the top row, while the binary frames after the encoding and decoding process are shown in the bottom row. This visualization allows you to observe the objects or regions identified by the autoencoder-based labeling process.

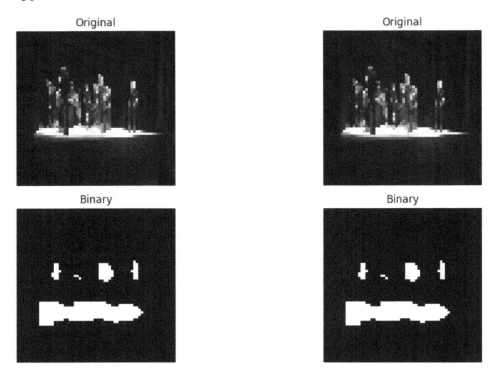

Figure 9.6 – The original images and binary images after encoding and decoding

The autoencoder model you have trained can be used for various tasks such as video classification, clustering, and anomaly detection. Here's a brief overview of how you can use the autoencoder model for these tasks:

- **Video classification**:

  - You can use the autoencoder to extract meaningful features from video frames. The encoded representations obtained from the hidden layer of the autoencoder can serve as a compact and informative representation of the input data.

  - Train a classifier (e.g., a simple feedforward neural network) on these encoded representations to perform video classification.

- **Clustering**:

  - Utilize the encoded representations to cluster videos based on the similarity of their features. You can use clustering algorithms such as k-means or hierarchical clustering.

  - Each cluster represents a group of videos that share similar patterns in their frames.

- **Anomaly detection**:

  - The autoencoder model is trained to reconstruct normal video frames accurately. Any deviation from the learned patterns can be considered an anomaly.

  - You can set a reconstruction error threshold, and frames with reconstruction errors beyond this threshold are flagged as anomalies.

Now, let's see a how to extract the encoded representations from the training dataset for video classification, using transfer learning.

Transfer learning

Using a pre-trained autoencoder model to extract representations from new data can be considered a form of transfer learning. In transfer learning, knowledge gained from training on one task or dataset is applied to a different but related task or dataset. Autoencoders, in particular, are often used as feature extractors in transfer learning scenarios.

Here's how we can break down the process:

1. **A pre-trained autoencoder**: When you train an autoencoder on a specific dataset or task (e.g., the reconstruction of input data), the learned weights in the encoder part of the autoencoder capture meaningful representations of the input data.

2. **Feature extraction for new data**: After training, you can use the pre-trained encoder as a feature extractor for new, unseen data. This means passing new data through the encoder to obtain a compressed representation (latent space) of the input.

3. **Transfer learning aspect**: The knowledge encoded in the weights of the autoencoder, learned from the original task, is transferred to the new task of encoding representations for the new data.

This approach can be beneficial in situations where labeled data for the new task is limited. Instead of training an entirely new model from scratch, you leverage the knowledge embedded in the pre-trained autoencoder to initialize or enhance the feature extraction capabilities.

In summary, using a pre-trained autoencoder for feature extraction is a form of transfer learning, where the knowledge gained from the original task (reconstruction) is transferred to a related task (representation extraction).

Let's see the code implementation here:

```
#load the saved auto encoder model
from tensorflow import keras

# Load your autoencoder model
autoencoder = keras.models.load_model("autoencoder_model.h5")

# Print the names of all layers in the loaded autoencoder
for layer in autoencoder.layers:
print(layer.name)

# Access the encoder layer by its name
encoder_layer_name = 'conv2d_2' # Replace with the actual name you
find
encoder_layer = autoencoder.get_layer(encoder_layer_name)

# Extract encoded representations of the video frames using the
autoencoder
encoded_reps = encoder_layer(frames).numpy()
```

After obtaining the encoded representations for the dataset, you can proceed to split the data into training and test sets. Subsequently, you can construct a classifier using these encoded representations, similar to the example shown in the *Building a CNN model for labeling video data* section in this chapter.

This classifier is designed to categorize the video dataset based on the learned features. The comprehensive code for this example is accessible on GitHub, providing a detailed implementation for reference.

It's important to note that the code provided is a simplified example, and depending on the complexity of your video data and specific requirements, you may need to adjust the architecture, hyperparameters, and thresholding technique. Experimentation and fine-tuning are key to achieving accurate and reliable labeling results.

In conclusion, autoencoders are a versatile and powerful tool in video data analysis. In this section, we provided a comprehensive introduction to autoencoders, explaining their architecture, training process, and applications in video analysis and labeling. We have explored how autoencoders can capture meaningful representations of video data, enabling various tasks such as denoising, super-resolution, and anomaly detection. By understanding the fundamentals of autoencoders, you will be equipped with the knowledge to leverage autoencoders in their video data analysis and classification projects. Autoencoders offer a unique approach to extracting meaningful features and reducing the dimensionality of video data, enabling efficient processing and analysis for video data labeling.

Next, let us learn about video labeling using the Watershed algorithm.

Using the Watershed algorithm for video data labeling

The Watershed algorithm is a popular technique used for image segmentation, and it can be adapted to label video data as well.

It is particularly effective in segmenting complex images with irregular boundaries and overlapping objects. Inspired by the natural process of watersheds in hydrology, the algorithm treats grayscale or gradient images as topographic maps, where each pixel represents a point on the terrain. By simulating the flooding of basins from different regions, the Watershed algorithm divides the image into distinct regions or segments.

In this section, we will explore the concept of the Watershed algorithm in detail. We will discuss its underlying principles, the steps involved in the algorithm, and its applications in various fields. Additionally, we will provide practical examples and code implementations to illustrate how the Watershed algorithm can be applied to segment and label video data.

The algorithm works by treating an image as a topographic surface and considering the grayscale intensity or gradient information as the elevation. This algorithm uses the concept of markers, which are user-defined points that guide the flooding process and help define the regions in the image.

The preprocessing steps are noise removal and gradient computation, which are crucial for obtaining accurate segmentation results. In a marker-based Watershed, initial markers are placed on the image to guide the flooding process. This process iteratively fills basins and resolves conflicts between regions. Post-processing steps merge and refine the segmented regions to obtain the final segmentation result.

Let's see an example of Python code that demonstrates how to use the Watershed algorithm to label video data, using the Kinetics Human Action Video dataset.

A hands-on example to label video data segmentation using the Watershed algorithm

In this example code, we will implement the following steps:

1. Import the required Python libraries for segmentation.
2. Read the video data and display the original frame.
3. Extract frames from the video.
4. Apply the Watershed algorithm to each frame.
5. Save the segmented frame to the output directory and print the segmented frame.

Here's the corresponding code:

First, let's import the required libraries:

```
# Step 1: Importing the required python libraries
import cv2
import numpy as np
from matplotlib import pyplot as plt


# Step 2: Read the Video Data
```

Let's read the video data from the input directory, extract the frames for the video, and then print the original video frame:

```
video_path = "<your_path>/datasets/Ch9/Kinetics/dance/dance3.mp4"

# Check if the file exists
if os.path.exists(video_path):
    cap = cv2.VideoCapture(video_path)
# Continue with your video processing logic here
else:
    print(f"The file '{video_path}' does not exist.")
```

In this step, we specify the path to the video file and create an instance of the `VideoCapture` class from OpenCV to read the video data:

```
# Step 3: Extract Frames from the Video
frames = []
while True:
    ret, frame = cap.read()
    if not ret:
        break
    frames.append(frame)
cap.release()
```

This step involves iterating through the video frames using a loop. We use the `cap.read()` method to read each frame. The loop continues until there are no more frames left in the video. Each frame is then stored in the `frames` list for further processing:

```
# Display the first one original frame for sample
plt.imshow(cv2.cvtColor(frames[0], cv2.COLOR_BGR2RGB))
plt.title('Original Frame')
plt.axis('off')
plt.show()
# Step 4: Apply Watershed Algorithm to Each Frame
```

This step involves applying the Watershed algorithm to each frame of the video. Here's a breakdown of the sub-steps:

1. Convert the frame to grayscale using `cv2.cvtColor(frame, cv2.COLOR_BGR2GRAY)`. This simplifies the subsequent processing steps.

2. Apply thresholding to obtain a binary image. This is done using `cv2.threshold()` with the `cv2.THRESH_BINARY_INV+cv2.THRESH_OTSU` flag. The Otsu thresholding method automatically determines the optimal threshold value.

3. Perform morphological operations to remove noise and fill holes in the binary image. Here, we use `cv2.morphologyEx()` with the `cv2.MORPH_OPEN` operation and a 3x3 kernel. This helps to clean up the image.

4. Apply the distance transform to identify markers. This is done using `cv2.distanceTransform()`. The distance transform calculates the distance of each pixel to the nearest zero-valued pixel in the binary image.

Let's take a look at the code for the aforementioned sub-steps:

```
labeled_frames = []
for frame in frames:
    # Convert the frame to grayscale
    gray = cv2.cvtColor(frame, cv2.COLOR_BGR2GRAY)
```

The input frame is converted to grayscale (gray), which simplifies the subsequent image-processing steps:

```
    # Apply thresholding to obtain a binary image
    _, thresh = cv2.threshold(gray, 0, 255, \
        cv2.THRESH_BINARY_INV+cv2.THRESH_OTSU)
```

A binary image (`thresh`) is created using Otsu's method, which automatically determines an optimal threshold for image segmentation. The `cv2.THRESH_BINARY_INV` flag inverts the binary image, making foreground pixels white:

```
    # Perform morphological operations to remove noise and fill holes
    kernel = np.ones((3, 3), np.uint8)
    opening = cv2.morphologyEx(thresh, cv2.MORPH_OPEN, kernel,
iterations=2)
    sure_bg = cv2.dilate(opening, kernel, iterations=3)
```

Morphological opening is applied to the binary image (`thresh`). `opening` is a sequence of dilation followed by erosion. It is useful for removing noise and small objects while preserving larger structures. `kernel` is a 3x3 matrix of ones, and the opening operation is iterated twice (`iterations=2`). This helps smooth out the binary image and fill small gaps or holes.

The result of the opening operation (`opening`) is further dilated (`cv2.dilate`) three times using the same kernel. This dilation increases the size of the white regions and helps to create a clear distinction between the background and the foreground. The resulting image is stored as `sure_bg`.

The overall purpose of these steps is to preprocess the image and create a binary image (`sure_bg`) that serves as a basis for further steps in the watershed algorithm. It helps to distinguish the background from potential foreground objects, contributing to the accurate segmentation of the image:

```
# Apply the distance transform to identify markers
dist_transform = cv2.distanceTransform(opening, cv2.DIST_L2, 5)
_, sure_fg = cv2.threshold(dist_transform, \
    0.7*dist_transform.max(), 255, 0)
```

The distance transform is applied to the opening result. This transform calculates the distance of each pixel to the nearest zero (background) pixel. This is useful for identifying potential markers. The result is stored in `dist_transform`.

A threshold is applied to the distance transform, creating the sure foreground markers (`sure_fg`). Pixels with values higher than 70% of the maximum distance transform value are considered part of the foreground:

```
# Combine the background and foreground markers
sure_fg = np.uint8(sure_fg)
unknown = cv2.subtract(sure_bg, sure_fg)

# Apply the watershed algorithm to label the regions
_, markers = cv2.connectedComponents(sure_fg)
markers = markers + 1
markers[unknown == 255] = 0
markers = cv2.watershed(frame, markers)
```

In this code snippet, the `markers = markers + 1` operation increments the values in the markers array by 1. In the watershed algorithm, markers are used to identify different regions or basins. By incrementing the marker values, you create unique labels for different regions, helping the algorithm distinguish between them.

`markers[unknown == 255] = 0` sets the markers to 0, where the unknown array has a value of 255. In watershed segmentation, the unknown regions typically represent areas where the algorithm is uncertain or hasn't made a decision about the segmentation. Setting these markers to 0 indicates that these regions are not assigned to any particular basin or region. This is often done to prevent the algorithm from over-segmenting or misinterpreting uncertain areas.

In summary, these operations are part of the process of preparing the marker image for the watershed algorithm. The incrementation helps to assign unique labels to different regions, while the second operation helps handle uncertain or unknown regions. The specifics may vary depending on the implementation, but this is a common pattern in watershed segmentation:

```
# Colorize the regions for visualization
frame[markers == -1] = [0, 0, 255]


labeled_frames.append(frame)

#Step 5: save the segmented frame to output directory.
 and print the segmented frame.
# Save the first segmented frame to the output folder
cv2.imwrite('<your_path>/datasets/Ch9/Kinetics/watershed/segmentation.
jpg', labeled_frames[0])
```

Now, let's print the first segmented video frame:

```
plt.imshow(cv2.cvtColor(labeled_frames[0], cv2.COLOR_BGR2RGB))
plt.title('first Segmented Frame')
plt.axis('off')
plt.show()
```

We get the following results:

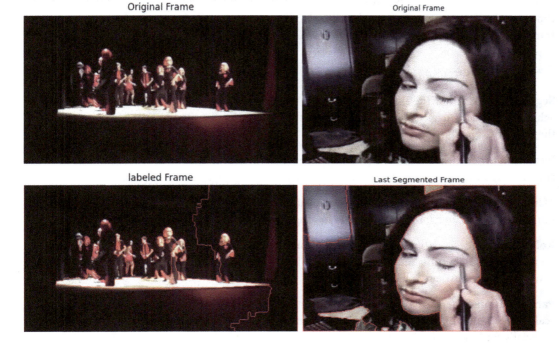

Figure 9.7 – The original, labeled, and segmented frames

The Watershed algorithm is a powerful tool in image segmentation, capable of handling complex and challenging segmentation tasks. In this section, we have introduced the Watershed algorithm, explaining its principles, steps, and applications. By understanding the underlying concepts and techniques, you will be equipped with the knowledge to apply the Watershed algorithm to segment and label video data effectively. Whether it is for medical imaging, quality control, or video analysis, the Watershed algorithm offers a versatile and reliable solution for extracting meaningful regions and objects from images and videos. Now, let's see some real-world examples in the industry using video data labeling.

The Watershed algorithm is a region-based segmentation technique that operates on grayscale images. Its computational complexity depends on several factors, including the size of the input image, the number of pixels, and the characteristics of the image itself.

Computational complexity

Time complexity: The basic Watershed algorithm has a time complexity of $O(N \log N)$, where N is the number of pixels in the image. This complexity arises from the sorting operations involved in processing the image gradient.

Space complexity: The space complexity is also influenced by the number of pixels and is generally $O(N)$, due to the need to store intermediate data structures.

Scalability for long videos: The Watershed algorithm can be applied to long videos, but scalability depends on the resolution and duration of the video. As the algorithm processes each frame independently, the time complexity per frame remains the same. However, processing long videos with high-resolution frames may require substantial computational resources and memory.

Performance metrics

Segmentation quality: The algorithm's success is often evaluated based on the quality of segmentation achieved. Metrics such as precision, recall, and the F1 score can be used to quantify the accuracy of the segmented regions.

Execution time: The time taken to process a video is a critical metric, especially for real-time or near-real-time applications. Lower execution times are desirable for responsive segmentation.

Memory usage: The algorithm's efficiency in managing memory resources is crucial. Memory-efficient implementations can handle larger images or longer videos without causing memory overflow issues.

Robustness: The algorithm's ability to handle various types of videos, including those with complex scenes, is essential. Robustness is measured by how well the algorithm adapts to different lighting conditions, contrasts, and object complexities.

Parallelization: Watershed algorithm implementations can benefit from parallelization, which enhances scalability. Evaluating the algorithm's performance in parallel processing environments is relevant, especially for large-scale video processing.

It's important to note that the specific implementation details, hardware specifications, and the nature of the video content greatly influence the algorithm's overall performance.

Real-world examples for video data labeling

Here are some real-world companies from various industries along with their use cases for video data analysis and labeling:

- **A retail company – a Walmart use case**: Walmart utilizes video data analysis for customer behavior tracking and optimizing store layouts. By analyzing video data, it gains insights into customer traffic patterns, product placement, and overall store performance.

- **A finance company – a JPMorgan Chase & Co. use case**: JPMorgan Chase & Co. employs video data analysis for fraud detection and prevention. By analyzing video footage from ATMs and bank branches, it can identify suspicious activities, detect fraud attempts, and enhance security measures.

- **An e-commerce company – an Amazon use case**: Amazon utilizes video data analysis for package sorting and delivery optimization in its warehouses. By analyzing video feeds, it can track packages, identify bottlenecks in the sorting process, and improve overall operational efficiency.

- **An insurance company – a Progressive case**: Progressive uses video data analysis for claims assessment and risk evaluation. By analyzing video footage from dashcams and telematics devices, it can determine the cause of accidents, assess damages, and determine liability accurately.

- **A telecom company – an AT&T use case**: AT&T utilizes video data analysis for network monitoring and troubleshooting. By analyzing video feeds from surveillance cameras installed in network facilities, it can identify equipment failures, security breaches, and potential network issues.

- **A manufacturing company – a General Electric (GE) use case**: GE employs video data analysis for quality control and process optimization in manufacturing plants. By analyzing video footage, it can detect defects, monitor production lines, and identify areas for improvement to ensure product quality.

- **An automotive company – a Tesla use case**: Tesla uses video data analysis for driver assistance and autonomous driving. By analyzing video data from onboard cameras, it can detect and classify objects, recognize traffic signs, and assist in **advanced driver-assistance system (ADAS)** features.

Now, let's see the recent developments in video data labeling and how generative AI can be leveraged for video data analysis to apply to various use cases.

Advances in video data labeling and classification

The field of video data labeling and classification is rapidly evolving, with continuous advancements. **Generative AI** can be applied to video data analysis and labeling in various use cases, providing innovative solutions and enhancing automation. Here are some potential applications:

- **A video synthesis for augmentation use case – training data augmentation**:

  Application: Generative models can generate synthetic video data to augment training datasets. This helps improve the performance and robustness of machine learning models by exposing them to a more diverse range of scenarios.

- **An anomaly detection and generation use case – security surveillance**:

  Application: Generative models can learn the normal patterns of activities in a video feed and generate abnormal or anomalous events. This is useful for detecting unusual behavior or security threats in real-time surveillance footage.

- **A content generation for video games use case – video game development**:

  Application: Generative models can be used to create realistic and diverse game environments, characters, or animations. This can enhance the gaming experience by providing dynamic and varied content.

- **A video captioning and annotation use case – video content indexing**:

  Application: Generative models can be trained to generate descriptive captions or annotations for video content. This facilitates better indexing, searchability, and retrieval of specific scenes or objects within videos.

- **A deepfake detection use case – content authenticity verification**:

  Application: Generative models can be used to create deepfake videos, and conversely, other generative models can be developed to detect such deepfakes. This is crucial for ensuring the authenticity of video content.

- **An interactive video editing use case – video production**:

  Application: Generative models can assist video editors by automating or suggesting creative edits, special effects, or transitions. This speeds up the editing process and allows for more innovative content creation.

- **A simulated training environment use case – autonomous vehicles or robotics**:

  Application: Generative models can simulate realistic video data for training autonomous vehicles or robotic systems. This enables the models to learn and adapt to various scenarios in a safe and controlled virtual environment.

- **A human pose estimation and animation use case – motion capture and animation:**

  Application: Generative models can be trained to understand and generate realistic human poses. This has applications in animation, virtual reality, and healthcare for analyzing and simulating human movement.

Generative AI, particularly in the form of **generative adversarial networks** (**GANs**) and **variational autoencoders** (**VAEs**), continues to find diverse applications across industries, and its potential in video data analysis and labeling is vast. However, it's important to be mindful of ethical considerations, especially in the context of deepfake technology and privacy concerns.

While generative models can be trained in a self-supervised manner, not all generative AI is self-supervised, and vice versa. Generative models can be trained with or without labeled data, and they can use a variety of training paradigms, including supervised, unsupervised, or **self-supervised learning**:

- **Self-supervised learning:** Self-supervised learning techniques have emerged as a promising approach for video data labeling. Instead of relying on manually labeled data, self-supervised learning leverages the inherent structure or context within videos to create labels. By training models to predict missing frames, temporal order, or spatial transformations, they learn meaningful representations that can be used for downstream video classification tasks.

- **Transformer-based models:** Transformer models, initially popular in natural language processing, have shown remarkable performance in video data labeling and classification. By leveraging self-attention mechanisms, transformers can effectively capture long-range dependencies and temporal relationships in videos, leading to improved accuracy and efficiency.

- **Graph Neural Networks (GNNs):** GNNs have gained attention for video data labeling, especially in scenarios involving complex interactions or relationships among objects or regions within frames. By modeling the spatial and temporal dependencies as a graph structure, GNNs can effectively capture context and relational information for accurate video classification.

- **Weakly supervised learning:** Traditional video data labeling often requires fine-grained manual annotation of each frame or segment, which can be time-consuming and expensive. Weakly supervised learning approaches aim to reduce annotation efforts by utilizing weak labels, such as video-level labels or partial annotations. Techniques such as multiple instance learning, attention-based pooling, or co-training can be employed to train models with limited supervision.

- **Domain adaptation and few-shot learning:** Labeling video data in specific domains or with limited labeled samples can be challenging. Domain adaptation and few-shot learning techniques address this issue by leveraging labeled data from a different but related source domain, or by learning from a small number of labeled samples. These techniques enable the effective transfer of knowledge and generalize well to new video data.

- **Active learning**: Active learning techniques aim to optimize the labeling process by actively selecting the most informative samples for annotation. By iteratively selecting unlabeled samples that are likely to improve the model's performance, active learning reduces annotation efforts while maintaining high classification accuracy.

Summary

In this chapter, we explored the world of video data classification, its real-world applications, and various methods for labeling and classifying video data. We discussed techniques such as frame-based classification, 3D CNNs, auto encoders, transfer learning, and Watershed methods. Additionally, we examined the latest advances in video data labeling, including self-supervised learning, transformer-based models, GNNs, weakly supervised learning, domain adaptation, few-shot learning, and active learning. These advancements contribute to more accurate, efficient, and scalable video data labeling and classification systems, enabling breakthroughs in domains such as surveillance, healthcare, sports analysis, autonomous driving, and social media. By keeping up with the latest developments and leveraging these techniques, researchers and practitioners can unlock the full potential of video data and derive valuable insights from this rich and dynamic information source.

In the next chapter, we will explore the different methods for audio data labeling.

10
Exploring Audio Data

Imagine a world without music, without the sound of your favorite movie's dialog, or without the soothing tones of a friend's voice on a phone call. Sound is not just background noise; it's a fundamental part of our lives, shaping our emotions, experiences, and memories. But have you ever wondered about the untapped potential hidden within the waves of sound?

Welcome to the realm of audio data analysis, a fascinating journey that takes you deep into the heart of sound. In this chapter, we'll embark on an exploration of the power of sound in the context of machine learning. We'll unveil the secrets of extracting knowledge from audio, turning seemingly random vibrations in the air into structured data that machines can understand, interpret, and even make predictions from.

In the era of artificial intelligence and machine learning, audio data analysis has emerged as a transformative force. Whether it's recognizing speech commands on your smartphone, understanding the sentiment in a customer service call, or classifying genres in your music library, audio data analysis is the silent hero behind the scenes.

This chapter is your guide to understanding the core concepts, techniques, and tools that bring the world of audio data analysis to life. We'll dive into the fundamental elements of sound, demystify complex terms such as spectrograms, mel spectrograms, and MFCCs, and explore the art of transforming sound into meaningful information.

Together, we'll uncover the magic of extracting patterns, features, and insights from audio data, paving the way for a myriad of applications, from automatic speech recognition to audio fingerprinting, music recommendation, and beyond. A compelling real-life example involves recording conversations between doctors and patients. Training AI models on these recordings allows for the generation of patient history summaries, providing doctors with a convenient overview for review and prescription. Understanding the various features and patterns of audio data is critical for the labeling of audio data, which we will see in the next chapter.

In this chapter, we'll cover the following topics:

- Real-life applications for labeling audio data

- Audio data fundamentals

- Loading and analyzing audio data

- Extracting features from audio data

- Visualizing audio data

By the end of this chapter, you'll be equipped with the knowledge and practical skills needed to embark on your audio data analysis journey. Librosa will be your trusted ally in unraveling the mysteries hidden within the realm of sound, whether you're a music enthusiast, a researcher, or a data analyst.

Let's dive in and unlock the potential of audio data with Librosa!

Technical requirements

The complete Python code notebook and datasets used in this chapter are available on GitHub here:

- `https://github.com/PacktPublishing/Data-Labeling-in-Machine-Learning-with-Python/tree/main/code/Ch10`

- `https://github.com/PacktPublishing/Data-Labeling-in-Machine-Learning-with-Python/tree/main/datasets/Ch10`

Let us start exploring audio data (`.wav` or `.mp3`) and understand some basic terminology in audio engineering.

Real-life applications for labeling audio data

Audio data is utilized in various real-life applications across industries. Here are some examples of how audio data is leveraged in machine learning and AI:

- **Voice assistants and speech recognition**: Platforms such as Azure AI Speech, Amazon Alexa, Google Assistant, and Apple's Siri utilize audio data for natural language processing and speech recognition. Users can interact with devices through voice commands, enabling tasks such as setting reminders, playing music, and controlling smart home devices.

- **Healthcare diagnostics**: Audio data analysis is employed in healthcare for tasks such as detecting respiratory disorders. For instance, analyzing cough sounds can help diagnose conditions such as asthma or pneumonia. Researchers are exploring the use of audio patterns for the early detection of neurological disorders.

Student researcher and Rise Global Winner Chandra Suda invented a tool in 2023 for screening tuberculosis using cough audio and published a paper on it. The paper describes a machine learning model that analyzes cough audio samples from smartphones' microphones to detect tuberculosis.

- **Automotive safety and autonomous vehicles**: In the automotive industry, audio data is used for driver monitoring and safety. Systems can analyze driver speech to detect signs of drowsiness or distraction. Additionally, autonomous vehicles utilize audio sensors to interpret sounds from the environment for improved situational awareness.

- **Security and surveillance**: Audio data is employed in security systems for detecting and recognizing specific sounds, such as breaking glass, gunshots, or unusual noises. This is crucial for enhancing the capabilities of surveillance systems in identifying potential threats.

- **Music and entertainment**: Music recommendation systems leverage audio features for personalized song recommendations based on user preferences. Audio fingerprinting is used to identify and categorize music on streaming platforms.

- **Environmental monitoring**: Audio data is utilized in environmental monitoring to analyze sounds from natural habitats. For example, monitoring bird sounds in forests can provide insights into biodiversity, and analyzing underwater sounds can help study marine life.

- **Call center analytics**: Beyond emotion recognition, call centers use audio data analysis for various purposes, including sentiment analysis to understand customer satisfaction, identifying trends, and optimizing customer interactions for better service.

- **Language learning apps**: Language learning applications use audio data for pronunciation evaluation. Machine learning models can analyze users' spoken language, provide feedback on pronunciation, and offer personalized language learning exercises.

- **Fraud detection**: In financial services, audio data is sometimes used for fraud detection. Voice biometrics and behavioral analysis can help verify the identity of individuals during phone transactions.

- **Smart cities**: Audio sensors in smart cities can be employed for various purposes, such as monitoring traffic patterns, detecting emergency situations (e.g., sirens, gunshots), and analyzing urban noise levels for environmental planning.

These examples showcase the versatility of audio data in diverse domains, highlighting the potential for machine learning and AI to extract valuable insights and enhance various aspects of our lives. Let's look at some other applications that integrate audio data with other data types, such as video data and text data.

The integration of audio analysis with other data types allows for the development of comprehensive AI applications that leverage multiple modalities. Here are some real-world applications where the integration of audio analysis with other data types is beneficial:

- **Multimodal emotion recognition**: Applications include customer service and user experience enhancement.

  Integration: We can combine the audio analysis of speech prosody and sentiment with video analysis of facial expressions to understand users' emotions during customer service interactions. This integration helps in providing a more personalized and empathetic response.

- **Audio-visual scene understanding**: Applications include smart surveillance and security.

  Integration: We can combine the audio analysis of environmental sounds with video analysis to detect and understand activity in a scene. For example, detecting a breaking-glass sound in conjunction with corresponding visual cues could trigger an alert for potential security issues.

- **Cross-modal music recommendation**: One application would be personalized content recommendations.

  Integration: We can combine the audio features of user-listened music with textual data from social media posts or reviews to provide personalized music recommendations. The system considers both the user's musical preferences and contextual information from text data.

- **Voice-driven intelligent assistants**: One application would be virtual assistants.

  Integration: We can combine the audio analysis of voice commands with the **natural language processing** (**NLP**) of textual data to create intelligent voice-driven assistants. This integration allows for more natural and context-aware interactions.

- **Healthcare monitoring and diagnosis**: One application would be remote health monitoring.

  Integration: We can combine the audio analysis of speech patterns with textual data from electronic health records to monitor patients remotely. This multimodal approach can aid in the early detection of health issues and provide more comprehensive insights for healthcare professionals.

- **Multimodal content moderation**: One application would be social media and content platforms.

  Integration: We can combine the audio analysis of spoken content with textual and visual data to enhance content moderation efforts. This approach helps in identifying and moderating harmful or inappropriate content more effectively.

- **Autonomous vehicles**: One application would be smart transportation.

  Integration: We can combine the audio analysis of surrounding sounds (e.g., sirens, honks) with video analysis and sensor data to enhance the perception capabilities of autonomous vehicles. This integration improves safety and situational awareness.

- **Cross-modal fraud detection**: One application would be financial services.

  Integration: We can combine the audio analysis of customer calls with textual data from transaction logs to detect potentially fraudulent activities. Integrating multiple modalities improves the accuracy of fraud detection systems.

- **Educational technology**: One application would be online learning platforms.

  Integration: We can combine the audio analysis of spoken content in educational videos with textual data from lecture transcripts and user interactions. This integration enhances the understanding of students' engagement and learning patterns.

- **Multimodal human-computer interaction**: Applications include gaming and virtual reality.

  Integration: We can combine the audio analysis of spoken commands and environmental sounds with visual and sensor data to create immersive and responsive virtual environments. This integration enhances the overall user experience in gaming and virtual reality applications.

These real-world applications demonstrate how the integration of audio analysis with other data types contributes to building more intelligent and context-aware AI systems across various domains. The combined use of multiple modalities often results in more robust and nuanced AI solutions. Now let's learn about the fundamentals of audio data for analysis.

Audio data fundamentals

First, let us understand some basic terminology in audio data analysis:

- **Amplitude**: Sound is made up of waves, and the height of those waves is called the amplitude. The bigger the amplitude, the louder the sound. Amplitude refers to the maximum extent of a vibration or oscillation, measured from the position of equilibrium. Imagine a swinging pendulum. The distance the pendulum moves from its resting position (middle point) to one extreme is its amplitude. Think of a person on a swing. The higher they swing, the greater the amplitude of their motion.

- **RMS calculation**: To find the loudness using RMS, we square the amplitude values of the sound waves. This is done because it helps us focus on the positive values (removing any negative values) and because loudness should reflect the intensity of the sound.

- **Average power**: After squaring the amplitudes, we calculate the average (mean) of these squared values. It's like finding the typical size of the sound waves.

- **Square root**: To get the final loudness measurement, we take the square root of that average power. This is the RMS, which tells us how intense the sound is on average.

- **RMS energy**: In practical terms, when you look at a loudness value given in **decibels** (**dB**), it's often calculated from the RMS energy. A higher RMS value means a louder sound, while a lower RMS value means a quieter sound.

So, RMS energy is a way to take the raw amplitudes of an audio signal, square them to focus on their intensity, find the average of these squared values, and then take the square root to get a measure of how loud the sound is overall. It's a useful tool for understanding and comparing the loudness of different audio signals.

Frequency: Think of frequency as how fast something vibrates. In sound, it's how quickly air moves back and forth to create a pitch. High frequency means a high-pitched sound, such as a whistle, and low frequency means a low-pitched sound, such as a bass drum. Think of ocean waves hitting the shore. The more waves that arrive in a given time frame, the higher the frequency.

- **Spectrogram**: A spectrogram is like a picture that shows how loud different frequencies are in sound. It's often used for music or speech analysis. Imagine a graph where time is on the x axis, frequency (pitch) is on the y axis, and color represents how loud each frequency is at a certain moment. Consider a musical score with notes over time. The position of the notes on the score represents their frequency, and the intensity of the notes represents their amplitude.

- **Mel spectrogram**: A mel spectrogram is a special type of spectrogram that tries to show how humans hear sound. It's like a picture of sound that's been adjusted to match how we perceive pitch. It's helpful for tasks such as music and speech recognition.

- **Mel-frequency cepstral coefficients** (**MFCCs**): MFCCs are like a special way to describe the features of sound. They take the mel spectrogram and turn it into a set of numbers that a computer can understand. It's often used in voice recognition and music analysis.

- **Binary cross-entropy** (**BCE**): BCE is a way to measure how well a computer is doing a "yes" or "no" task, such as telling whether a picture has a cat in it or not. It checks whether the computer's answers match the real answers and gives a score.

- **AMaxP** (`.95 f1`, `.96 acc`): AMaxP is a way to find the best answer among many choices. Imagine you have a test with multiple questions, and you want the highest score. `.95 f1` and `.96 acc` are like scores that tell you how well you did. `f1` is about finding a balance between being right and not missing anything, while `acc` is just about how many answers you got right.

Now let us learn about the most used libraries for audio data analysis.

Librosa is a versatile Python library that empowers researchers, data scientists, and engineers to explore and manipulate audio data with ease. It provides a range of tools and functions that simplify the complexities of audio analysis, making it accessible to both beginners and experts. Whether you're seeking to identify music genres, detect voice patterns, or extract meaningful features from audio recordings, Librosa is your go-to companion on this journey.

Apart from Librosa, there are several other libraries that cater to different aspects of audio processing and analysis. Here's a brief comparison with a few notable audio analysis libraries:

Library	Focus	Features
Librosa	Librosa is primarily focused on music and audio analysis tasks, providing tools for feature extraction, signal processing, and music information retrieval (MIR).	Comprehensive feature extraction for MIR tasks. Support for loading audio files and visualization. Integration with scikit-learn for machine learning applications.
pydub	pydub is a library specifically designed for audio manipulation tasks, such as editing, slicing, and format conversion.	Simple and intuitive API for common audio operations. Support for various audio formats. Easy conversion between different audio representations.
Essentia	Essentia is a C++ library with Python bindings, offering a wide range of audio analysis and processing algorithms for both music and general audio.	Extensive collection of audio analysis algorithms. Support for feature extraction, audio streaming, and real-time processing. Integration with other libraries such as MusicBrainz.
MIDIUtil	MIDIUtil is a library for creating and manipulating MIDI files, enabling the generation of music programmatically.	Creation and manipulation of MIDI files. Control over musical notes, tempo, and other MIDI parameters. Pythonic interface for generating music compositions.
TorchAudio (PyTorch)	TorchAudio is part of the PyTorch ecosystem and is designed for audio processing within deep learning workflows.	Integration with PyTorch for seamless model training. Tools for audio preprocessing, data augmentation, and feature extraction. Support for GPU acceleration.

Aubio	Aubio is a C library with Python bindings, specializing in audio segmentation and pitch detection tasks.	Pitch detection, beat tracking, and other segmentation algorithms.
		Efficient and lightweight for real-time applications.
		Suitable for music analysis and interactive audio applications.

Table 10.1 – Comparison of features of different audio analysis libraries

It's important to choose the library that best suits your specific needs and the nature of your audio data analysis task. Depending on the application, you may need to use a combination of libraries to cover different aspects of audio processing, from basic manipulation to advanced feature extraction and machine learning integration.

Hands-on with analyzing audio data

In this section, we'll dive deep into various operations that we can perform on audio data such as, cleaning, loading, analyzing, and visualizing it.

Example code for loading and analyzing sample audio file

Before diving into audio data analysis with Librosa, you'll need to install it. To install Librosa, you can use pip, Python's package manager:

```
pip install librosa
```

This will download and install Librosa, along with its dependencies.

Now that you have Librosa installed, let's begin by loading an audio file and performing some basic analysis on it. In this example, we'll analyze a sample audio file. We can read audio files using SciPy as follows:

```
from scipy.io import wavfile
import matplotlib.pyplot as plt

sample_rate, data = wavfile.read('cat_1.wav')
print(sample_rate)
print(data)

#Visulize the wave form
plt.figure(figsize=(8, 4))
plt.plot(data)
```

```
plt.title('Waveform')
plt.xlabel('Sample')
plt.ylabel('Amplitude')
plt.show()
```

We get the following result:

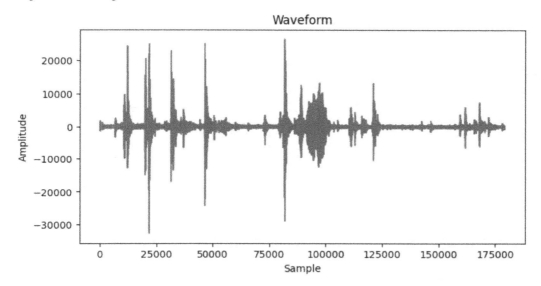

Figure 10.1 – Waveform visualization

The provided code is for loading an audio file in WAV format, extracting information about the audio, and visualizing its waveform using Python. Here's a step-by-step explanation of the code.

Importing libraries

from scipy.io import wavfile: This line imports the wavfile module from the scipy.io library, which is used to read WAV audio files.

import matplotlib.pyplot as plt: This line imports the pyplot module from the matplotlib library, which is used for creating plots and visualizations.

from IPython.display import Audio: IPython.display's Audio module allows audio playback integration within Jupyter notebooks.

Loading the audio file

`sample_rate, data = wavfile.read('cat_1.wav')`: This line loads an audio file named `cat_1.wav` and extracts two pieces of information:

- `sample_rate`: The sample rate, which represents how many samples (measurements of the audio signal) are taken per second. It tells you how finely the audio is represented.

- `data`: The audio data itself, which is an array of values representing the amplitude of the audio signal at each sample.

Printing sample rate and data

`print(sample_rate)`: This line prints the sample rate to the console. The sample rate is typically expressed in **hertz (Hz)**.

`print(data)`: This line prints the audio data, which is an array of amplitude values sampled at the given sample rate. The printed data may look like a long list of numbers, each representing the amplitude of the audio at a specific point in time.

Visualizing the waveform

`plt.figure(figsize=(8, 4))`: This line sets up a new figure for a plot of a specified size (8 inches in width and 4 inches in height).

`plt.plot(data)`: This line creates a line plot of the audio data. The *x* axis represents the sample index (time), and the *y* axis represents the amplitude of the audio at each sample. This plot is called the waveform.

`plt.title('Waveform')`: This line sets the title of the plot to `Waveform`.

`plt.xlabel('Sample')`: This line labels the *x* axis `Sample`, indicating the sample index.

`plt.ylabel('Amplitude')`: This line labels the *y* axis `Amplitude`, indicating the intensity or strength of the audio signal at each sample.

`plt.show()`: This line displays the plot on the screen.

The resulting visualization is a waveform plot that shows how the amplitude of the audio signal changes over time. It's a common way to get a visual sense of the audio data, allowing you to see patterns, peaks, and troughs in an audio signal.

Let us plot the audio player:

```
#   Audio player
audio_player = Audio(data=data, rate=sample_rate)
display(audio_player)
```

We have loaded audio data and extracted two pieces of information (sample rate and data) from an audio file. Next, let us see how to extract other important properties from audio data.

Best practices for audio format conversion

When working with audio data in the industry, there are several common best practices for converting audio to the correct format and performing cleaning or editing tasks. The following are some steps and recommendations.

- **File format conversion**:

  - **Use common formats**: Convert audio files to commonly used formats such as WAV, MP3, and FLAC. The choice of format depends on the specific requirements of your application.

  - **Use lossless formats for editing**: When editing or processing audio, consider using lossless formats such as WAV and FLAC to preserve the original quality during modifications.

  Tools for conversion include FFmpeg, a powerful multimedia processing tool that can be used for audio format conversion, and Audacity, a piece of open source audio editing software that supports various formats.

- **Audio cleaning**:

  - **Noise reduction**: Apply noise reduction techniques to remove unwanted background noise. Libraries such as Librosa in Python can be helpful.

  - **High-pass/low-pass filtering**: Use filtering to remove frequencies outside the desired range. This can be helpful for removing low-frequency humming or high-frequency noise.

  - **Normalization**: Normalize audio levels to ensure consistent loudness. This can be done to prevent distortion and ensure uniform volume across different recordings.

  - **Editing tools**: Audacity provides a user-friendly interface for various audio editing tasks, including noise reduction and filtering.

- **Snipping and segmentation**:

  - **Segmentation**: Divide longer audio recordings into segments or snippets based on specific criteria. This could be time-based or event-based segmentation.

  - **Identify key events**: Use audio analysis techniques or manual inspection to identify key events or boundaries within the audio data.

  - **Tools for snipping**: These include Audacity, which allows users to easily select and cut portions of audio, and Librosa, for audio processing and segmentation.

- **Quality assurance**:

  - **Listen to the output**: Always listen to the audio after processing to ensure that the modifications meet the desired quality standards.

  - **Automated checks**: Implement automated checks to identify potential issues, such as clipping or distortion, during processing.

- **Documentation**:

  - **Metadata**: Keep track of metadata such as sampling rate, bit depth, and any processing steps applied. This documentation is crucial for reproducibility.

  - **Version control**: Use version control systems to track changes to audio files and processing scripts.

Remember to adapt these best practices based on the specific requirements of your project and the characteristics of the audio data you are working with. Always document your processing steps to maintain transparency and reproducibility.

Example code for audio data cleaning

Audio data cleanup is essential to enhance the quality and accuracy of subsequent analyses or applications. It helps remove unwanted artifacts, background noise, or distortions, ensuring that the processed audio is more suitable for tasks such as speech recognition, music analysis, and other audio-based applications, ultimately improving overall performance and interpretability.

Cleaning audio data often involves techniques such as background noise removal. One popular approach is using a technique called **spectral subtraction**. Python provides several libraries that can be used for audio processing, and one of the commonly used ones is Librosa.

The following code utilizes the Librosa library for audio processing to demonstrate background noise removal.

Loading the audio file

The code begins by loading an audio file using Librosa. The file path is specified as `audio_file_path`, and the `librosa.load` function returns the audio signal (`y`) and the sampling rate (`sr`):

```
# Load the audio file
audio_file_path = "../PacktPublishing/DataLabeling/ch10/cats_dogs/
cat_1.wav"

# Replace with the path to your audio file
y, sr = librosa.load(audio_file_path)
```

Displaying the original spectrogram

The original spectrogram of the audio signal is computed using the **short-time Fourier transform (STFT)** and displayed using librosa.display.specshow. This provides a visual representation of the audio signal in the frequency domain:

```
D_original = librosa.amplitude_to_db(np.abs(librosa.stft(y)), ref=np.max)
plt.figure(figsize=(12, 8))
librosa.display.specshow(D_original,sr=sr, x_axis='time', y_axis='log')
plt.colorbar(format='%+2.0f dB')
plt.title('Original Spectrogram')
plt.show()
```

Applying background noise removal

Harmonic-percussive source separation (librosa.effects.hpss) is applied to decompose the audio signal into harmonic and percussive components. Background noise is then estimated by subtracting the harmonic component, resulting in y_noise_removed:

```
# Apply background noise removal
y_harmonic, y_percussive = librosa.effects.hpss(y)
y_noise_removed = y - y_harmonic
```

Displaying the spectrogram after background noise removal

The cleaned audio's spectrogram is computed and displayed, allowing a comparison with the original spectrogram. This step visualizes the impact of background noise removal on the frequency content of the audio signal:

```
# Display the spectrogram after background noise removal
D_noise_removed = librosa.amplitude_to_db( \
    np.abs(librosa.stft(y_noise_removed)), ref=np.max)
plt.figure(figsize=(12, 8))
librosa.display.specshow(D_noise_removed, sr=sr, \
    x_axis='time', y_axis='log')
plt.colorbar(format='%+2.0f dB')
plt.title('Spectrogram after Background Noise Removal')
plt.show()
```

Saving the cleaned audio file

The cleaned audio signal (`y_noise_removed`) is saved as a new WAV file specified by `output_file_path` using the `scipy.io.wavfile.write` function:

```
# Convert the audio signal to a NumPy array
y_noise_removed_np = np.asarray(y_noise_removed)

# Save the cleaned audio file
output_file_path = "../PacktPublishing/DataLabeling/ch10/cleaned_
audio_file.wav"
write(output_file_path, sr, y_noise_removed_np)
```

We have now seen an example of how Librosa can be utilized for preprocessing and cleaning audio data, particularly for removing background noise from an audio signal.

Extracting properties from audio data

In this section, we will learn how to extract the properties from audio data. Librosa provides many tools for extracting features from audio. These features are useful for audio data classification and labeling. For example, the MFCCs feature is used to classify cough audio data and predict whether a cough indicates tuberculosis.

Tempo

The term *tempo* in the context of audio and music refers to the speed or pace of a piece of music. It's a fundamental characteristic of music, and it's often measured in **beats per minute (BPM)**.

In the context of audio data analysis with Librosa, when we estimate tempo, we are using mathematical techniques to figure out how fast or slow a piece of music is without having to listen and count the beats ourselves. For example, to extract the tempo of the audio, you can use the following code:

```
import librosa
import librosa.display
import matplotlib.pyplot as plt

# Load an audio file
audio_file = "cat_1.wav"
y, sr = librosa.load(audio_file)
# Extract the tempo
tempo, _ = librosa.beat.beat_track(y=y, sr=sr)
print(f"Tempo: {tempo} BPM")
```

Output:

```
Tempo: 89.10290948275862 BPM
```

This code utilizes `librosa.beat.beat_track()` to estimate the tempo of the audio.

Application: Music genre classification.

Example: Determining the tempo of a music track can help classify it into genres. Fast tempos might indicate genres such as rock or dance, while slower tempos could suggest classical or ambient genres.

Chroma features

Chroma features represent the energy distribution of pitch classes (notes) in an audio signal. This can help us identify the musical key or tonal content of a piece of music. Let's calculate the chroma feature for our audio:

```
# Calculate chroma feature
chroma = librosa.feature.chroma_stft(y=y, sr=sr)

# Display the chromagram
plt.figure(figsize=(12, 4))
librosa.display.specshow(chroma, y_axis='chroma', x_axis='time')
plt.title("Chromagram")
plt.colorbar()
plt.show()
```

Here's the output:

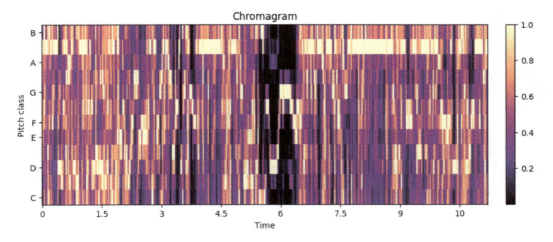

Figure 10.2 –A chromagram

In this code, `librosa.feature.chroma_stft()` is used to compute the chroma feature, and `librosa.display.specshow()` displays it.

Application: Chord recognition in music.

Example: Chroma features represent the 12 different pitch classes. Analyzing chroma features can help identify chords in a musical piece, aiding in tasks such as automatic chord transcription.

Mel-frequency cepstral coefficients (MFCCs)

MFCCs are a widely used feature for audio analysis. It captures the spectral characteristics of an audio signal. In speech and music analysis, MFCCs are commonly used for tasks such as speech recognition. Here's how you can compute and visualize MFCCs:

```
# Calculate MFCC
mfccs = librosa.feature.mfcc(y=y, sr=sr)

# Display the MFCCs
plt.figure(figsize=(12, 4))
librosa.display.specshow(mfccs, x_axis='time')
plt.title("MFCCs")
plt.colorbar()
plt.show()
```

Here is the output:

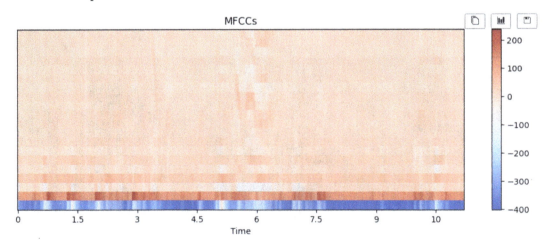

Figure 10.3 – Plotting MFCCs

`librosa.feature.mfcc()` calculates the MFCCs, and `librosa.display.specshow()` displays the MFCCs.

Application: Speech recognition.

Example: Extracting MFCCs from audio signals is common in speech recognition. The unique representation of spectral features in MFCCs helps us identify spoken words or phrases.

Zero-crossing rate

The zero-crossing rate measures how rapidly the signal changes from positive to negative or vice versa. It's often used to characterize noisiness in audio. Here's how you can calculate it:

```
# Calculate zero-crossing rate
zero_crossings_rate = librosa.feature.zero_crossing_rate(y)
plt.figure(figsize=(12, 4))
plt.semilogy(zero_crossings_rate.T)
plt.title("Zero-Crossing Rate")
plt.show()
```

Here is the output:

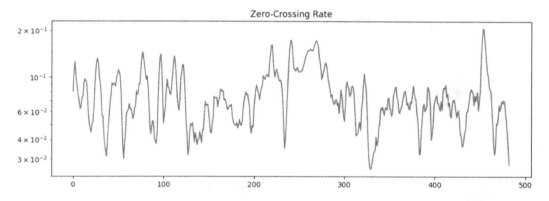

Figure 10.4 – Zero-crossing rate graph plot

In this code, `librosa.feature.zero_crossing_rate()` computes the zero-crossing rate, and we use `plt.semilogy()` to visualize it.

Application: Speech and audio segmentation

Example: The zero-crossing rate is useful for identifying transitions between different sounds. In speech analysis, it can be applied to segment words or phrases.

Spectral contrast

Spectral contrast measures the difference in amplitude between peaks and valleys in the audio spectrum. It can help identify the timbre or texture of the audio signal. Here's how to compute and display it:

```
# Calculate spectral contrast
spectral_contrast = librosa.feature.spectral_contrast(y=y, sr=sr)

# Display the spectral contrast
plt.figure(figsize=(12, 4))
librosa.display.specshow(spectral_contrast, x_axis='time')
plt.title("Spectral Contrast")
plt.colorbar()
plt.show()
```

We get the output as follows:

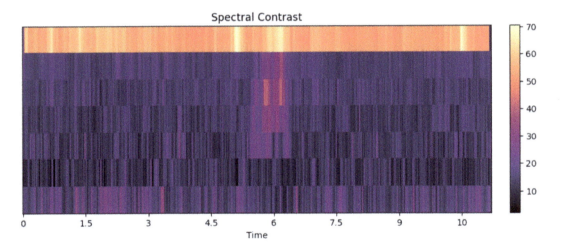

Figure 10.5 – A spectral contrast plot

`librosa.feature.spectral_contrast()` calculates the spectral contrast, and `librosa.display.specshow()` displays it.

In this section, we've explored more audio analysis features with Librosa, including chroma features, MFCCs, tempo estimation, zero-crossing rate, and spectral contrast. These features are essential tools for understanding and characterizing audio data, whether it's for music, speech, or any other sound-related applications.

As you continue your journey into audio data analysis, keep experimenting with these features and combine them to solve interesting problems. Audio analysis can be used in music classification, speech recognition, emotion detection, and much more. Have fun exploring the world of audio data! In the following section, let's dive into the visualization aspect of the audio data.

Application: Environmental sound classification.

Example: Spectral contrast measures the difference in amplitude between peaks and valleys in the spectrum. It can be employed in classifying environmental sounds, distinguishing between, for instance, a bird's chirp and background noise.

Another example where we use a combination of features is emotion recognition in speech. For instance, a blend of tempo, MFCCs, and zero-crossing rate is utilized, leveraging rhythmic patterns, spectral characteristics, and signal abruptness to enhance the identification of emotional states in spoken language.

Considerations for extracting properties

Model training: In real-world applications, these features are often used as input features for machine learning models. The model is trained to recognize patterns in these features based on labeled data.

Multimodal applications: These features can be combined with other modalities (text, image) for multimodal applications such as video content analysis, where audio features complement visual information.

Real-time processing: Some applications require real-time processing, such as voice assistants using MFCCs for speech recognition or music recommendation systems analyzing tempo and chroma features on the fly.

These examples demonstrate the versatility of audio features in various domains, showcasing their significance in tasks ranging from music classification to emotion recognition in speech.

Visualizing audio data with matplotlib and Librosa

Visualizations play a crucial role in understanding and interpreting audio data. Here's a comparison of different types of visualizations for audio data and their uses in various scenarios. The choice of visualization depends on the specific goals of the analysis, the nature of the audio data, and the intended application. Combining multiple visualizations can provide a comprehensive understanding of complex audio signals.

This section demonstrates how to visualize audio data, an essential skill in audio analysis.

Waveform visualization

A waveform is a simple plot that shows how the audio signal changes over time. It's like looking at the ups and downs of the audio as a line graph. In other words, a waveform represents the amplitude of the audio signal over time:

```python
import librosa
import librosa.display
import matplotlib.pyplot as plt

# Load an audio file
audio_file = "sample_audio.wav"
y, sr = librosa.load(audio_file)

# Create a waveform plot
plt.figure(figsize=(12, 4))
librosa.display.waveshow(y, sr=sr)
plt.title("Audio Waveform")
plt.xlabel("Time (s)")
plt.ylabel("Amplitude")
plt.show()
```

In this code, we load an audio file using `librosa.load()`. We create a waveform plot using `librosa.display.waveshow()`. The *x* axis represents time in seconds, and the *y* axis represents the amplitude of the audio signal.

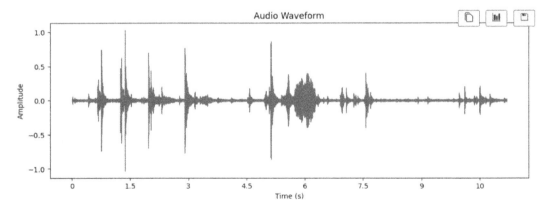

Figure 10.6 – An audio waveform

Use case: General signal overview

Purpose: Provides a visual representation of the audio signal's amplitude changes, useful for general analysis and identifying patterns.

Loudness visualization

To visualize the loudness of an audio signal, you can create a loudness curve, which shows how the loudness changes over time. The loudness curve is essentially a plot of loudness against time. You can use the librosa library to compute loudness and Matplotlib to visualize it. Here's a sample code snippet:

```
import librosa
import librosa.display
import matplotlib.pyplot as plt

# Load an audio file
audio_file = "cat_1.wav"
y, sr = librosa.load(audio_file)

# Calculate loudness using the RMS (Root Mean Square) energy
loudness = librosa.feature.rms(y=y)

# Convert the loudness to dB (decibels)
loudness_db = librosa.power_to_db(loudness)

# Create a loudness curve plot
plt.figure(figsize=(12, 4))
librosa.display.waveshow(loudness_db, sr=sr, x_axis='time')
plt.title("Loudness Curve")
plt.xlabel("Time (s)")
plt.ylabel("Loudness (dB)")
plt.show()
```

In this code, we load an audio file using librosa.load(). We calculate loudness using the RMS energy, which provides a measure of the amplitude or loudness of the audio.

To make the loudness values more interpretable, we convert them to dB using librosa.power_to_db(). We create a loudness curve plot using librosa.display.waveshow(). The x axis represents time in seconds, and the y axis represents loudness in dB.

This loudness curve can help you visualize how the loudness changes over the duration of the audio. It's a valuable tool for understanding the dynamics and intensity of an audio signal.

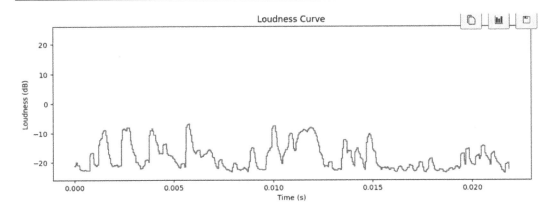

Figure 10.7 – Loudness visualization

Loudness visualization serves as a versatile tool, offering valuable insights and benefits across a spectrum of applications and scenarios.

Scenario: Audio production and mixing.

Purpose: Assists audio engineers in understanding and adjusting the volume levels of different elements within a mix to achieve a balanced and pleasing sound.

Benefits: Enhances the quality and consistency of audio mixes by visualizing loudness dynamics.

Spectrogram visualization

A **spectrogram** is a more advanced visualization that shows how the audio's frequency content changes over time. It's like a heat map, where different colors represent different frequencies:

```
# Generate a spectrogram
spectrogram = librosa.feature.melspectrogram(y=y, sr=sr)
db_spectrogram = librosa.power_to_db(spectrogram, ref=np.max)

# Create a spectrogram plot
# Create a spectrogram plot with the y_axis set to 'hz' for Hertz
plt.figure(figsize=(12, 4))
librosa.display.specshow(db_spectrogram, x_axis='time', y_axis='hz')
plt.title("Spectrogram")
plt.colorbar(format='%+2.0f dB')
plt.show()
```

In this code, we generate a spectrogram using `librosa.feature.melspectrogram()`. We convert the spectrogram to dB for better visualization with `librosa.power_to_db()`. We create a spectrogram plot using `librosa.display.specshow()`. The *x* axis represents time, and the *y* axis represents frequency.

These visualizations help you see the audio data and can reveal patterns and structures in the sound. Waveforms are great for understanding amplitude changes, and spectrograms are excellent for understanding the frequency content, which is particularly useful for tasks such as music analysis, speech recognition, and sound classification.

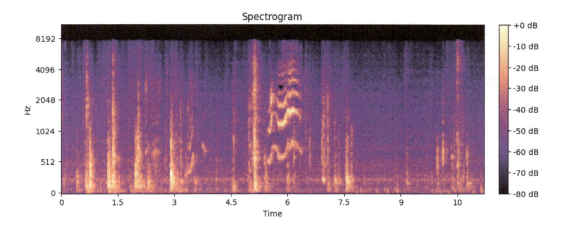

Figure 10.8 – A spectrogram

Scenario: Frequency analysis.

Purpose: Reveals the distribution of frequencies in the signal. Useful for identifying components such as harmonics and analyzing changes in frequency content.

Mel spectrogram visualization

A **mel spectrogram** is a type of spectrogram that uses the **mel scale** to represent frequencies, which closely mimics how humans perceive pitch. It's a powerful tool for audio analysis and is often used in speech and music processing. Let's create a mel spectrogram and visualize it.

The following is a Python code example for generating a mel spectrogram using Librosa, along with an explanation of each step:

```
import librosa
import librosa.display
import matplotlib.pyplot as plt
```

```
# Load an audio file
audio_file = "sample_audio.wav"
y, sr = librosa.load(audio_file)

# Generate a mel spectrogram
spectrogram = librosa.feature.melspectrogram(y, sr=sr)

# Convert the spectrogram to decibels for better visualization
db_spectrogram = librosa.power_to_db(spectrogram, ref=np.max)

# Create a mel spectrogram plot
plt.figure(figsize=(12, 4))
librosa.display.specshow(db_spectrogram, x_axis='time', y_axis='mel')
plt.title("Mel Spectrogram")
plt.colorbar(format='%+2.0f dB')
plt.show()
```

Now, let's break down the code step by step:

1. We load an audio file using `librosa.load()`. Replace `"sample_audio.wav"` with the path to your audio file.

2. We generate a mel spectrogram using `librosa.feature.melspectrogram()`. The mel spectrogram is a representation of how the energy in different frequency bands (in mel scale) evolves over time.

3. To enhance the visualization, we convert the spectrogram to decibels using `librosa.power_to_db()`. This transformation compresses the dynamic range, making it easier to visualize.

4. We create a mel spectrogram plot using `librosa.display.specshow()`. The x axis represents time, the y axis represents the mel frequency bands, and the color indicates the intensity or energy in each band.

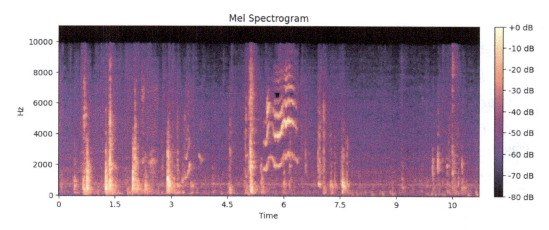

Figure 10.9 – A mel spectrogram

Mel spectrograms are especially valuable in tasks such as speech recognition, music genre classification, and audio scene analysis, as they capture the essence of the acoustic content in a way that's more aligned with human auditory perception.

By visualizing mel spectrograms, you can explore the frequency content and patterns in your audio data, which is crucial for many audio analysis applications.

The key difference between mel (mel frequency) and Hz (hertz) is how they represent frequency, especially in the context of audio and human perception:

- **Hertz (Hz)**: Hertz is the standard unit of measurement for frequency. It represents the number of cycles or vibrations per second. In the context of sound and music, Hertz is used to describe the fundamental frequency of a tone, the pitch of a note, or the frequency content of an audio signal. For example, the A4 note on a piano has a fundamental frequency of 440 Hz.

- **Mel (mel frequency)**: The mel scale is a scale of pitch perception that relates to how humans perceive pitch. It is a nonlinear scale, which means it doesn't represent frequency linearly like Hertz. Instead, it is designed to model how our ears perceive changes in pitch. The mel scale is often used in audio processing and analysis to better match human auditory perception.

In mel frequency, lower values represent smaller perceived changes in pitch, which is useful for speech and music analysis because it corresponds more closely to the way we hear differences in pitch. For example, a change from 100 Hz to 200 Hz in hertz space represents a smaller change in pitch than a change from 1,000 Hz to 1,100 Hz, but in mel space, these changes are more equal.

In audio analysis, the mel scale is often preferred when working with tasks related to human auditory perception, such as speech recognition and music analysis, as it aligns better with how we hear sound. The mel spectrogram is a common representation of audio data that utilizes the mel scale for its frequency bands.

Scenario: Speech and music analysis.

Purpose: Enhances the representation of audio features important for human perception, commonly used in speech and music analysis.

Considerations for visualizations

Multimodal integration: Visualizations can be combined with other modalities (text, image) for multimodal analysis, enhancing the understanding of audio data in various contexts.

Real-time applications: Some visualizations may be more suitable for real-time processing, crucial for applications such as live performance analysis or interactive systems.

Feature extraction: Visualizations often guide the selection of features for machine learning models, helping capture relevant patterns in the data.

User interaction: Interactive visualizations allow users to explore and interact with audio data dynamically, facilitating in-depth analysis.

Ethical implications of audio data

Handling audio data raises several ethical implications and challenges, and it's crucial to address them responsibly. Here are some key considerations:

- **Privacy concerns**:

    Audio surveillance: The collection and processing of audio data, especially in the context of voice recordings or conversations, can pose significant privacy risks. Users should be informed about the purpose of data collection, and explicit consent should be obtained.

    Sensitive information: Audio recordings may unintentionally capture sensitive information such as personal conversations, medical discussions, or confidential details. The careful handling and protection of such data is essential.

- **Informed consent**:

    Clear communication: Individuals should be informed about the collection, storage, and usage of their audio data. Transparency about how the data will be processed and for what purposes is crucial for obtaining informed consent.

    Opt-in mechanisms: Users should have the option to opt into data collection, and they should be able to withdraw their consent at any time.

- **Data security**:

    Storage and transmission: Audio data should be securely stored and transmitted to prevent unauthorized access or data breaches. Encryption and secure data transfer protocols are essential components of data security.

Anonymization: If possible, personal identifiers in audio data should be removed or anonymized to minimize the risk of re-identification.

- **Bias and fairness**:

Training data bias: Bias in training data used for machine learning models can lead to biased outcomes. Care must be taken to ensure diversity and representativeness in the training data to avoid reinforcing existing bias.

Algorithmic fairness: The development and deployment of audio processing algorithms should be guided by principles of fairness, ensuring that the technology does not disproportionately impact certain groups or individuals.

- **Accessibility**:

Ensuring inclusivity: Audio applications and technologies should be designed with inclusivity in mind. Considerations for users with disabilities or special needs should be taken into account.

- **Regulatory compliance**:

Legal requirements: Organizations handling audio data should comply with relevant data protection laws, such as the **General Data Protection Regulation (GDPR)** in the European Union or the **Health Insurance Portability and Accountability Act (HIPAA)** in the United States.

- **Dual-use concerns**:

Potential misuse: Audio technology, if used irresponsibly, has the potential for misuse, such as unauthorized surveillance or eavesdropping. Robust ethical guidelines and legal frameworks are necessary to prevent such abuses.

- **Long-term impact**:

Long-term consequences: The long-term impact of audio data collection and analysis on individuals and societies should be considered. This includes potential societal shifts, changes in behavior, and the evolving nature of privacy expectations.

Addressing these ethical challenges requires a multi-stakeholder approach involving technologists, policymakers, ethicists, and the general public. It is essential to strike a balance between technological advancements and the protection of individual rights and privacy. Ongoing discussions, awareness, and ethical frameworks are crucial in navigating these challenges responsibly.

Recent advances in audio data analysis

Audio data analysis is a rapidly evolving field, and recent developments include advancements in deep learning models, transfer learning, and the application of neural networks to various audio tasks. Here are some advanced topics and models in audio data analysis:

- **Deep learning architectures for audio**:

  WaveNet: Developed by DeepMind, WaveNet is a deep generative model for raw audio waveforms. It has been used for tasks like speech synthesis and has demonstrated the ability to generate high-quality, natural-sounding audio.

  VGGish: Developed by Google, VGGish is a deep convolutional neural network architecture designed for audio classification tasks. It extracts embeddings from audio signals and has been used for tasks such as audio event detection.

  Convolutional Recurrent Neural Network (CRNN): Combining convolutional and recurrent layers, CRNNs are effective for sequential data such as audio. They have been applied to tasks such as music genre classification and speech emotion recognition.

- **Transfer learning in audio analysis**:

  OpenL3: OpenL3 is an open source deep feature extraction library that provides pre-trained embeddings for audio signals. It enables transfer learning for various audio tasks, such as classification and similarity analysis.

  VGGish + LSTM: Combining the VGGish model with a **Long Short-Term Memory** (**LSTM**) network allows for effective transfer learning on audio tasks. This combination leverages both spectral features and sequential information

- **Environmental sound classification**:

  The ESC-50 dataset: This dataset contains 2,000 environmental audio recordings across 50 classes. Advanced models, including deep neural networks, have been applied to this dataset for tasks such as environmental sound classification.

  Detection and Classification of Acoustic Scenes and Events (DCASE): DCASE challenges focus on various audio tasks, including sound event detection and acoustic scene classification. Participants use advanced models to compete on benchmark datasets.

- **Voice synthesis and voice cloning**:

  Tacotron and WaveNet-based models: Tacotron and its variations, along with WaveNet-based vocoders, are used for end-to-end text-to-speech synthesis. These models have significantly improved the quality of synthesized voices.

  Voice cloning with transfer learning: Transfer learning approaches, such as fine-tuning pre-trained models, have been explored for voice cloning tasks. This allows the creation of personalized synthetic voices with limited data.

- **Music generation and style transfer**:

  Magenta Studio: Magenta Studio, an open source research project by Google, explores the intersection of creativity and artificial intelligence. Magenta Studio includes models for music generation, style transfer, and more.

  Generative adversarial networks (GANs) for music: GANs have been applied to music generation, enabling the creation of realistic and novel musical compositions.

- **Speech enhancement and separation**:

  Speech Enhancement Generative Adversarial Network (SEGAN): SEGAN uses GANs for speech enhancement, aiming to remove noise from speech signals while preserving the naturalness of the speech.

  Deep clustering for speech separation: Deep clustering techniques involve training neural networks to separate sources in a mixture, addressing challenges in speech separation and source localization.

- **Multimodal approaches**:

  Audio-visual fusion: Combining audio and visual information has shown promise in tasks such as speech recognition and emotion recognition. Multimodal models leverage both audio and visual cues for improved performance.

  Cross-modal learning: Cross-modal learning involves training models across different modalities (e.g., audio and text) to enhance performance on specific tasks.

These advanced topics and models represent a snapshot of the current state of audio data analysis. As the field continues to evolve, researchers are exploring novel architectures, training techniques, and applications for audio-related tasks.

Troubleshooting common issues during data analysis

Troubleshooting common issues during audio data analysis involves identifying and addressing problems that may arise at various stages of the analysis pipeline. Here are some common issues and guidance on troubleshooting:

- **Data preprocessing issues**:

  Problem: Noisy or inconsistent audio quality.

  Guidance: Check the audio recording conditions and equipment. Consider using noise reduction techniques or applying filters to enhance audio quality. If possible, collect additional high-quality samples.

- **Feature extraction issues**:

  Problem: Extracted features do not capture relevant information.

  Guidance: Review the feature extraction methods. Experiment with different feature representations (e.g., spectrograms, MFCCs) and parameters. Ensure that the chosen features are relevant to the analysis task.

- **Model training issues**:

  Problem: Poor model performance.

  Guidance: Analyze the training data for class imbalance, bias, or insufficient diversity. Experiment with different model architectures, hyperparameters, and optimization algorithms. Monitor loss curves and validation metrics during training.

- **Overfitting or underfitting**:

  Problem: Overfitting (model performs well on training data but poorly on new data) or underfitting (model performs poorly on both training and new data).

  Guidance: Adjust the model complexity and regularization techniques, or collect more diverse training data. Utilize techniques such as dropout, early stopping, and cross-validation to address overfitting.

- **Data labeling issues**:

  Problem: Incorrect or insufficient labels.

  Guidance: Double-check the labeling process. If possible, use multiple annotators for quality control. Consider refining the annotation guidelines or conducting additional labeling to improve the dataset quality.

- **Deployment issues**:

  Problem: Model does not generalize well to new data.

  Guidance: Evaluate the model on diverse test data to ensure generalization. Fine-tune the model on additional relevant data if needed. Consider deploying the model as a part of an ensemble or incorporating transfer learning.

- **Interpreting model decisions**:

  Problem: Lack of model interpretability.

  Guidance: Explore interpretability techniques such as feature importance analysis, layer-wise relevance propagation, or attention mechanisms. Choose models with inherent interpretability or leverage model-agnostic interpretability methods.

- **Computational resources**:

  Problem: Insufficient computing power or memory.

  Guidance: Optimize the model architecture for efficiency. Consider using model quantization, reducing the input size, and utilizing cloud-based services with greater computational resources.

- **Software/library compatibility**:

  Problem: Compatibility issues with audio processing libraries or versions.

  Guidance: Ensure that the software libraries and dependencies are up to date. Check for compatibility issues between different library versions. Refer to documentation or community forums for guidance.

- **Ethical considerations**:

  Problem: Ethical concerns regarding data privacy or bias.

  Guidance: Review the ethical implications of your analysis. Implement privacy-preserving techniques, address biases in the data or model, and consider the broader societal impact of your work.

Remember that troubleshooting can involve a combination of technical expertise, domain knowledge, and iterative experimentation. Additionally, seeking support from relevant communities, forums, or experts can be valuable when encountering challenging issues during audio data analysis.

Troubleshooting common installation issues for audio libraries

Here are some troubleshooting steps for common installation issues related to Librosa and other commonly used audio libraries in Python:

- **Librosa installation issues**: *Missing dependencies*: Librosa relies on several external libraries (such as NumPy, SciPy, and others). Missing dependencies can cause installation issues.

  Troubleshooting steps:

  - **Check dependencies**: Ensure that all required dependencies are installed. You can install them using `pip install numpy scipy numba audioread`.

  - **Install Librosa**: After installing dependencies, try installing Librosa again with `pip install librosa`.

  - **Virtual environment**: If you're using a virtual environment, activate it before installing Librosa.

- **pydub installation issues**: *FFmpeg not found*: pydub requires FFmpeg for audio file conversions.

  Troubleshooting steps:

  - **Install FFmpeg**: Install FFmpeg using the system package manager or download it from the official website.

  - **Set the FFmpeg path**: Add the path to the FFmpeg executable to your system's `PATH` variable.

  - **Install pydub**: After installing FFmpeg, try installing pydub with `pip install pydub`.

- **TorchAudio installation issues**: *PyTorch version mismatch*: TorchAudio compatibility depends on the PyTorch version.

  Troubleshooting steps:

  - **Check the PyTorch version**: Ensure that you have the correct version of PyTorch installed. Check the TorchAudio documentation for compatibility information.

  - **Install TorchAudio**: Install TorchAudio using `pip install torchaudio`.

- **Soundfile installation issues**: *C library missing*: Soundfile relies on the `libsndfile` C library.

  Troubleshooting steps:

  - **Install the C library**: Install the `libsndfile` C library using your system's package manager.

  - **Install Soundfile**: After installing the C library, install Soundfile using `pip install soundfile`.

- **Aubio installation issues**: *Cython dependency*: Aubio requires Cython for compilation.

  Troubleshooting steps:

  - **Install Cython**: Install Cython using `pip install cython`.

  - **Install Aubio**: After installing Cython, install Aubio using `pip install aubio`.

- **General tips**:

  - **Check system requirements**: Ensure that your system meets the requirements specified by each library.

  - **Use virtual environments**: Consider using virtual environments to isolate library installations.

  - **Check the Python version**: Verify that you are using a compatible Python version for the libraries you're installing.

  - **Consult the documentation**: Refer to the documentation of each library for specific installation instructions and troubleshooting tips.

  - **Community forums**: If you encounter persistent issues, check community forums or GitHub repositories for discussions and solutions.

By following these troubleshooting steps and paying attention to library-specific requirements, you can address common installation issues related to audio libraries in Python.

Summary

In this chapter, we have delved into the fundamentals of audio data, including the concept of waveforms, sample rates, and the discrete nature of audio. These fundamentals provide the building blocks for audio analysis. We analyzed the difference between spectrograms and mel spectrograms in audio analysis and visualized how audio signals change over time and how they relate to human perception. Visualization is a powerful way to gain insights into the structure and characteristics of audio. With the knowledge and techniques gained in this chapter, we are better equipped to explore the realms of speech recognition, music classification, and countless other applications where sound takes center stage.

In the next chapter, we will learn how to label audio data using CNNs and speech recognition using the Whisper model and Azure Cognitive Services.

11
Labeling Audio Data

In this chapter, we will embark on this transformative journey through the realms of real-time audio capture, cutting-edge transcription with the Whisper model, and audio classification using a **convolutional neural network** (**CNN**), with a focus on spectrograms. Additionally, we'll explore innovative audio augmentation techniques. This chapter not only equips you with the tools and techniques essential for comprehensive audio data labeling but also unveils the boundless possibilities that lie at the intersection of AI and audio processing, redefining the landscape of audio data labeling.

Welcome to a journey through the intricate world of audio data labeling! In this chapter, we embark on an exploration of cutting-edge techniques and technologies that empower us to unravel the richness of audio content. Our adventure unfolds through a diverse set of topics, each designed to enhance your understanding of audio processing and labeling.

Our journey begins with the dynamic realm of real-time audio capture using microphones. We delve into the art of voice classification, using the random forest classifier to discern and categorize distinct voices in the captured audio.

Then, we introduce the groundbreaking Whisper model, a powerful tool for transcribing uploaded audio data. Witness the seamless integration of the Whisper model with OpenAI for accurate transcriptions, followed by a meticulous labeling process. As we unfold the capabilities of the Whisper model, we draw insightful comparisons with other open source models dedicated to audio data analysis.

Our journey takes a visual turn as we explore the creation of spectrograms, visually capturing the intricate details of sound. The transformative CNNs come into play, elevating audio classification through visual representations. Learn the art of labeling spectrograms, unraveling a new dimension in audio processing.

Prepare to expand your horizons as we venture into the realm of augmented data for audio labeling. Discover the transformative impact of noise augmentation, time-stretching, and pitch-shifting on audio data. Uncover the techniques to enhance the robustness of your labeled audio datasets.

Our exploration culminates in the innovative domain of Azure Cognitive Services. Immerse yourself in the capabilities of Azure to transform speech to text and achieve speech translation. Witness the seamless integration of Azure Cognitive Services, revolutionizing the landscape of audio processing.

We are going to cover the following topics:

- Capturing real-time voice using a microphone and classifying voices using the random forest classifier

- Uploading audio data and transcribing an audio file using OpenAI's Whisper model and then labeling the transcription.

- A comparison of the Whisper model with other open source models for audio data analysis

- Creating a spectrogram for audio data and then labeling the spectrogram, using CNN for audio classification

- Augmenting audio data such as noise augmentation, time-stretching, and pitch-shifting

- Azure Cognitive Services for speech-to-text and speech translation

Technical requirements

We are going to install the following Python libraries.

openai-whisper is the Python library provided by OpenAI, offering access to the powerful Whisper **Automatic Speech Recognition** (**ASR**) model. It allows you to transcribe audio data with state-of-the-art accuracy:

```
%pip install openai-whisper
```

librosa is a Python package for music and audio analysis. It provides tools for various tasks, such as loading audio files, extracting features, and performing transformations, making it a valuable library for audio data processing:

```
%pip install librosa
```

pytube is a lightweight, dependency-free Python library for downloading YouTube videos. It simplifies the process of fetching video content from YouTube, making it suitable for various applications involving YouTube data:

```
%pip install pytube
```

transformers is a popular Python library developed by Hugging Face. It provides pre-trained models and various utilities for **natural language processing** (**NLP**) tasks. This includes transformer-based models such as BERT and GPT:

```
%pip install transformers
```

joblib is a Python library for lightweight pipelining in Python. It is particularly useful for parallelizing and caching computations, making it efficient for tasks involving parallel processing and job scheduling:

```
%pip install joblib
```

Downloading FFmpeg

FFmpeg is a versatile and open source multimedia framework that facilitates the handling, conversion, and manipulation of audio and video files (`https://ffmpeg.org/download.html`).

To download FFmpeg for macOS, select `static FFmpeg binaries for macOS 64-bit` from `https://evermeet.cx/ffmpeg/`. Download `ffmpeg-6.1.1.7z` and extract and copy it to your `<home directory>/<new folder>/bin`. Change **System preferences | Security and privacy| General**, and then select **Open anyway**. Then, double-click the `ffmpeg` executable file.

To download FFmpeg for a Windows OS, select Windows builds by BtbN: `https://github.com/BtbN/FFmpeg-Builds/releases`. Download `ffmpeg-master-latest-win64-gpl.zip`. Extract and set the `path` environment variable of the extracted `ffmpeg` bin folder.

The code for this chapter is available at GitHub here: `https://github.com/PacktPublishing/Data-Labeling-in-Machine-Learning-with-Python/tree/main/code/Ch11`.

Azure Machine Learning

If you want to explore the Whisper model along with other machine learning models available in the Azure Machine Learning model catalog, you can create a free Azure account at `https://azure.microsoft.com/en-us/free`. Then, you can try Azure Machine Learning for free at `https://azure.microsoft.com/en-us/products/machine-learning/`.

Real-time voice classification with Random Forest

In an era marked by the integration of advanced technologies into our daily lives, real-time voice classification systems have emerged as pivotal tools across various domains. The Python script in this section, showcasing the implementation of a real-time voice classification system using the Random Forest classifier from scikit-learn, is a testament to the versatility and significance of such applications.

The primary objective of this script is to harness the power of machine learning to differentiate between positive audio samples, indicative of human speech (voice), and negative samples, representing background noise or non-vocal elements. By employing the Random Forest classifier, a robust and widely used algorithm from the scikit-learn library, the script endeavors to create an efficient model capable of accurately classifying real-time audio input.

The real-world applications of this voice classification system are extensive, ranging from enhancing user experiences in voice-controlled smart devices to enabling automated voice commands in robotics. Industries such as telecommunications, customer service, and security can leverage real-time voice classification to enhance communication systems, automate processes, and bolster security protocols.

Whether it involves voice-activated virtual assistants, hands-free communication in automobiles, or voice-based authentication systems, the ability to classify and understand spoken language in real time is pivotal. This script provides a foundational understanding of the implementation process, laying the groundwork for developers and enthusiasts to integrate similar voice classification mechanisms into their projects and contribute to the evolution of voice-centric applications in the real world.

Let's see the Python script that demonstrates a real-time voice classification system, using the Random Forest classifier from scikit-learn. The goal is to capture audio samples, distinguish between positive samples (voice) and negative samples (background noise or non-voice), and train a model for voice classification.

Let's us see the Python code that provides a simple framework to build a real-time voice classification system, allowing you to collect your own voice samples to train and test the model:

Import the Python libraries: First, let's import the requisite libraries using the following code snippet:

```
import numpy as np
import sounddevice as sd
from sklearn.model_selection import train_test_split
from sklearn.ensemble import RandomForestClassifier
from sklearn.metrics import accuracy_score
```

Capture audio samples: The `capture_audio` function uses the `sounddevice` library to record real-time audio. The user is prompted to speak, and the function captures audio for a specified duration (the default is five seconds):

```
# Function to capture real-time audio
def capture_audio(duration=5, sampling_rate=44100):
    print("Recording...")
    audio_data = sd.rec(int(sampling_rate * duration), \
        samplerate=sampling_rate, channels=1, dtype='int16')
    sd.wait()
    return audio_data.flatten()
```

Collect training data: The `collect_training_data` function gathers training data for voice and non-voice samples. For positive samples (voice), the user is prompted to speak, and audio data is recorded using the `capture_audio` function. For negative samples (background noise or non-voice), the user is prompted to create ambient noise without speaking:

```
# Function to collect training data
def collect_training_data(num_samples=10, label=0):
    X = []
```

```
    y = []

    for _ in range(num_samples):
        input("Press Enter and speak for a few seconds...")
    audio_sample = capture_audio()
    X.append(audio_sample)
    y.append(label)

    return np.vstack(X), np.array(y)

# Main program
class VoiceClassifier:
    def __init__(self):
        self.model = RandomForestClassifier()

    def train(self, X_train, y_train):
        self.model.fit(X_train, y_train)

    def predict(self, X_test):
        return self.model.predict(X_test)

# Collect positive samples (voice)
positive_X, positive_y = collect_training_data(num_samples=10, label=1)

# Collect negative samples (background noise or non-voice)
negative_X, negative_y = collect_training_data(num_samples=10, label=0)
```

Combine and shuffle data: Positive and negative samples are combined into feature vectors (X) and corresponding labels (y). The data is shuffled to ensure a balanced distribution during training:

```
# Combine and shuffle the data
X = np.vstack([positive_X, negative_X])
y = np.concatenate([positive_y, negative_y])
```

Split data into training and testing sets: The data is split into training and testing sets using the train_test_split function from scikit-learn:

```
# Split the data into training and testing sets
X_train, X_test, y_train, y_test = train_test_split(X, y, \
    test_size=0.2, random_state=42)
```

Train the voice classifier: A `VoiceClassifier` class is defined, encapsulating the random forest model. An instance of the `VoiceClassifier` is created, and the model is trained using the positive and negative training data:

```
# Train the voice classifier model
voice_classifier = VoiceClassifier()
voice_classifier.train(X_train, y_train)
```

Make predictions: The trained model predicts labels for the test set:

```
# Make predictions on the test set
predictions = voice_classifier.predict(X_test)
```

Evaluate model accuracy: The accuracy of the model is evaluated using scikit-learn's `accuracy_score` function, comparing predicted labels with actual labels:

```
# Evaluate the model
accuracy = accuracy_score(y_test, predictions)
print(f"Model Accuracy: {accuracy * 100:.2f}%")
```

When you run this code, it prompts with the following pop-up window to enter and speak.

Press Enter and speak for a few seconds... (Press 'Enter' to confirm or 'Escape' to cancel)

Figure 11.1 – Prompt to start speaking

Then, you speak a few sentences that will be recorded:

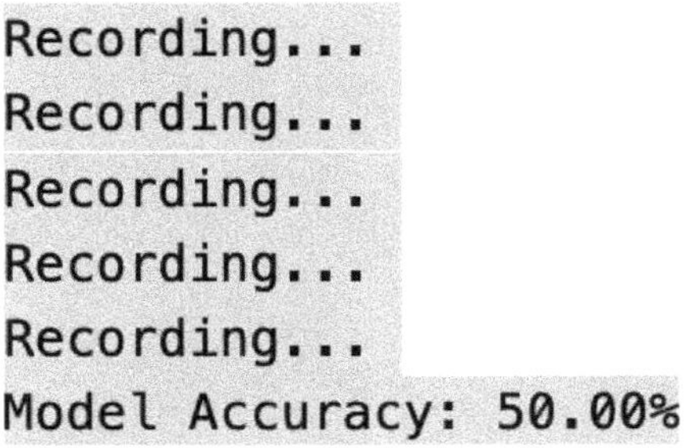

```
Recording...
Recording...
Recording...
Recording...
Recording...
Model Accuracy: 50.00%
```

Figure 11.2 – Trained model accuracy

Inference: Let's see the practical application of a pre-trained voice classification model for real-time voice inference. Leveraging the scikit-learn library's `RandomForestClassifier`, the model was previously trained to discern between positive samples (voice) and negative samples (non-voice or background noise).

The primary objective of this script is to demonstrate the seamless integration of the pre-trained voice classification model into a real-time voice inference system. You are prompted to provide audio input by pressing *Enter* and speaking for a few seconds, after which the model predicts whether the input contains human speech or non-voice elements:

```python
import joblib
# Save the trained model during training
joblib.dump(voice_classifier, "voice_classifier_model.pkl")


import numpy as np
import sounddevice as sd
from sklearn.ensemble import RandomForestClassifier
#from sklearn.externals import joblib # For model persistence


# Load the pre-trained model
voice_classifier = joblib.load("voice_classifier_model.pkl")


# Function to capture real-time audio
def capture_audio(duration=5, sampling_rate=44100):
    print("Recording...")
    audio_data = sd.rec(int(sampling_rate * duration), \
        samplerate=sampling_rate, channels=1, dtype='int16')
    sd.wait()
    return audio_data.flatten()


# Function to predict voice using the trained model
def predict_voice(audio_sample):
    prediction = voice_classifier.predict([audio_sample])
    return prediction[0]


# Main program for real-time voice classification
def real_time_voice_classification():
    while True:
        input("Press Enter and speak for a few seconds...")

        # Capture new audio
        new_audio_sample = capture_audio()

        # Predict if it's voice or non-voice
        result = predict_voice(new_audio_sample)

        if result == 1:
            print("Voice detected!")
        else:
```

```
        print("Non-voice detected.")

if __name__ == "__main__":
    real_time_voice_classification()
```

The output is as follows:

```
Recording...
Voice detected!
```

Figure 11.3 – Inference output

In a similar manner, we can use this model to label a voice as male or female to analyze customer calls and understand target customers.

We have seen the real-time voice classification inference that holds significant relevance in numerous scenarios, including voice-activated applications, security systems, and communication devices. By loading a pre-trained model, users can experience the instantaneous and accurate classification of voice in real-world situations.

Whether applied to enhance accessibility features, automate voice commands, or implement voice-based security protocols, this script serves as a practical example of deploying machine learning models for voice classification in real-time scenarios. As technology continues to advance, the seamless integration of voice inference models contributes to the evolution of user-friendly and responsive applications across various domains.

Now, let's see how to transcribe audio using the OpenAI Whisper model.

Transcribing audio using the OpenAI Whisper model

In this section, we are going to see how to transcribe audio file to text using the **OpenAI Whisper** model and then label the audio transcription using the OpenAI **large language model** (**LLM**).

Whisper is an open source ASR model developed by OpenAI. It is trained on nearly 700,000 hours of multilingual speech data and is capable of transcribing audio to text in almost 100 different languages. According to OpenAI, Whisper "approaches human level robustness and accuracy on English speech recognition."

In a recent benchmark study, Whisper was compared to other open source ASR models, such as wav2vec 2.0 and Kaldi. The study found that Whisper performed better than wav2vec 2.0 in terms of accuracy and speed across five different use cases, including conversational AI, phone calls, meetings, videos, and earnings calls.

Whisper is also known for its affordability, accuracy, and features. It is best suited for audio-to-text use cases and is not well-suited for text-to-audio or speech synthesis tasks.

The Whisper model can be imported as a Python library. The other option is to use the Whisper model available in the model catalog at **Azure Machine Learning studio**.

Let's see the process of transcribing audio using the OpenAI Whisper ASR using the Python library now. It's crucial to ensure the existence and accessibility of the specified audio file for successful transcription. The transcribed text is likely stored in `text['text']`, as indicated by the `print` statement.

First, we need to install the whisper model, as mentioned in the *technical requirements* section. Then, we import the OpenAI Whisper model.

Step 1 – importing the Whisper model

Let us import the required Python libraries:

```
import whisper
Import pytube
```

The `whisper` library is imported, which is the library providing access to the OpenAI Whisper ASR model. The `pytube` library is imported to download YouTube videos.

Step 2 – loading the base Whisper model

Let us load the base Whisper model:

```
model = whisper.load_model("base")
```

The Whisper model is loaded using the `whisper.load_model` function with the `"base"` argument. This loads the base version of the Whisper ASR model.

Let us download the audio stream from a YouTube video. Even though we are using a video file, we are only focusing on the audio of the YouTube video and downloading an audio stream from it. Alternatively, you can directly use any audio file:

```
#we are importing Pytube library
import pytube
#we are downloading YouTube video from YouTube link
video = "https://youtu.be/g8Q452PEXwY"
data = pytube.YouTube(video)
```

The YouTube video URL is specified. Using the `pytube.YouTube` class, the video data is fetched:

```
# Converting and downloading as 'MP4' file
audio = data.streams.get_audio_only()
audio.download()
```

This code utilizes the `pytube` library to download the audio stream from a video hosted on a platform such as YouTube. Let's examine the preceding code snippet:

- `audio = data.streams.get_audio_only()`: This line fetches the audio stream of the video. It uses the `get_audio_only()` method to obtain a stream containing only the audio content.

- `audio.download()`: Once the audio stream is obtained, this line downloads the audio content. The download is performed in the default format, which is typically an MP4 file containing only the audio data.

In summary, the code extracts the audio stream from a video and downloads it as an MP4 file, preserving only the audio content.

Step 3 – setting up FFmpeg

Whisper is designed to transcribe audio, but it requires a specific format for processing. The format required by Whisper for processing audio is WAV format. Whisper is designed to transcribe audio in WAV format, and it may not directly support other formats. Therefore, audio data that needs to be processed by Whisper should be provided in the WAV format. FFmpeg acts as a bridge by converting various audio formats (such as MP3, WAV, or AAC) into a format that Whisper can handle.

For example, if the input is in the MP3 format, FFmpeg can convert it to a format suitable for Whisper. Whisper typically requires audio data in WAV format, so FFmpeg can convert the input MP3 file to WAV during the process. This conversion allows the audio data to be in a format compatible with the requirements of the Whisper model.

Without this conversion, Whisper wouldn't be able to process the audio effectively.

In scenarios where real-time transcription is needed (such as streaming a **real-time messaging protocol** (**RTMP**) feed), FFmpeg helps segment the audio stream. It splits the continuous audio into smaller chunks (e.g., 30-second segments) that can be processed individually. Each segment is then passed to Whisper for transcription:

```
# Set the FFMPEG environment variable to the path of your ffmpeg
executable
os.environ['PATH'] = '/<your_path>/audio-orchestrator-ffmpeg/bin:' +
os.environ['PATH']
```

The code sets the FFmpeg environment variable to the path of the `ffmpeg` executable. This is necessary for handling audio and video files.

Step 4 – transcribing the YouTube audio using the Whisper model

Now, let's transcribe the YouTube audio using the Whisper model:

```
model = whisper.load_model('base')
text = model.transcribe('Mel Spectrograms with Python and Librosa
Audio Feature Extraction.mp4')
#printing the transcribe
text['text']
```

Here's the output:

```
" Hello, in this video we'll go over an important audio feature to extract, called Mel Spectrum
```

Figure 11.4 – A snippet of the code output

The Whisper model is loaded again to ensure that it uses the base model. The transcribe function is called on the model with the filename of the audio file as an argument. The resulting transcribed text is printed using `text['text']`.

> **Note**
> The provided filename in `model.transcribe` is `Mel Spectrograms with Python and Librosa Audio Feature Extraction.mp4`. Make sure this file exists and is accessible for the code to transcribe successfully.

Now, let's see another code example on how to transcribe an audio file to text:

```
model = whisper.load_model('base')
text = model.transcribe('/Users/<username>/PacktPublishing/
DataLabeling/Ch11/customer_call_audio.m4a')
#printing the transcribe
text['text']
```

Here is the output:

```
' Hello, I have not received the product yet. I am very disappointed.
Are you going to replace if my product is damaged or missed? I will be
happy if you replace with your product in case I miss the product due
to incorrect shipping address.'
```

Now, let's perform sentiment analysis to label this text transcribed from a customer call.

Classifying a transcription using Hugging Face transformers

Now, let's use Hugging Face transformers to classify the output text from the previous customer call audio transcription and perform sentiment analysis to label it.

The following code snippet utilizes Hugging Face's transformers library to perform sentiment analysis on a given text. It begins by importing the necessary module, and then it loads a pre-trained sentiment analysis pipeline from Hugging Face's transformers. The code defines an example text that expresses dissatisfaction with a product not yet received. Subsequently, the sentiment analysis pipeline is applied to classify the sentiment of the text, and the result is displayed by printing it to the console. The sentiment analysis model outputs a label indicating the sentiment, such as positive or negative, along with a confidence score.

Let's import the Python library:

```
from transformers import pipeline

# Load the sentiment analysis pipeline
sentiment_classifier = pipeline('sentiment-analysis')

# text for sentiment analysis

text="Hello, I have not received the product yet. I am very
disappointed.are you going to replace if my product is damaged or
missed.I will be happy if you replace with new product incase i missed
the product die to incorrect shipping address"

# Perform sentiment analysis
result = sentiment_classifier(text)

# Display the result
print(result)
```

Here is the output:

```
No model was supplied, defaulted to distilbert-base-uncased-finetuned-
sst-2-english and revision af0f99b (https://huggingface.co/distilbert-
base-uncased-finetuned-sst-2-english). Using a pipeline without
specifying a model name and revision in production is not recommended.
[{'label': 'NEGATIVE', 'score': 0.9992625117301941}]
```

Hands-on – labeling audio data using a CNN

In this section, we will see how to train the CNN network on audio data and use it to label the audio data.

The following code demonstrates the process of labeling audio data using a CNN. The code outlines how to employ a CNN to label audio data, specifically training the model on a dataset of cat and dog audio samples. The goal is to classify new, unseen audio data as either a cat or a dog. Let's take the cat and dog sample audio data and train the CNN model. Then, we will send new unseen data to the model to predict whether it is a cat or a dog:

1. **Load and pre-process the data**: The audio data for cats and dogs is loaded from the specified folder structure using the `load_and_preprocess_data` function. The `load_and_preprocess_data` function processes the audio data, converting it into mel spectrograms and resizing them for model compatibility.

2. **Split data into training and testing sets**: The loaded and pre-processed data is split into training and testing sets using `train_test_split`, and labels are converted to one-hot encoding.

3. **Create a neural network model**: A CNN model is created using TensorFlow and Keras, comprising convolutional layers, pooling layers, and fully connected layers.

4. **Compile the model**: The model is compiled with an Adam optimizer, categorical cross-entropy loss, and accuracy as the evaluation metric.

5. **Train the model**: The CNN model is trained on the training data for a specified number of epochs.

6. **Evaluate the accuracy of the model**: The accuracy of the trained model is evaluated on the testing set.

7. **Save the trained model**: The trained model is saved for future use.

8. **Test the new audio file**: Finally, the saved model is loaded, and a new audio file (in this case, a cat meow) is processed and classified, with class probabilities and accuracy displayed for each class.

In summary, this code provides a comprehensive guide on using a CNN to label audio data, from data loading and preprocessing to model training, evaluation, and prediction on new audio samples.

Let's import all the required Python modules as the first step:

```
import os
import librosa
import numpy as np
import tensorflow as tf
from tensorflow.keras.layers import Input, Conv2D, MaxPooling2D,
Flatten, Dense
from tensorflow.keras.models import Model
from tensorflow.keras.optimizers import Adam
from sklearn.model_selection import train_test_split
from tensorflow.keras.utils import to_categorical
from tensorflow.image import resize
from tensorflow.keras.models import load_model
```

Step 1: Load and preprocess data: Now, let's load and pre-process the data for cats and dogs. The source of this dataset is https://www.kaggle.com/datasets/mmoreaux/audio-cats-and-dogs:

```
# Define your folder structure
data_dir = '../cats_dogs/data/'
classes = ['cat', 'dog']
```

This code establishes the folder structure for a dataset containing the 'cat' and 'dog', categories, with the data located at the specified directory, '../cats_dogs/data/'. Next, let's pre-process the data:

```
# define the function for Load and preprocess audio data
def load_and_preprocess_data(data_dir, classes, target_shape=(128,
128)):
data = []
labels = []
for i, class_name in enumerate(classes):
    class_dir = os.path.join(data_dir, class_name)
    for filename in os.listdir(class_dir):
        if filename.endswith('.wav'):
            file_path = os.path.join(class_dir, filename)
            audio_data, sample_rate = librosa.load(file_path, sr=None)
            # Perform preprocessing (e.g., convert to Mel spectrogram
and resize)
            mel_spectrogram = \
                librosa.feature.melspectrogram( \
                    y=audio_data, sr=sample_rate)
            mel_spectrogram = resize( \
                np.expand_dims(mel_spectrogram, axis=-1), \
                target_shape)
            print(mel_spectrogram)
            data.append(mel_spectrogram)
        labels.append(i)
return np.array(data), np.array(labels)
```

This code defines a function named load_and_preprocess_data that loads and preprocesses audio data from a specified directory. It iterates through each class of audio, reads .wav files, and uses the Librosa library to convert the audio data into a mel spectrogram. We learned about the mel spectrogram in *Chapter 10* in the *Visualizing audio data with Matplotlib and Librosa – spectrogram visualization* section.

The mel spectrogram is then resized to a target shape (128x128) before being appended to the data list, along with the corresponding class labels. The function returns the preprocessed data and labels as NumPy arrays.

Step 2: Split data into training and testing sets: This code segment divides the preprocessed audio data and corresponding labels into training and testing sets. It utilizes the `load_and_preprocess_data` function to load and preprocess the data. The labels are then converted into one-hot encoding using the `to_categorical` function. Finally, the data is split into training and testing sets with an 80–20 ratio using the `train_test_split` function, ensuring reproducibility with a specified random seed:

```
# Split data into training and testing sets
data, labels = load_and_preprocess_data(data_dir, classes)
labels = to_categorical(labels, num_classes=len(classes)) # Convert
labels to one-hot encoding
X_train, X_test, y_train, y_test = train_test_split(data, \
    labels, test_size=0.2, random_state=42)
```

Step 3: Create a neural network model: This code defines a neural network model for audio classification. The model architecture includes convolutional layers with max pooling for feature extraction, followed by a flattening layer. Subsequently, there is a dense layer with ReLU activation for further feature processing. The final output layer utilizes softmax activation to produce class probabilities. The model is constructed using the Keras functional API, specifying the input and output layers, and is ready to be trained on the provided data:

```
# Create a neural network model
input_shape = X_train[0].shape
input_layer = Input(shape=input_shape)
x = Conv2D(32, (3, 3), activation='relu')(input_layer)
x = MaxPooling2D((2, 2))(x)
x = Conv2D(64, (3, 3), activation='relu')(x)
x = MaxPooling2D((2, 2))(x)
x = Flatten()(x)
x = Dense(64, activation='relu')(x)
output_layer = Dense(len(classes), activation='softmax')(x)
model = Model(input_layer, output_layer)
```

Step 4: Compile the model: This code compiles the previously defined neural network model using the Adam optimizer, with a learning rate of `0.001`, categorical cross-entropy as the loss function (suitable for multi-class classification), and accuracy as the evaluation metric. The `model.summary()` command provides a concise overview of the model's architecture, including the number of parameters and the structure of each layer:

```
# Compile the model
model.compile(optimizer=Adam(learning_rate=0.001), \
    loss='categorical_crossentropy', metrics=['accuracy'])

model.summary()
```

Here is the output:

Layer (type)	Output Shape	Param #
input_1 (InputLayer)	[(None, 128, 128, 1)]	0
conv2d (Conv2D)	(None, 126, 126, 32)	320
max_pooling2d (MaxPooling2 D)	(None, 63, 63, 32)	0
conv2d_1 (Conv2D)	(None, 61, 61, 64)	18496
max_pooling2d_1 (MaxPoolin g2D)	(None, 30, 30, 64)	0
flatten (Flatten)	(None, 57600)	0
dense (Dense)	(None, 64)	3686464
dense_1 (Dense)	(None, 2)	130

```
Total params: 3705410 (14.14 MB)
Trainable params: 3705410 (14.14 MB)
Non-trainable params: 0 (0.00 Byte)
```

Figure 11.5 – Model summary

Step 5: Train the model: This code initiates the training of the neural network model using the training data (X_train and y_train) for 20 epochs, with a batch size of 32. The validation data (X_test and y_test) is used to evaluate the model's performance during training:

```
# Train the model
model.fit(X_train, y_train, epochs=20, batch_size=32, \
    validation_data=(X_test, y_test))
```

Step 6: Test the accuracy of the model: After training completion, it calculates the test accuracy of the model on the separate test set and prints the accuracy score, providing insights into the model's effectiveness in classifying audio data:

```
#Test  the accuracy of model
test_accuracy=model.evaluate(X_test,y_test,verbose=0)
print(test_accuracy[1])
```

Here is the output:

0.9464285969734192

Figure 11.6 – Accuracy of the model

Step 7: Save the trained model:

```
# Save the model
model.save('audio_classification_model.h5')
```

Step 8: Test the new audio file: Let's classify the new audio file and label it using this saved model:

```
# Load the saved model
model = load_model('audio_classification_model.h5')

# Define the target shape for input spectrograms
target_shape = (128, 128)

# Define your class labels
classes = ['cat', 'dog']

# Function to preprocess and classify an audio file
def test_audio(file_path, model):
# Load and preprocess the audio file
audio_data, sample_rate = librosa.load(file_path, sr=None)
mel_spectrogram = librosa.feature.melspectrogram( \
    y=audio_data, sr=sample_rate)
mel_spectrogram = resize(np.expand_dims(mel_spectrogram, \
    axis=-1), target_shape)
mel_spectrogram = tf.reshape(mel_spectrogram, (1,) + target_shape +
(1,))
```

This code defines a function, test_audio, to preprocess and classify an audio file. It loads and preprocesses the audio data from the specified file path using Librosa, generating a mel spectrogram. The spectrogram is then resized and reshaped to match the input dimensions expected by the model. This function is designed to prepare audio data for classification using a neural network model, providing a streamlined way to apply the trained model to new audio files for prediction.

Now, let's make **predictions**. In this code segment, predictions are made using the trained neural network model on a specific audio file (./cat-meow-14536.mp3). The test_audio function is employed to preprocess the audio file and obtain class probabilities and the predicted class index.

The model.predict method generates predictions, and the class probabilities are extracted from the result. The predicted class index is determined by identifying the class with the highest probability. This process demonstrates how the trained model can be utilized to classify new audio data, providing insights into the content of the tested audio file:

```
# Make predictions
predictions = model.predict(mel_spectrogram)
# Get the class probabilities
class_probabilities = predictions[0]
# Get the predicted class index
predicted_class_index = np.argmax(class_probabilities)
return class_probabilities, predicted_class_index

# Test an audio filetest_audio_file = '../Ch10/cat-meow-14536.mp3'
class_probabilities, predicted_class_index = test_audio( \
    test_audio_file, model)
```

The following code snippet iterates through all the classes in the model and prints the predicted probabilities for each class, based on the audio file classification. For each class, it displays the class label and its corresponding probability, providing a comprehensive view of the model's confidence in assigning the audio file to each specific category:

```
# Display results for all classes
for i, class_label in enumerate(classes):
    probability = class_probabilities[i]
    print(f'Class: {class_label}, Probability: {probability:.4f}')
```

The following code calculates and reveals the predicted class and accuracy of the audio file classification. It identifies the predicted class using the index with the highest probability, retrieves the corresponding class label and accuracy from the results, and then prints the predicted class along with its associated accuracy. This provides a concise summary of the model's prediction for the given audio file and the confidence level associated with the classification. Calculate and display the predicted class and accuracy:

```
predicted_class = classes[predicted_class_index]
accuracy = class_probabilities[predicted_class_index]
print(f'The audio is labeled Spectrogram Visualization
as: {predicted_class}')
print(f'Accuracy: {accuracy:.4f}')
```

This is the output we get:

```
Class: cat, Probability: 0.5721
Class: dog, Probability: 0.4279
The audio is labeled as: cat
Accuracy: 0.5721
```

Figure 11.7 – Output showing probabilities and accuracy of the model

We have seen how to transcribe audio data using machine learning. Now, let's see how to do audio data augmentation and train a model with augmented data. Finally, we will see and compare the accuracy with and without augmented data.

Exploring audio data augmentation

Let's see how to manipulate audio data by adding noise, using NumPy.

Adding noise to audio data during training helps the model become more robust in real-world scenarios, where there might be background noise or interference. By exposing a model to a variety of noisy conditions, it learns to generalize better.

Augmenting audio data with noise prevents a model from memorizing specific patterns in the training data. This encourages the model to focus on more general features, which can lead to better generalization on unseen data:

```
import numpy as np
def add_noise(data, noise_factor):
    noise = np.random.randn(len(data))
    augmented_data = data + noise_factor * noise
    # Cast back to same data type
    augmented_data = augmented_data.astype(type(data[0]))
    return augmented_data
```

This code defines a function named add_noise that adds random noise to an input data array. The level of noise is controlled by the noise_factor parameter. The function generates random noise using NumPy, adds it to the original data, and then returns the augmented data. To ensure the data type consistency, the augmented data is cast back to the same type as the elements in the original data array. This function can be used for data augmentation, a technique commonly employed in machine learning to enhance model robustness by introducing variations in the training data.

Let's test this function using sample audio data, as follows:

```
# Sample audio data
sample_data = np.array([0.1, 0.2, 0.3, 0.4, 0.5])

# Sample noise factor
```

```
sample_noise_factor = 0.05

# Apply augmentation
augmented_data = add_noise(sample_data, sample_noise_factor)

# Print the original and augmented data
print("Original Data:", sample_data)
print("Augmented Data:", augmented_data)
```

Here is the output:

```
Original Data: [0.1 0.2 0.3 0.4 0.5]
Augmented Data: [0.10100212 0.27209387 0.24770854 0.38437647 0.42163954]
```

Figure 11.8 – Representation of the augmented data

Now, let's retrain our CNN model using data augmentation for the classification of dogs and cats sounds that we saw in the *Hands-on – labeling audio data using a CNN* section:

```
# Load and preprocess audio data
def load_and_preprocess_data(data_dir, classes, target_shape=(128,
128)):
    data = []
    labels = []
    noise_factor = 0.05
    for i, class_name in enumerate(classes):
    class_dir = os.path.join(data_dir, class_name)
    for filename in os.listdir(class_dir):
    if filename.endswith('.wav'):
    file_path = os.path.join(class_dir, filename)
    audio_data, sample_rate = librosa.load(file_path, sr=None)
    # Apply noise manipulation
    noise = np.random.randn(len(audio_data))
    augmented_data = audio_data + noise_factor * noise
    augmented_data = augmented_data.astype(type(audio_data[0]))

    # Perform preprocessing (e.g., convert to Mel spectrogram and
resize)
    mel_spectrogram = librosa.feature.melspectrogram( \
        y=augmented_data, sr=sample_rate)
    mel_spectrogram = resize( \
        np.expand_dims(mel_spectrogram, axis=-1), target_shape)
    print(mel_spectrogram)
    data.append(mel_spectrogram)
```

```
        labels.append(i)
    return np.array(data), np.array(labels)
```

In this code, we introduced data augmentation by adding random noise (`noise_factor *
noise`) to the audio data before spectrogram conversion. This helps improve the model's robustness
by exposing it to varied instances of the same class during training:

```
test_accuracy=model.evaluate(X_test,y_test,verbose=0)
print(test_accuracy[1])
```

Here is the output:

0.9642857313156128

Figure 11.9 – Accuracy of the model

By using this noise-augmented audio data, the model accuracy increased from 0.946 to 0.964.
Depending on the data, we can apply data augmentation and test the accuracy to decide whether
data augmentation is required.

Let's see three more data augmentation techniques applied to an original audio file – time-stretching,
pitch-shifting, and dynamic range compression.

The following Python script employs the librosa library for audio processing, loading an initial audio
file that serves as the baseline for augmentation. Subsequently, functions are defined to apply each
augmentation technique independently. Time-stretching alters the temporal duration of the audio,
pitch-shifting modifies the pitch without affecting speed, and dynamic range compression adjusts
the volume dynamics.

The augmented waveforms are visually presented side by side with the original waveform using Matplotlib.
This visualization aids in understanding the transformative impact of each augmentation technique on
the audio data. Through this script, you will gain insights into the practical implementation of audio
augmentation, a valuable practice for creating diverse and robust datasets for machine learning models.

As audio data labeling becomes increasingly integral to various applications, mastering the art of
augmentation ensures the generation of comprehensive datasets, thereby enhancing the effectiveness of
machine learning models. Whether applied to speech recognition, sound classification, or voice-enabled
applications, audio augmentation is a powerful technique for refining and enriching audio datasets:

```
import librosa
import librosa.display
import numpy as np
import matplotlib.pyplot as plt
from scipy.io.wavfile import write
```

```
# Load the audio file
audio_file_path = "../ch10/cats_dogs/cat_1.wav"
y, sr = librosa.load(audio_file_path)

# Function for time stretching augmentation
def time_stretching(y, rate):
    return librosa.effects.time_stretch(y, rate=rate)

# Function for pitch shifting augmentation
def pitch_shifting(y, sr, pitch_factor):
    return librosa.effects.pitch_shift(y, sr=sr, n_steps=pitch_factor)

# Function for dynamic range compression augmentation
def dynamic_range_compression(y, compression_factor):
    return y * compression_factor

# Apply dynamic range compression augmentation
compression_factor = 0.5 # Adjust as needed
y_compressed = dynamic_range_compression(y, compression_factor)

# Apply time stretching augmentation
y_stretched = time_stretching(y, rate=1.5)

# Apply pitch shifting augmentation
y_pitch_shifted = pitch_shifting(y, sr=sr, pitch_factor=3)

# Display the original and augmented waveforms
plt.figure(figsize=(12, 8))

plt.subplot(4, 1, 1)
librosa.display.waveshow(y, sr=sr)
plt.title('Original Waveform')

plt.subplot(4, 1, 2)
librosa.display.waveshow(y_stretched, sr=sr)
plt.title('Time Stretched Waveform')

plt.subplot(4, 1, 3)
librosa.display.waveshow(y_pitch_shifted, sr=sr)
plt.title('Pitch Shifted Waveform')
```

```
plt.subplot(4, 1, 4)
librosa.display.waveshow(y_compressed, sr=sr)
plt.title('Dynamic Range Compressed Waveform')

plt.tight_layout()
plt.show()
```

Here is the output:

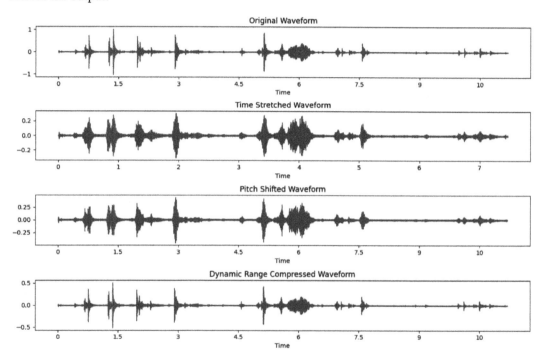

Figure 11.10 – Data augmentation techniques – time stretching,
pitch shifting, and dynamic range compression

Now, let's move on to another interesting topic in labeling audio data in the next section.

Introducing Azure Cognitive Services – the speech service

Azure Cognitive Services offers a comprehensive set of speech-related services that empower developers to integrate powerful speech capabilities into their applications. Some key speech services available in Azure AI include the following:

- **Speech-to-text (speech recognition)**: This converts spoken language into written text, enabling applications to transcribe audio content such as voice commands, interviews, or conversations.

- **Speech Translation**: This translates spoken language into another language in real time, facilitating multilingual communication. This service is valuable for applications requiring language translation for global audiences.

These Azure Cognitive Services speech capabilities cater to a diverse range of applications, from accessibility features and voice-enabled applications to multilingual communication and personalized user experiences. Developers can leverage these services to enhance the functionality and accessibility of their applications through seamless integration of speech-related features.

Creating an Azure Speech service

Let's create a speech service using the Azure portal, as follows.

Go to the Azure portal at `https://portal.azure.com`, search for `speech service`, and then create a new service.

As shown in the following screenshot, enter the project details such as your resource group speech service name and region details. Then, click on the **Review + create** button to create a speech service in an Azure environment.

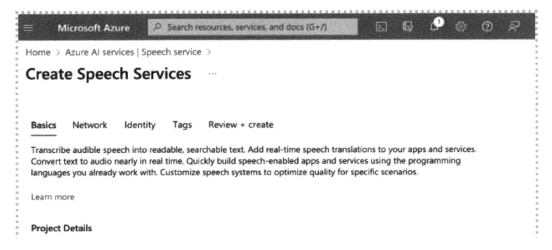

Figure 11.11 – Create Speech Services

Now, your Azure speech service is deployed, and you can go to that speech service resource by clicking on the **Go to resource** button on the deployment screen. Then, on the speech service resource screen, click on **Go to speech studio**. In **Speech Studio**, you can see various services for captioning with speech to text, post call transcription and analytics, and a live chat avatar, as shown in the following screenshot.

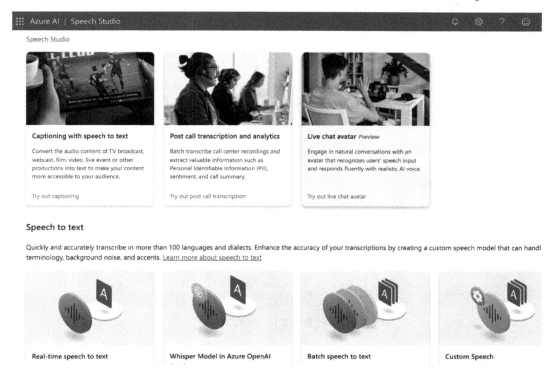

Figure 11.12 – Speech Studio

Speech to text

Now, let's try to use the speech to text service. As shown in the following screenshot, you can drag and drop an audio file or upload it, and record audio with microphone. You can see the corresponding **Text** or **JSON** tabs on the right-side window for the uploaded audio file, as shown in the following screenshot.

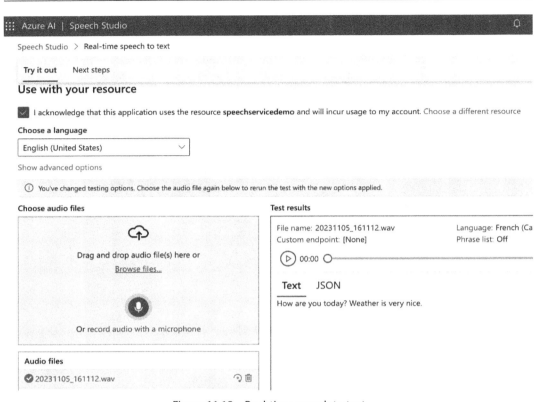

Figure 11.13 – Real-time speech to text

Speech translation

Now, let's see how to translate the speech. On the following screen, we are translating from English to French. Let's choose a spoken language and a target language.

Then, speak in English and record the audio with a microphone. The translated text in French is shown on the right side of the window, as shown in the following screenshot.

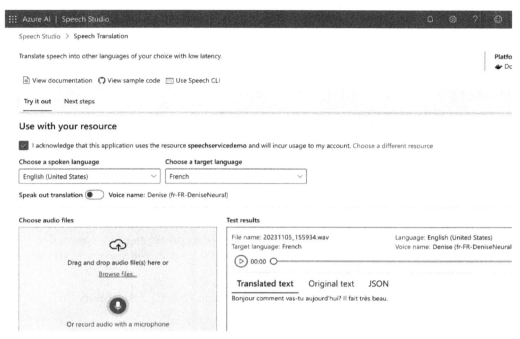

Figure 11.14 – Translated text test results

We can also see the original text on the **Original text** tab, as shown in the following screenshot:

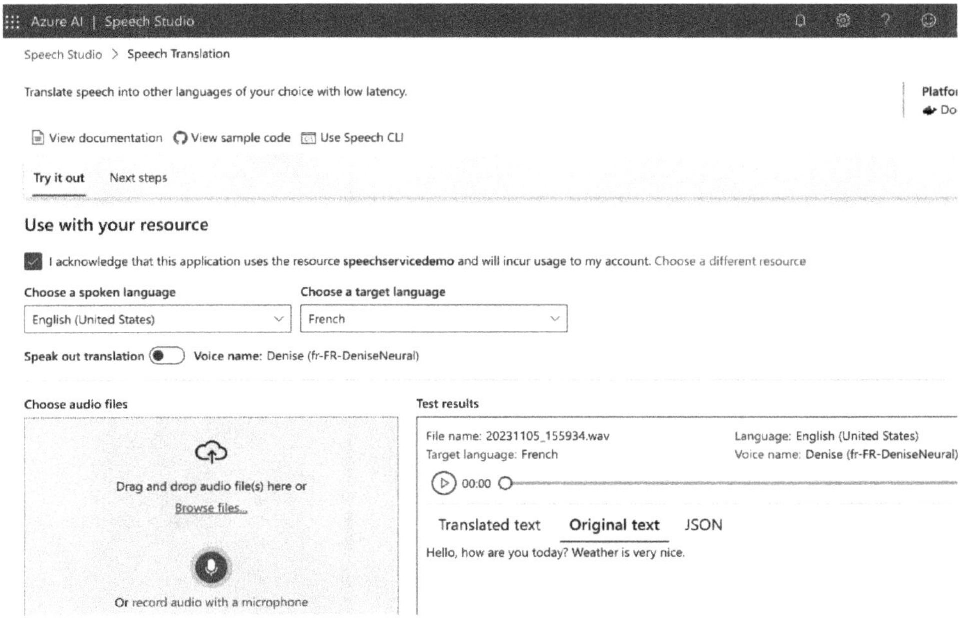

Figure 11.15 – Original text in test results

We have seen how to transcribe from speech to text and translate from English to French using Azure speech services. Aside from this, there are many other Azure speech services in Azure Speech Studio that you can apply, based on your requirements.

Summary

In this chapter, we explored three key sections that delve into the comprehensive process of handling audio data. The journey began with the upload of audio data, leveraging the Whisper model for transcription, and subsequently labeling the transcriptions using OpenAI. Following this, we ventured into the creation of spectrograms and employed CNNs to label these visual representations, unraveling the intricate details of sound through advanced neural network architectures. The chapter then delved into audio labeling with augmented data, thereby enhancing the dataset for improved model training. Finally, we saw the Azure Speech service for speech to text and speech translation. This multifaceted approach equips you with a holistic understanding of audio data processing, from transcription to visual representation analysis and augmented labeling, fostering a comprehensive skill set in audio data labeling techniques.

In the next and final chapter, we will explore different hands-on tools for data labeling.

12

Hands-On Exploring Data Labeling Tools

In the dynamic landscape of machine learning and artificial intelligence, effective data annotation plays a pivotal role in enhancing model performance and fostering accurate predictions. As we delve into the intricacies of image, text, video, and audio annotation, we find ourselves immersed in the realm of the **Azure Machine Learning** service and its robust **data labeling** capabilities. This chapter serves as a comprehensive guide to leveraging Azure Machine Learning data labeling tools to create precise and meaningful annotations.

We will also look at another open source data labeling tool, **Label Studio**, for annotating image, video, and text data. Label Studio empowers data scientists, developers, and domain experts to collaboratively annotate various data types such as images, video, and text.

We also see how to annotate data using **pyOpenAnnotate**, and finally, we will explore **Computer Vision Annotation Tool (CVAT)**, an open source, collaborative data labeling platform for streamlining the annotation process across various data types.

We will cover the following topics in this chapter:

- Labeling image, text, and audio data using Azure Machine Learning
- Labeling image, video, and text data using Label Studio
- Labeling image and video data using pyOpenAnnotate and CVAT

Join us as we navigate the intricacies of data labeling with Azure Machine Learning, empowering you to harness the full potential of annotated datasets and propel your machine learning endeavors to new heights.

Technical requirements

Let's understand the prerequisites needed for each tool we'll discuss for you to follow along in this chapter.

Azure Machine Learning data labeling

Azure Machine Learning provides labeling tools to rapidly prepare data for machine learning projects. Let's create an Azure subscription and Azure Machine Learning workspace as follows:

- **Azure subscription**: You can create a free Azure subscription at `https://azure.microsoft.com/en-us/free`.

- **Azure Machine Learning workspace**: Once your Azure subscription is ready, you can create an Azure Machine Learning workspace in that subscription.

Label Studio

Install the `label-studio` Python library using your Python editor:

```
%pip install label-studio
```

Then, start the Label Studio development server using the following shell command:

```
!label-studio start
```

pyOpenAnnotate

pyOpenAnnotate is a simple tool that helps to label and annotate images and videos using OpenCV.

Let's install this tool using the Python editor as follows:

```
%pip install pyOpenAnnotate
```

The dataset and code used in this chapter are available on GitHub:

- **Dataset**: `https://github.com/PacktPublishing/Data-Labeling-in-Machine-Learning-with-Python/tree/main/datasets/Ch12`

- **Code**: `https://github.com/PacktPublishing/Data-Labeling-in-Machine-Learning-with-Python/tree/main/code/Ch12`

Data labeling using Azure Machine Learning

With an increasing demand for sophisticated models capable of understanding diverse data types, the importance of accurate annotations cannot be overstated. Azure Machine Learning offers a powerful solution, providing a data labeling interface designed to streamline the annotation process for images, text, and audio. Azure Machine Learning's data labeling capability facilitates the process of creating, managing, and monitoring data labeling projects and enables seamless collaboration among data scientists, domain experts, and annotators.

Let's look at the benefits of data labeling with Azure Machine Learning.

Benefits of data labeling with Azure Machine Learning

Data labeling is used to train machine learning models and helps to improve the accuracy of these models. Azure Machine Learning data labeling tools can be used to create image, text, and audio labeling projects.

Azure Machine Learning data labeling tools provide the ability to manage and monitor labeling projects seamlessly from within the studio web experience and reduce the back-and-forth process of labeling data offline.

After labeling the data in an Azure Machine Learning data labeling project, the labeled data can be exported to Azure Blob storage using the **Export** option in the project. From there, this labeled data can be integrated as a dataset in the Azure Machine Learning pipeline for training machine learning models.

Data that is labeled on-premises using other open source tools, such as Label Studio and pyOpenAnnotate, also can be integrated with Azure Machine Learning by creating a dataset from local files.

Let us see how to create a labeling project, how to upload data, how to create a labeling task, and how to manage and monitor the labeling project using Azure Machine Learning data labeling tools.

Data labeling steps using Azure Machine Learning

Here is an overview of the steps to create image, text, and audio labeling projects using Azure Machine Learning data labeling tools:

1. **Create a labeling project**: Sign into Azure Machine Learning and create a new labeling project. You can choose to create an image, text, or audio labeling project.

2. **Create a labeling task for your data**: You can choose to create a classification, object detection, instance segmentation, or semantic segmentation task.

3. **Upload data**: Upload the data you want to label to your labeling project. You can upload data from your local machine or from a cloud storage account.

4. **Label your data**: Use the labeling tool to label your data. In the case of machine learning-assisted data labeling, machine learning algorithms may be triggered to assist with the data labeling task. After some data has been labeled manually, machine learning algorithms automatically group similar images on the screen with the suggested label name.

5. **Manage and monitor your labeling project**: Monitor the progress of your labeling project and tasks from within the studio web experience. You can also export your labeled data as an Azure Machine Learning dataset.

In the following sections, we are going to discuss data labeling for image, text, and audio data using Azure Machine Learning.

Image data labeling with Azure Machine Learning

Azure Machine Learning is an industry-leading machine learning and AI platform designed to build and deploy machine learning and AI applications. Data scientists, machine learning engineers, and software engineers can use it in their day-to-day work for training, deploying their models, and managing the machine learning project life cycle.

Preparing good data is key for any machine learning project. Azure Machine Learning provides the capability to prepare labeled data for training. Let us first see how to label images using Azure Machine Learning.

Azure Machine Learning can be used to label images at a large scale and automate the data labeling process. We will see simple image data labeling for the following image. We will label this image with the labels man and bike. This image is available in the Datasets folder in the GitHub path specified in the *Technical requirements* section:

Figure 12.1 – Bike_riding_man image

Let's go through the steps to label images with Azure Machine Learning.

Step 1 – Create an Azure Machine Learning workspace

Before creating a labeling project, you need to create an Azure Machine Learning workspace if you have not already created one, as mentioned in the *Technical requirements* section.

Go to `portal.azure.com`. Under **Azure services**, you will see the **Create a resource** option. Click on + **Create a resource**, as shown in the following screenshot:

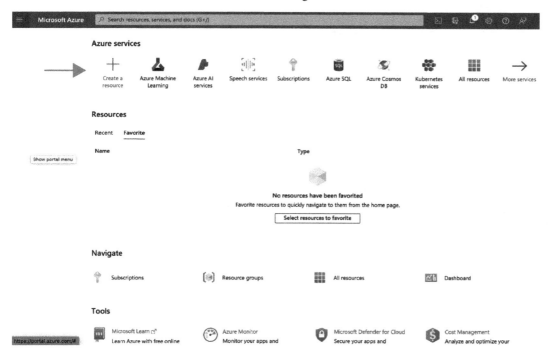

Figure 12.2 – Create a resource

Then, on the following **Marketplace** screen, search for `azure machine learning` in the search box. Click on **Azure Machine Learning**, create an Azure Machine Learning service, and follow the prompts to enter a name for it.

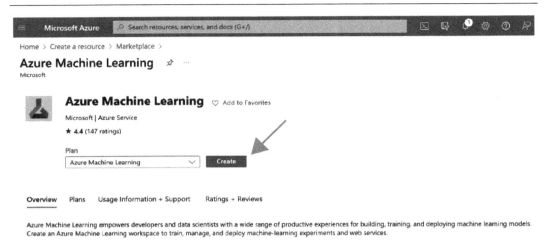

Figure 12.3 – Creating an Azure Machine Learning service from Marketplace

Then, click on the Azure Machine Learning workspace that you created. In the following screenshot, you can see that the name of the Azure Machine Learning workspace is `azuremllabelling`:

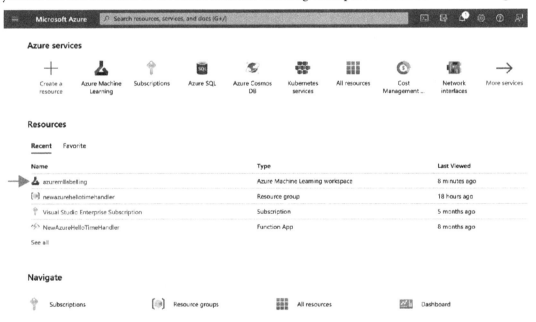

Figure 12.4 – Azure services

When you click on your Azure Machine Learning workspace name, `azuremllabelling`, you will see the following screen. Launch the Azure Machine Learning studio by clicking on the blue **Launch studio** button:

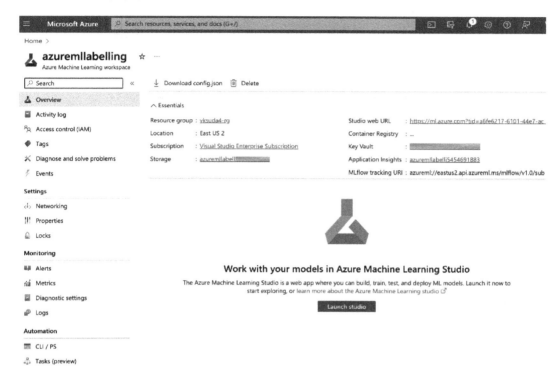

Figure 12.5 – Azure Machine Learning workspace

Step 2 – Create a data labeling project

We want to create a data labeling project so that we can upload images and label them or assign them to labelers and manage the workflow effectively.

In your Azure Machine Learning Studio, on the left-hand side, under **Manage**, you will see a **Data labeling** option; click on this.

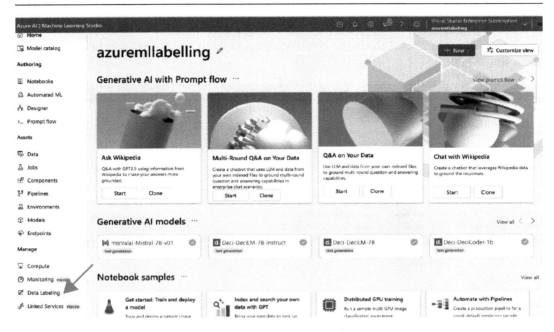

Figure 12.6 – Azure ML studio

Enter a name for your data labeling project and select **Image** for **Media type**. You also need to select a **Labeling task type** option from five different types for image labeling, as shown in *Figure 12.7*.

Depending on your scenario, choose a labeling task type that suits your needs:

- If you want to label an image with only one category from a list of options, choose **Image Classification Multi-class**.

- If you want to label an image with multiple categories from a list of options, choose **Image Classification Multi-label**. For instance, a picture of a dog could have both `dog` and `daytime` labels.

- If you want to label each object in an image with a category and a bounding box, choose **Object Identification (Bounding Box)**.

- If you want to label each object in an image with a category and a polygon outline, choose **Polygon (Instance Segmentation)**.

- If you want to label each pixel in an image with a category and a mask, choose **Semantic Segmentation (Preview)**.

Enter the project name `Image_data_labeling_project`. Select the **Object Identification (Bounding Box)** labeling task type, as shown in the following screenshot:

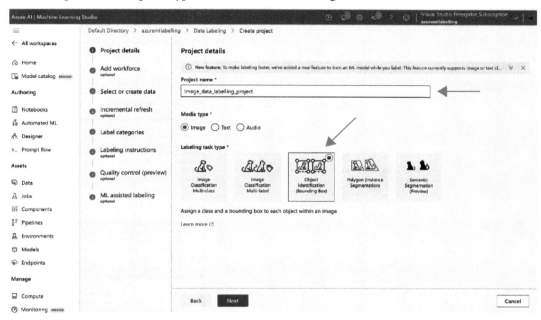

Figure 12.7 – Selecting the labeling task type

After entering the project details, the next step is **Add workforce**, which we can skip for this example. This step is only required if you want to add any vendor or labeling company from the Azure Marketplace to this labeling project.

Step 3 – Upload your data

There are two options to create a data asset. You can either create a data asset by uploading your files from Azure Blob storage, or you can directly create a data asset by uploading your local files.

You can find detailed steps to create a data asset from Azure Blob storage or by uploading local files at `https://learn.microsoft.com/en-us/azure/machine-learning/how-to-create-image-labeling-projects?view=azureml-api-2#specify-the-data-to-label`.

To upload data, first, let's create a data asset with the name `bike_riding_man`, as shown in the following screenshot:

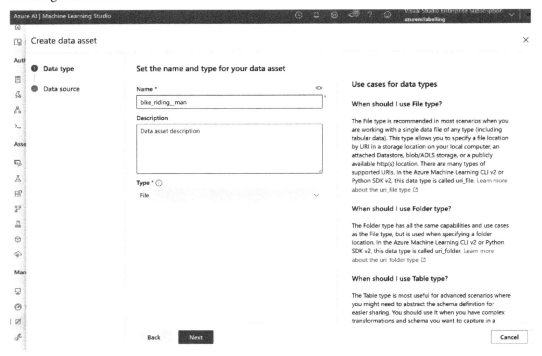

Figure 12.8 – Creating a data asset

Next, select the data source and create a data asset using one of the following two options.

Option 1 – Create a data asset from files in Azure Blob storage

Generate a data asset using an Azure datastore. While local file uploads are common, Azure Storage Explorer offers a more efficient method for transferring large data assets. It is recommended as the default tool for file movement.

For the data source, select **From Azure storage** to upload files from Azure Blob storage and create the data asset.

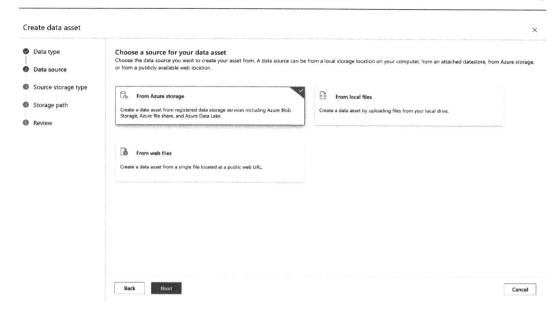

Figure 12.9 – Creating a data asset from Azure Blob storage

Option 2 – Create a data asset from files on your local system

You can upload files from your local system and create a data asset, as shown in the following screenshot:

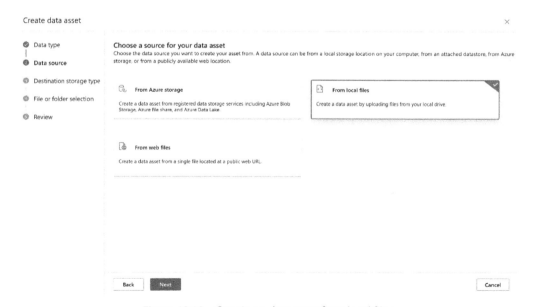

Figure 12.10 – Creating a data asset from local files

For this example, I have uploaded data from the local filesystem as the data asset size is small and available on the local system.

Step 4 – Label image data

Now, select the `bike_riding_man` data asset that we created in the previous step:

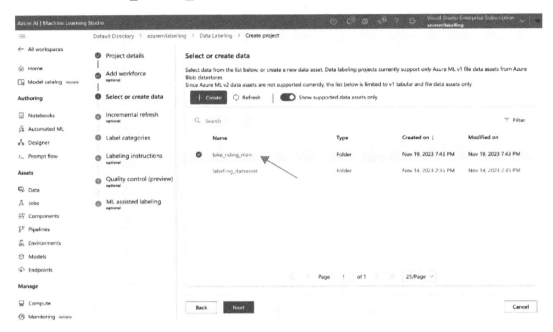

Figure 12.11 – Selecting the data asset

After selecting the data asset, click on **Next**. The **Incremental refresh** step is optional. This is required if we want to automatically refresh new data in the labeling project. For this example, let us skip this optional step and click **Next** again.

You will land on the following **Label categories** screen. Let's add the label categories `Bike` and `person` for this example.

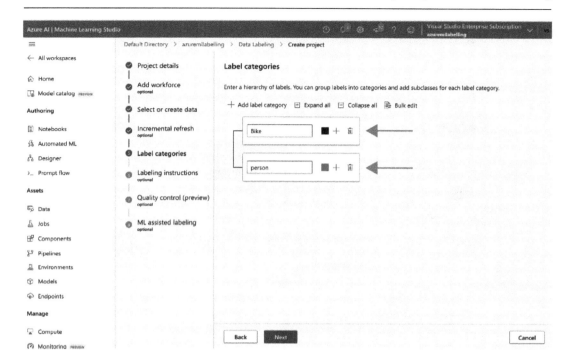

Figure 12.12 – Adding label categories

After adding the categories, click on **Next**. You will land on the **Labeling instructions** page. Let's skip this optional step and click on **Next** again. You will now be on the **Quality control (preview)** page. This is currently in preview. It is used to send labels to multiple labelers to get more accurate labels. Skip this by clicking on **Next**. You will now be on the **ML assisted labeling** page.

This step is optional. If you want to train a model to pre-label the data, then you can use this, but beware that it incurs additional compute costs.

If **ML assisted labeling** is enabled, after manually labeling the configured number of items, then the ML model will automatically label the rest of the items and provide suggestions for human review.

The threshold for the number of manually labeled items to commence ML assisted labeling isn't fixed and can significantly vary between labeling projects. In some instances, pre-labeling or cluster tasks may appear after manually labeling around 300 items. This threshold depends on how similar your dataset is to the dataset that the ML model was already trained on.

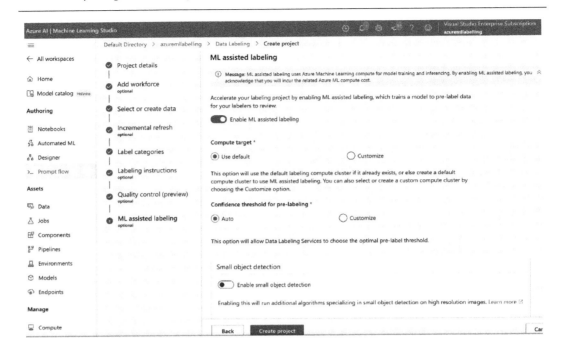

Figure 12.13 – ML assisted labeling

Finally, click on **Create project** on the **ML assisted labeling** page. Our labeling project, Image_
data_labeling_project, has been created on the **Data labeling** page.

Click on the project, and it will open the next screen. Click on **Label data** to start labeling the data
that you uploaded:

Figure 12.14 – Label data

When you click on **Label data**, it will show the images that you uploaded, and you can now start labeling those images.

Labeling the person

Select the `person` tag and then create a bounding box for the person in the image:

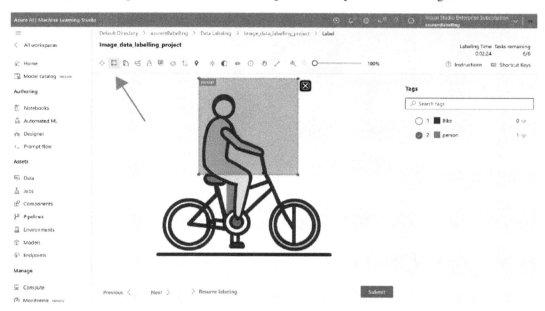

Figure 12.15 – Labeling the person

Labeling the bike

Similarly, select the `Bike` tag, draw the bounding box around the bike to label it, and click on the **Submit** button. This will take you to the next image. You can continue this process for all your images. You can navigate to images using the **Previous** and **Next** buttons on this screen.

Figure 12.16 – Labeling the bike

Similarly, you can label all other images and click **Submit**. All the images labeled by the labelers will be shown on the dashboard under **Review labels**, as shown in the following screenshot, and here the reviewer can review and approve those labels by clicking on the **Approve** button:

Figure 12.17 – Review labels

Finally, you can export the labeled data using the **Label export** option on the **Details** tab, as shown in the following screenshot, and use that exported data in machine learning experiments for training:

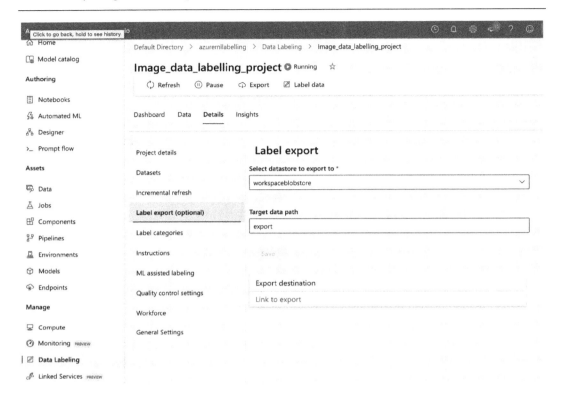

Figure 12.18 – Exporting the labels

You have seen how to create a project for image data labeling and then label the image data in Azure Machine Learning. Now, let's see how to label text data using Azure Machine Learning.

Text data labeling with Azure Machine Learning

In this section, let's see how to label text documents with Azure Machine Learning. To do this, select **Text** for **Media type**, as shown in the following screenshot:

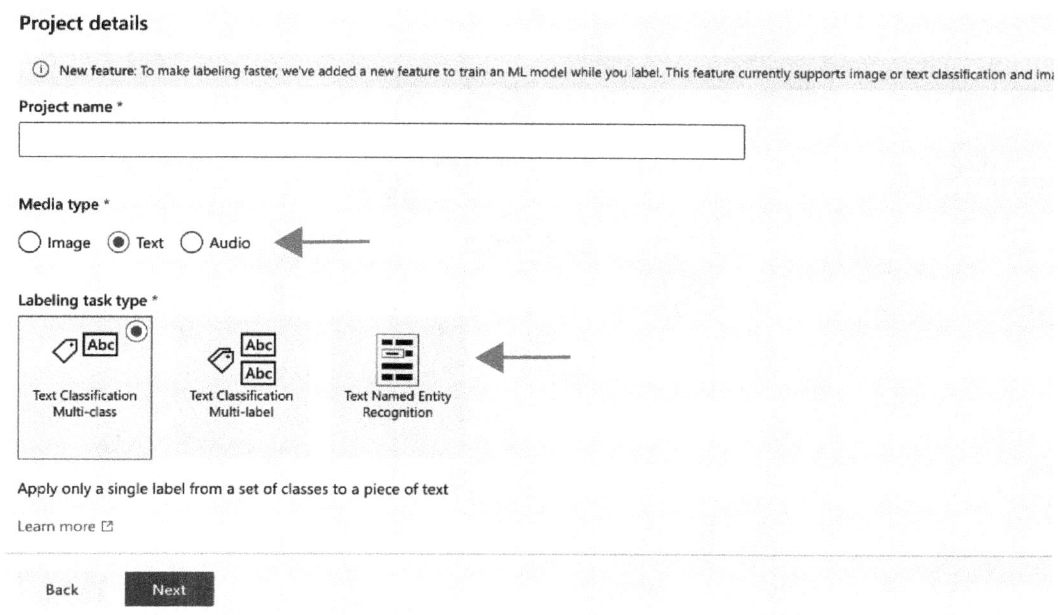

Project details

ⓘ New feature: To make labeling faster, we've added a new feature to train an ML model while you label. This feature currently supports image or text classification and ima

Project name *

Media type *

○ Image ◉ Text ○ Audio ◀━━━━━━━

Labeling task type *

[Abc] ◉	[Abc] [Abc]	▤
Text Classification Multi-class	Text Classification Multi-label	Text Named Entity Recognition

◀━━━

Apply only a single label from a set of classes to a piece of text

Learn more ↗

Back Next

Figure 12.19 – Text data labeling

In Azure Machine Learning data labeling, you can label the text in three different ways:

- You can label using a single tag.
- You can label using two tags.
- You can annotate entities in a text. For example, entities can be the name of the person, location, or organization in the text.

Choose the appropriate labeling task type based on your scenario from the following:

- **Text Classification Multi-class**: In this case, you will assign only one label from a set of classes to the entire text entry.
- **Text Classification Multi-label**: In this case, you can assign two labels to the entire text entry, as shown in the following figure.

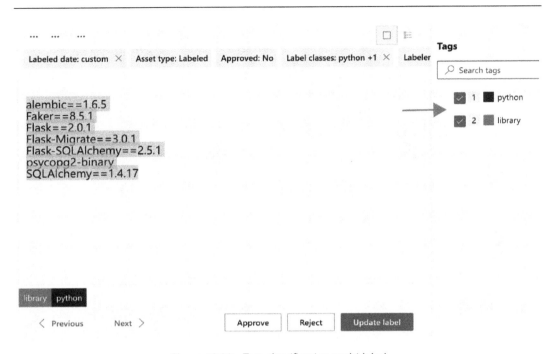

Figure 12.20 – Text classification multi-label

- **Text Named Entity Recognition**: For example, in a sentence, if we want to identify a person or organization entity, then we can select this task type.

We will see more about this in the following steps. Let's start creating a text labeling project in Azure Machine Learning.

Step 1 – Create a text data labeling project

On the Azure Machine Learning page, the steps are similar to when we created a labeling project for image data labeling in the previous section but with a few exceptions, such as the **Labeling task type** step.

Click on **Add project** on the **Data Labeling** page:

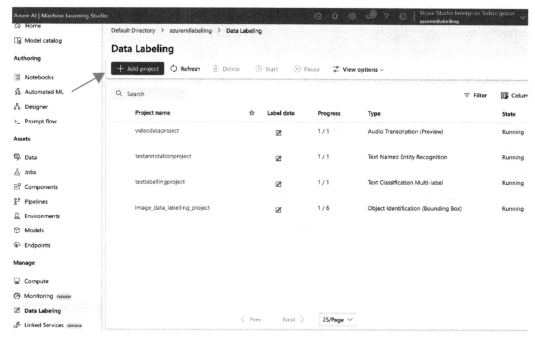

Figure 12.21 – Add project

Enter the project name for the text data labeling project, select **Text** for **Media type**, and select the labeling task type as shown in the following screenshot:

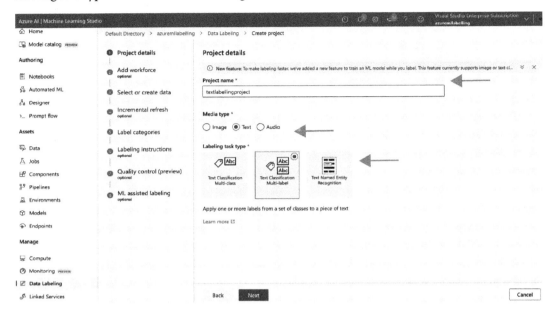

Figure 12.22 – Project details

Step 2 – Create data asset

As we saw in the previous section for the image data labeling project, we can create a data asset with two options: either from Azure Blob storage or from local files.

After selecting the data asset, click on **Next**. The next step, **Incremental refresh**, is optional. This is required if we want to automatically refresh new data in the labeling project. For this example, skip this optional step and click **Next**.

Then, you will land on the following **Label categories** screen.

Step 3 – Select the label category

On the **Label categories** page, add the label categories that you want to use for labeling your text data.

For this exercise, add the `animal`, `person`, and `location` label categories to label the text documents.

Figure 12.23 – Adding label categories

Click on **Next**, skip the optional steps as discussed in the previous section, and create the labeling project for text data.

You have now created the `textannotationproject` project and can see it on the **Data Labeling** page, as shown in the following screenshot:

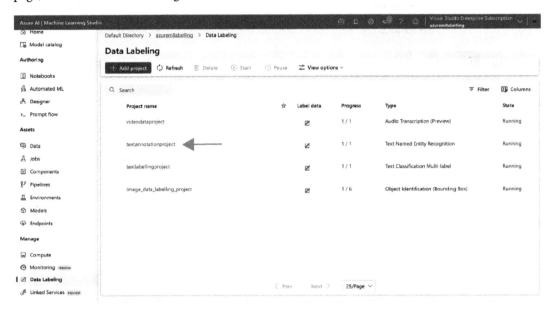

Figure 12.24 – The textannotationproject project

Step 5 – Label the text data

Now, click on the project name. On the following page, click on the **Label data** option under **textannotationproject**:

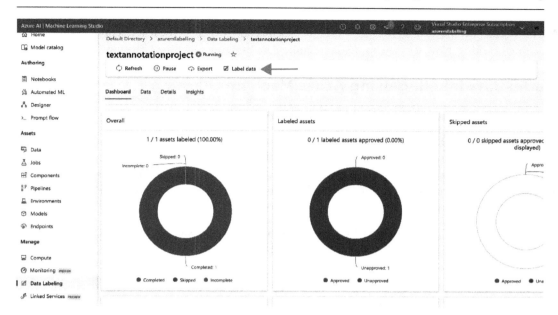

Figure 12.25 – Dashboard – Label data option

Finally, you can annotate your text data here:

Figure 12.26 – Annotating the text data

We have seen how to create a project for text data labeling and then label the text documents in Azure Machine Learning. Now, let's see how to label audio data in Azure Machine Learning.

Audio data labeling using Azure Machine Learning

In this section, let's see how to label audio data using Azure Machine Learning.

In Azure Machine Learning, we can annotate pieces of audio using text labels. We are going to use the `cat_1.wav` audio dataset for this. We will play the audio in Azure Machine Learning and use the `cat` label for that audio. This file is located in the `Datasets/Ch12` folder at the GitHub path specified in the *Technical requirements* section. The same process can be followed to label the required number of audio files.

After labeling, we are going to export the labeled audio files to Azure storage, and from there, we can consume them in the Azure Machine Learning pipeline as a dataset.

Similar to image data and text data, first, we will create a labeling project for audio data.

All the steps all similar to the previous section, except the labeling task type, for creating a new audio project.

Let's create the project first for audio data labeling in Azure Machine Learning.

Step 1 – Create the project

Let's create an audio project by following the same steps that we have seen in the previous section for creating image and text data labeling projects.

Enter the project name, select **Audio** for **Media type**, and select **Audio Transcription (Preview)** for **Labeling task type**:

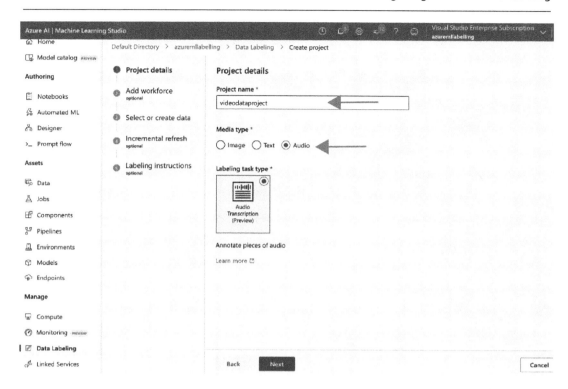

Figure 12.27 – Creating a project for audio transcription

The sample audio dataset that we are going to label is `cat_1.wav`. This is available in the GitHub repository.

Once the project is created, go to the **Data Labeling** page and click on the project name. On the project page, click on **Label data** in the same manner that we saw for the text labeling project.

Step 2 – Label the audio data

You will now be on the audio page where you can play the audio and enter the tag name in text format in the **Transcription** area under the audio.

Now, you need to add the transcription label for your audio data. As shown in the following screenshot, there is a **Play** tab to play the audio:

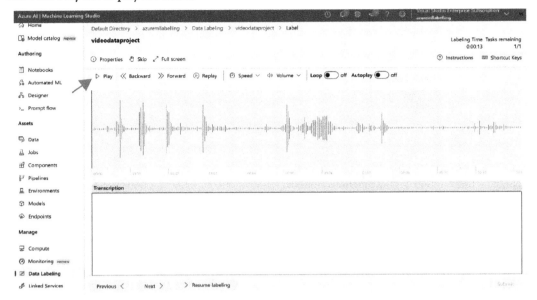

Figure 12.28 – Playing the audio

Select the cat label for this audio, as shown here:

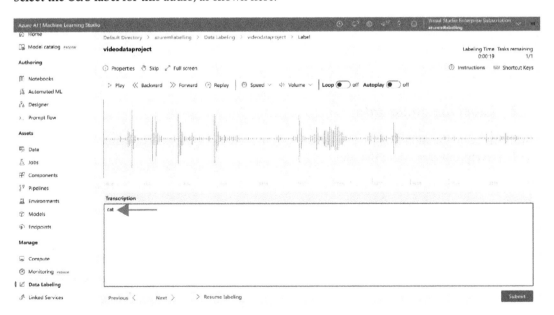

Figure 12.29 – Labeling the text for a piece of audio

You have seen how to create a project for audio data and label the audio data in Azure Machine Learning. Let's now see how to integrate this labeled data for training ML models in the Azure Machine Learning pipeline.

Integration of the Azure Machine Learning pipeline with the labeled dataset

To integrate labeled data from Azure Machine Learning data labeling into machine learning pipelines, you can follow these general steps:

1. **Set up the Azure Machine Learning workspace**: Ensure you have an Azure Machine Learning workspace set up. You can create one using the Azure portal.

2. **Data labeling**: Use the Azure Machine Learning data labeling capabilities to label your data. You can use Azure Machine Learning Studio to create labeling projects, upload data, and manage labeling tasks.

3. **Store the labeled data**: After data labeling is complete, the labeled data is typically stored in storage. You can create a dataset in Azure Machine Learning that points to the location of your labeled data.

4. **Define the machine learning pipeline**: Create an Azure Machine Learning pipeline that includes steps for data preprocessing, model training, and evaluation. You can use the Azure Machine Learning SDK to define these steps in a Python script.

5. **Reference the labeled dataset**: In the pipeline, reference the labeled dataset you created in the *Data labeling* step. This dataset will be used for training your machine learning model.

6. **Run the pipeline**: Execute the pipeline in your Azure Machine Learning workspace. This will trigger the data preprocessing, model training, and evaluation steps consistently and repeatably.

7. **Monitor and Iterate**: Monitor the pipeline execution and evaluate model performance. If necessary, iterate on the pipeline to improve your model by adjusting hyperparameters or using different algorithms.

Here is a simplified example using the Azure Machine Learning SDK to give you an idea:

```
from azureml.core import Dataset, Workspace
from azureml.core.experiment import Experiment
from azureml.core.runconfig import RunConfiguration
from azureml.core.conda_dependencies import CondaDependencies

# Load your Azure ML workspace
ws = Workspace.from_config()

# Reference the labeled dataset
labeled_dataset = Dataset.get_by_name(ws, name='your_labeled_dataset_
name')
```

```
# Define a machine learning experiment
experiment_name = 'your_experiment_name'
experiment = Experiment(workspace=ws, name=experiment_name)

# Define a run configuration with necessary dependencies
run_config = RunConfiguration()
run_config.environment.python.user_managed_dependencies = False
run_config.environment.python.conda_dependencies = CondaDependencies.
create(conda_packages=['your_required_packages'])

# Define your machine learning pipeline steps
# ...

# Reference the labeled dataset in your pipeline steps
# ...

# Submit the pipeline run
pipeline_run = experiment.submit(pipeline)
```

Remember to replace placeholders such as `'your_labeled_dataset_name'` and `'your_required_packages'` with your actual dataset name and required Python packages.

Adjust the pipeline steps according to your specific use case and requirements. The Azure Machine Learning SDK documentation provides detailed information on how to define and run pipelines, as ML pipeline implementation is beyond the scope of this book.

Now, let's see how to label the data using the open source tool Label Studio.

Exploring Label Studio

Label Studio (`https://labelstud.io/`) is an open source data labeling and annotation platform designed to streamline the process of labeling diverse data types, including images, text, and audio. With a user-friendly interface, Label Studio empowers machine learning practitioners and data scientists to efficiently label and annotate datasets for training and evaluating models. Its versatility, collaborative features, and support for multiple labeling tasks make it a valuable tool in the development of robust and accurate machine learning models.

In this section, we are going to label four types of data: image, video, text, and audio.

Labeling the image data

Let us label the image data using Label Studio.

Once you have installed the Label Studio tool using the `pip` command as given in the *Technical requirements* section, start Label Studio, go to the browser, and type in the following URL: `http://localhost:8080/`. As we have deployed Label Studio using the Python `pip` command, our Label Studio UI is running on the local system on port `8080`. This is our Label Studio UI application, and we can access the same from the browser to label our data.

For this exercise, we are going to use the same bike riding image that we used in the *Image data labeling using Azure Machine Learning* section.

Here's an overview of the steps for labeling images using Label Studio:

1. **Installation**: Download and install Label Studio on your local machine or server. Follow the installation instructions provided by Label Studio.

2. **Initialization**: Start the Label Studio application either through a command line or by using the provided interface.

3. **Account creation**: Create user accounts within Label Studio to facilitate project management. These accounts will be used to oversee and organize labeling projects.

4. **Project setup**: Define the labeling requirements for your dataset. Specify the type of labeling tasks needed (e.g., image classification or object detection) and configure project settings such as task distribution and completion criteria.

5. **Interface configuration**: Customize the labeling interface according to your project's needs. Add and define the labels that annotators will apply during the labeling process. Tailor the interface to ensure efficient and accurate annotations.

6. **Data import**: Import your dataset into Label Studio as labeling tasks. This involves uploading images or linking to data sources to create a set of tasks for annotators.

7. **Labeling and annotation**: Annotators use the configured interface to label and annotate the images according to the defined tasks. The labeling process involves applying the specified labels to regions or objects within the images.

8. **Export the labeled data**: Once labeling is complete, export the labeled data or annotations. Depending on your needs, you may export the data in various formats suitable for further analysis or integration with other tools and platforms.

By following these steps, you can effectively use Label Studio to manage and execute image labeling projects. Let's see a few important steps next.

Creating a new project

First, go to **Projects** to create a new project using the Label Studio UI as follows:

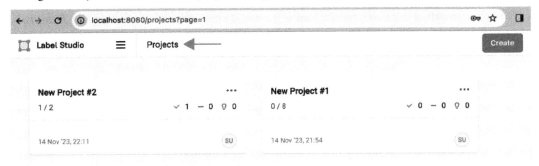

Figure 12.30 – Label Studio

Enter the project name:

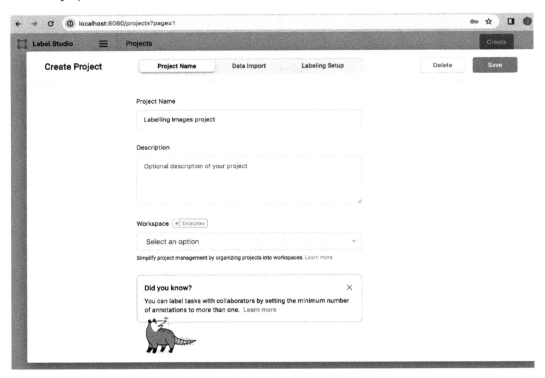

Figure 12.31 – Entering the project name

After you create a project, import data into Label Studio. You can import many types of data, including text, time series, audio, and image data. The file types supported depend on the type of data. Now, select the label template for labeling the dataset.

Selecting the label template

Go to **Settings | Labeling Interface**. Here, you can select a template from the available templates in Label Studio as shown in the project. Select **Image Classification**.

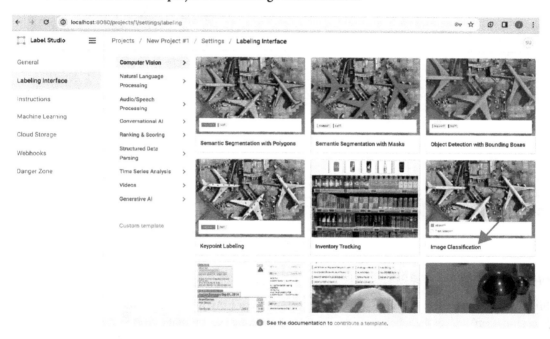

Figure 12.32 – Selecting the template

Once you have selected the label template, you need to set up the label names `bicycle` and `person`:

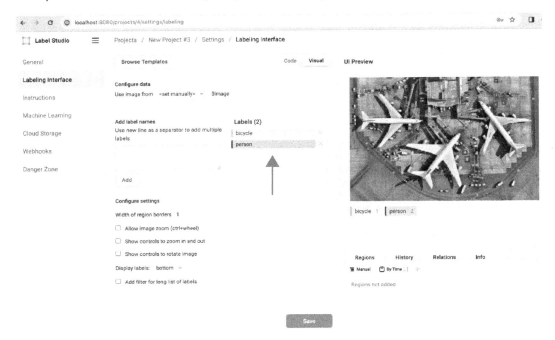

Figure 12.33 – Adding label names

Applying labels in Label Studio

Finally, go to **Labeling** and apply the labels to the images. As per the selected template (**Image Classification**), select the label and then draw the bounding box on that object in the image:

Figure 12.34 – Applying labels in Label Studio

You can label the next image in a similar fashion.

We have now seen how to create a project, select a template, and label the images in Label Studio. Now, let's see how to label text data in Label Studio.

Labeling the text data

In this section, let's see how to label text data using Label Studio.

For text data labeling, there are various natural language templates available in Label Studio, such as text classification templates and named entity recognition templates to identify the entity (person, organization, etc.) in the given sentence.

We will follow the same steps that we used for labeling image data in Label Studio. First, we create a project, then we import the data and select an appropriate label template. We have added the labels `Title` and `person` manually for this exercise. Finally, we apply the labels to the text. We have applied the labels `Title` and `person` to the entities in the sentence `"This is vijay text annotation"` for this example.

For more detailed documentation, go to `https://labelstud.io/`.

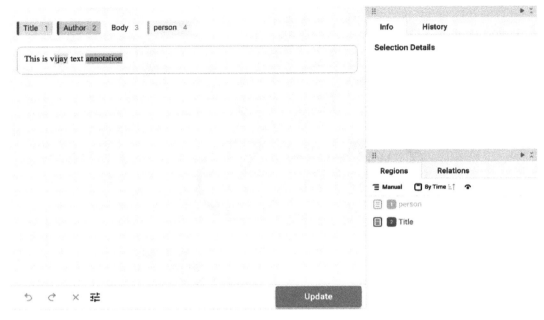

Figure 12.35 – Text annotation

We have now seen how to annotate the sample text using labels in Label Studio. Similarly, we can label the next piece of text data that we uploaded using Label Studio.

Labeling the video data

In this section, let's see how to label video data.

All the steps are similar to the image data labeling steps, except the template used for video data labeling. First, we will create the project in Label Studio and then import the video data files and select the appropriate template. Finally, we apply the labels to the video.

Now, let's add annotations to the project. Here, we are adding dog and Man labels manually for this exercise. Now, we go to the video annotation project and start labeling the video in Label Studio. We have created bounding boxes for the dog and Man objects shown in this video. We apply these labels to the video frames.

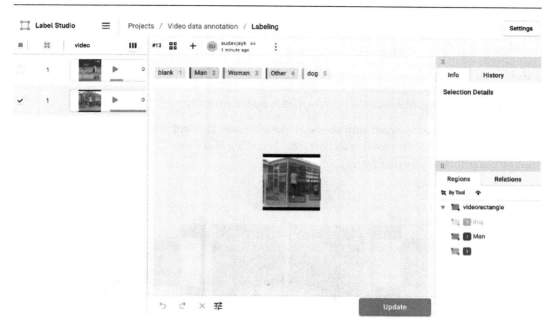

Figure 12.36 – Video data labeling

We have now seen how to label video data in Label Studio. All the steps are similar for image data labeling, text data labeling, and video data labeling, except for the label template. These labels can be exported from Label Studio and saved to the local computer. From there, a dataset can be created using local files in Azure Blob storage. This dataset can be used in the Azure Machine Learning pipeline for training the ML models.

As well as Label Studio, there are many other open source Python libraries available for data labeling. Now, let's see about another Python-based open source labeling tool, pyOpenAnnotate. The choice of tool depends on the availability of skilled resources, the volume of the data, and the format of the data.

pyOpenAnnotate

pyOpenAnnotate is an open source Python-based annotation tool that automates the image annotation pipeline using OpenCV. It is particularly well-suited for annotating simple datasets, such as images with plain backgrounds or infrared images. pyOpenAnnotate is a single-class automated annotation tool that can help you label and annotate images and videos using computer vision techniques. It is built by harnessing the power of OpenCV. You can check out the Python library documentation to understand how pyOpenAnnotate has been designed: https://pypi.org/project/pyOpenAnnotate/.

You can load your images in a directory and then run the following command to start labeling the bounding boxes for your images:

```
!annotate --img /path/to/directory/Images
```

The following image is available in the book's GitHub path for this chapter.

You can replace the directory path with your own dataset path. This will prompt the tool to label the objects in your image and you can drag and drop the bounding boxes around the objects (blue-colored bounding boxes in the following figure):

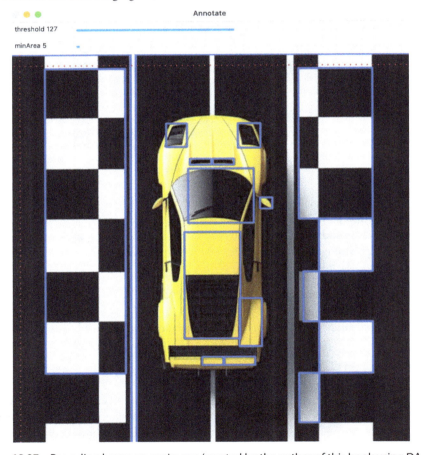

Figure 12.37 – Bounding boxes on car image (created by the author of this book using DALL-E)

Similarly, we can annotate videos using this pyOpenAnnotate tool. We can extract the frames for the video as shown in *Chapter 8*, and then provide the path of that video frame for drawing bounding boxes to the video frames. Now, let's see another popular tool to label the image data, CVAT.

Computer Vision Annotation Tool

CVAT is a free, open source tool that is widely used in various industries for annotating images to facilitate the training of machine learning models. This tool is designed to handle a large volume of images for labeling. Setting up and using CVAT for annotating images involves several steps. The following is a guide that covers the process.

Step 1 – Install Docker

CVAT is containerized using Docker, so you'll need to have Docker installed on your machine. Follow the installation instructions for your operating system on the official Docker website: `https://docs.docker.com/get-docker/`.

Step 2 – Install Docker Compose

CVAT has multiple components, including a web server, a database, and a worker for background tasks. Docker Compose allows you to define and manage the dependencies between these components in a single configuration file (`docker-compose.yml`).

Docker Compose simplifies the management of multi-container Docker applications. Install Docker Compose by following the instructions on the official Docker Compose installation page: `https://docs.docker.com/compose/install/`.

Step 3 – Clone the CVAT repository

Clone the CVAT repository from GitHub:

```
git clone https://github.com/openvinotoolkit/cvat.git
```

Step 4 – Configure CVAT environment variables

Navigate to the CVAT directory and create a `.env` file with configuration settings:

```
cd cvat
cp env_example .env
```

Edit the `.env` file to customize settings if needed.

You will typically need to customize the `docker-compose.yml` file to configure various aspects of CVAT, such as database credentials and port numbers.

Step 5 – Build and run CVAT

Build and run the CVAT containers using Docker Compose:

```
docker-compose up -d
```

Now we have completed deploying the CVAT tool using Docker on your local environment. Let's start labeling the images using the CVAT now.

Step 6 – Access the CVAT web interface

CVAT's web interface is accessible at `http://localhost:8080`. Open a web browser and navigate to this URL.

Step 7 – Create a new annotation task

Create a free account and log in to the CVAT web interface. Create a new task by clicking on the **Tasks** tab, then click the **Create Task** button. Enter the task details, such as name, labels, and mode (image or video). Configure additional settings based on your annotation requirements.

Next, upload images or video files for annotation. For images and videos, use the **Data** tab in the **Tasks** menu.

Now, annotate the data by selecting the task from the list and clicking **Go to the task**. Use the annotation tools to draw bounding boxes and polygons, or to annotate text.

Step 8 – Stop and remove CVAT containers

After you have finished the annotation tasks, stop and remove CVAT containers.

This step-by-step guide should help you set up and use CVAT for annotating images and videos. Adjustments can be made based on specific requirements and preferences, and CVAT's documentation provides comprehensive details for advanced use cases. However, this is beyond the scope of this book. You can explore CVAT's documentation for advanced features, customization, and troubleshooting at `https://opencv.github.io/cvat/docs/`.

Comparison of data labeling tools

Here is a table depicting the comparison of the tools on various features:

Tool	Pros	Cons	Cost	Labeling Features Support	Scalability
Azure Machine Learning labeling	Rapid data preparation for machine learning projects. Assisted machine learning.	Limited to Microsoft ecosystem. Limited support for custom labeling interfaces.	Azure services may have associated costs depending on the usage	Images, text documents, and audio	Ability to scale labeling tasks with the power of Azure cloud services

Label Studio	Open source and multi-type data labeling tool	Limited documentation. Limited support for video data.	Label Studio is available as open source software as well as an Enterprise cloud service	Images, text documents, and video	May require additional configuration for large-scale projects
CVAT	Web-based and collaborative. Easy to use with intuitive shortcuts.	Limited support for custom labeling interfaces. Users need to set up and host the tool themselves.	Open source. No direct cost for software; users only pay for hosting and infrastructure.	Images and videos	Large-scale projects may require additional configuration
pyOpen Annotate	Supports multiple annotation formats. Supports custom annotation interfaces.	Limited documentation. Limited support for video data.	Free and open source	Images and videos	Large-scale projects may require additional configuration

Table 12.1 – Comparison of data labeling and annotation tools

The cost of each tool may vary depending on the number of labeling tasks and the features required. It is recommended to evaluate each tool based on your specific requirements before deciding on the labeling tool.

Advanced methods in data labeling

Active learning and semi-automated learning are popular machine learning techniques that help overcome the challenge of data labeling. Both involve presenting uncertain or challenging labels to human annotators for feedback; the key difference lies in the overall strategy and decision-making process. Let's break down the distinction.

Active learning

Active learning is a machine learning paradigm in which a model is trained on a subset of the data, and then the model actively selects the most informative examples for labeling to improve its performance. The following list discusses various features of this method:

- **Workflow**: The initial model is trained on a small labeled dataset. The model identifies instances where it is uncertain or likely to make errors. These uncertain or challenging instances are presented to human annotators for labeling. The model is updated with the new labeled data, and the process iterates.

- **Benefits**: It reduces the amount of labeled data needed for model training and focuses annotation efforts on examples that are challenging for the current model.

- **Challenges**: It requires an iterative process of model training and annotation. The selection of informative instances is crucial for success.

- **Decision-making by the model**: In active learning, the model takes an active role in selecting which instances it finds most uncertain or challenging. The model employs specific query strategies to identify instances that, when labeled, are expected to improve its performance the most.

- **Iterative process**: The initial model is trained on a small labeled dataset. The model selects instances for annotation based on its uncertainty or expected improvement. Human annotators label the selected instances. The model is updated with the new labels, and the process iterates.

Semi-automated labeling

Semi-automated labeling involves a combination of automated tools and human intervention to label datasets. Automated methods assist human annotators in the labeling process but may not fully replace human input. The following list discusses various features of this method:

- **Workflow**: Automated algorithms perform an initial labeling of data. Human annotators review and correct the automated labels. The corrected labels are used to refine the model or dataset.

- **Benefits**: It speeds up the labeling process by leveraging automation. It maintains the accuracy and quality of labels through human review.

- **Challenges**: It is dependent on the accuracy of automated algorithms. It requires a balance between automation and human expertise.

- **Decision-making by automation**: In semi-automated labeling, automated algorithms are involved in the initial labeling of data. The automation might include pre-labeling based on algorithms, heuristics, or rules.

- **Human review and correction**: Human annotators review the automated labels and correct them as needed. Annotators might also add or modify labels based on their expertise. The corrected labels contribute to refining the dataset or model.

Key points of distinction between these two methods are as follows:

- **Initiation of labeling**: In active learning, the model actively initiates the process by selecting instances for labeling. In semi-automated labeling, automation takes the lead in the initial labeling, and human annotators review and correct the labels afterward.

- **Query strategies**: Active learning involves specific query strategies designed to maximize information gain for the model. Semi-automated labeling might rely on heuristics or algorithms for initial labeling, but the emphasis is on human correction rather than model-driven query strategies.

- **Decision responsibility**: Active learning places more decision-making responsibility on the model. Semi-automated labeling involves a more collaborative approach where both automated algorithms and human annotators contribute to decision-making.

While both approaches aim to make the most of human annotation efforts, the active learning process is more driven by the model's uncertainty and improvement goals, while semi-automated labeling focuses on a collaborative effort between automated tools and human expertise. The choice between them depends on the specific needs of the task and the available resources.

Summary

In this chapter, we have learned how to use Azure Machine Learning to label image, video, and audio data. We also learned about the open source annotation tool Label Studio for image, video, and text annotation. Finally, we learned about pyOpenAnnotate and CVAT for labeling image and video data. Now, you can try using these open source tools to prepare the labeled data for machine learning model training.

As we reach the final pages of this book, I extend my heartfelt congratulations to you on completing this insightful journey into the world of data labeling for image, text, audio, and video data. Your dedication and curiosity have paved the way for a deeper understanding of cutting-edge technologies. May the knowledge gained here continue to inspire your future endeavors. Thank you for being a part of this enriching experience!

Index

Packtpub.com

Subscribe to our online digital library for full access to over 7,000 books and videos, as well as industry leading tools to help you plan your personal development and advance your career. For more information, please visit our website.

Why subscribe?

- Spend less time learning and more time coding with practical eBooks and Videos from over 4,000 industry professionals

- Improve your learning with Skill Plans built especially for you

- Get a free eBook or video every month

- Fully searchable for easy access to vital information

- Copy and paste, print, and bookmark content

Did you know that Packt offers eBook versions of every book published, with PDF and ePub files available? You can upgrade to the eBook version at packtpub.com and as a print book customer, you are entitled to a discount on the eBook copy. Get in touch with us at customercare@packtpub.com for more details.

At www.packtpub.com, you can also read a collection of free technical articles, sign up for a range of free newsletters, and receive exclusive discounts and offers on Packt books and eBooks.

Other Books You May Enjoy

If you enjoyed this book, you may be interested in these other books by Packt:

Machine Learning for Imbalanced Data

Kumar Abhishek, Dr. Mounir Abdelaziz

ISBN: 978-1-80107-083-6

- Use imbalanced data in your machine learning models effectively
- Explore the metrics used when classes are imbalanced
- Understand how and when to apply various sampling methods such as over-sampling and under-sampling
- Apply data-based, algorithm-based, and hybrid approaches to deal with class imbalance
- Combine and choose from various options for data balancing while avoiding common pitfalls
- Understand the concepts of model calibration and threshold adjustment in the context of dealing with imbalanced datasets

Data-Centric Machine Learning with Python

Jonas Christensen, Nakul Bajaj

ISBN: 978-1-80461-812-7

- Learn the principles of data centricity and how they apply to real-world scenarios
- Understand the impact of input data quality vs. model selection and tuning
- Know why subject-matter experts are critical to good model development
- Implement best-practice data cleaning, labeling and augmentation
- Learn common synthetic data generation techniques and their application
- Get well versed with applying these techniques using common Python packages
- Detect and correct bias in a dataset using best-practice techniques
- Appreciate the need for reliable, responsible and ethical ML/AI

Packt is searching for authors like you

If you're interested in becoming an author for Packt, please visit `authors.packtpub.com` and apply today. We have worked with thousands of developers and tech professionals, just like you, to help them share their insight with the global tech community. You can make a general application, apply for a specific hot topic that we are recruiting an author for, or submit your own idea.

Share your thoughts

Now you've finished *Data Labeling in ML and AI with Python*, we'd love to hear your thoughts! Scan the QR code below to go straight to the Amazon review page for this book and share your feedback or leave a review on the site that you purchased it from.

`https://packt.link/r/1-804-61054-2`

Your review is important to us and the tech community and will help us make sure we're delivering excellent quality content.

Download a free PDF copy of this book

Thanks for purchasing this book!

Do you like to read on the go but are unable to carry your print books everywhere?

Is your eBook purchase not compatible with the device of your choice?

Don't worry, now with every Packt book you get a DRM-free PDF version of that book at no cost.

Read anywhere, any place, on any device. Search, copy, and paste code from your favorite technical books directly into your application.

The perks don't stop there, you can get exclusive access to discounts, newsletters, and great free content in your inbox daily

Follow these simple steps to get the benefits:

1. Scan the QR code or visit the link below

https://packt.link/free-ebook/9781804610541

2. Submit your proof of purchase
3. That's it! We'll send your free PDF and other benefits to your email directly

www.ingramcontent.com/pod-product-compliance
Lightning Source LLC
Chambersburg PA
CBHW080607060326
40690CB00021B/4620